Words - Sounds - Speech - men - memory
Thoughts - Fears - Emotions & Time, all
Related - ALL made From one ALL made
In one.

Blessed Be His Name.

Thought waves - Heat waves - ALL
Vibrations - ALL Paths Lead to God.

His way -- It is Lovely - It is Gracious
It is merciful,

Thank you God.

One Thought can Produce millions of
Vibrations and They All Go Back To
God - Everything Does -

Thank you God.

Have No Fear - Believe,

The universe Has many wonders - and
God is ALL.

Thoughts - Deeds - vibrations, Etc.
They all Go Back To God and He Cleanses
ALL.

He Is Gracious And Merciful.

Glory to God. God is so alive - God is,

ABOUT THE AUTHOR

Ashley Kahn is the author of *Kind of Blue: The Making of the Miles Davis Master-piece*. As a journalist and editor, he has contributed articles to *The New York Times*, *Rolling Stone*, *Mojo*, and many other publications. He also served as primary editor of *Rolling Stone: The Seventies* and primary contributor to *The Rolling Stone Jazz & Blues Album Guide*. He lives in Fort Lee, New Jersey.

Praise for *A Love Supreme: The Story of John Coltrane's Signature Album*

"Kahn is building a publishing career by detailing the circumstances surrounding the creation of classic jazz recordings. *A Love Supreme* follows *Kind of Blue*, his earlier take on the classic Miles Davis session of the late '50s, with a similarly thorough overview—with numerous photos—of a vital episode in the history of jazz recording."
—*Los Angeles Times*

"Jazz writing appears to be moving toward high art, with Kahn leading the way . . . this is absolutely essential jazz history for all libraries."
—*Library Journal* (starred review)

"Kahn's [*A Love Supreme*] continues what has turned out to be a great invention in music writing—a brilliantly thorough history of one record central to American musical culture. . . . This is little less than a stupendous piece of work—even greater than Kahn's portrait of the "Kind of Blue" sessions."
—*The Buffalo News*

"*A Love Supreme* vividly tells the story of a musical earthquake that most every serious music fan and musician alike felt the challenge to acknowledge and react to."
—*JazzWeek*

"Kahn describes the music with marvelous lucidity. . . . But his greatest triumph is to put the album in full context."
—*Entertainment Weekly*

"In a season of remarkable music writing, *A Love Supreme* arrives as one of the most satisfying books of 2002."
—*Seattle Weekly*

"Ashley Kahn's book is a trove of information both trivial and profound."
—*Down Beat*

A Love Supreme

A Love Supreme / John Coltrane

impulse! STEREO A-77

The Story of
John Coltrane's
Signature
Album

Ashley Kahn

Penguin Books

PENGUIN BOOKS
Published by the Penguin Group
Penguin Group (USA) Inc., 375 Hudson
Street, New York, New York 10014,
U.S.A. ■ Penguin Books Ltd, 80 Strand,
London WC2R 0RL, England ■ Penguin
Books Australia Ltd, 250 Camberwell
Road, Camberwell, Victoria 3124, Aus-
tralia ■ Penguin Books Canada Ltd, 10
Alcorn Avenue, Toronto, Ontario,
Canada M4V 3B2 ■ Penguin Books
India (P) Ltd, 11 Community Centre,
Panchsheel Park, New Delhi – 110 017,
India ■ Penguin Books (N.Z.) Ltd, Cnr
Rosedale and Airborne Roads, Albany,
Auckland, New Zealand ■ Penguin
Books (South Africa) (Pty) Ltd, 24
Sturdee Avenue, Rosebank, Johannes-
burg 2196, South Africa

Penguin Books Ltd, Registered Offices:
80 Strand, London WC2R 0RL, England

First published in 2002 by Viking Penguin, a member of Penguin Putnam Inc.
Published in Penguin Books 2003

10 9 8 7 6 5 4 3 2 1

IMAGE CREDITS:
Joe Alper/Courtesy of George Alper:
pages 74–75. Courtesy of ALS Publications: 201 (football fanzine). Author's
collection: xxiii, 180. Courtesy of
Coltrane family/JOWCOL Music: end-
papers, xiv, 79, 96, 137, 148, 164. Frank
Driggs Collection: 14. Esmond Edwards:
91. Lee Friedlander/Courtesy Fraenkel
Gallery, San Francisco: 35, 43. Courtesy
of Yasuhiro Fujioka: 189. Burt Goldblatt
and Katherine Holzman Goldblatt:
112–13, 125. Randi Hultin/Courtesy of
Wivi-Ann Wells: 166, 168. Courtesy of

Institute of Jazz Studies: 17. Courtesy of
Insitut National Audiovisuel (France):
171 (all). Sy Johnson: 18. Victor
Kalin/Courtesy of Katy Kalin: 151. Frank
Kofsky/Courtesy of Bonnie Kofsky: 174,
182, 199. Manfred Leber: viii–ix. Jean-
Pierre Leloir: xxvi, 2, 3, 5, 167, 169
(both), 172, 173, 218. Courtesy of
Marsalis Music: 209. Peter Max/VIA
MAX: 203 (bottom). Bob Parent/Cour-
tesy of Bob Parent Archive: 37, 42. Ray-
mond Ross: 69, 194, 196–97. Courtesy
of Saint Gregory the Great Church: 188.
Duncan P. Schiedt: 64–65. Don Schlitten: 28–29, 47, 48, 76–77. Riccardo
Schwamenthal: 40. Herb Snitzer: 56–57,
58. Courtesy of Sony Music: 203 (top).
Chuck Stewart: 82, 85, 93, 98, 117, 128,
130, 132, 134–35, 138, 140–41, 142, 178.
Bunny Styron/Courtesy of Mark Styron:
190. Lee Tanner/The Jazz Image: 62.
Courtesy of Creed Taylor: 53, 54 (bottom). Courtesy of Universal Music
Group: 201 (Chanté Moore CD). Courtesy of Rudy Van Gelder: 84. Jack Var-
toogian/Front Row Photos, Inc.: 206–7.
Courtesy of Verve Music Group: iii, xxiii,
54 (top), 70, 80, 92, 127, 141 (bottom),
145, 146, 152, 180, 201 (LP), 215, 216
(all), 217. Courtesy of Warner Books:
201 (photo book). Francis Wolff, ©
Mosaic Images: 89, 90, 143. The X Press
(UK): 201 (Pauline Hopkins book).

All excerpts from Ralph J. Gleason's
interview with John Coltrane from May
2, 1961, are © 1989, Jazz Casual Productions, Inc., and are used by permission. All rights reserved.

Both poems or excerpts on pages 78
and 79 are by John Coltrane, are ©
2002, JOWCOL Music, and are used by
permission. All rights reserved.
The image of Alice Coltrane's *World
Galaxy* LP on page 203 is © 2002, Peter

Max, and is used by permission. All
rights reserved. Peter Max wishes to
express that this image does not fully
represent the original, full-color work.

THE LIBRARY OF CONGRESS HAS CATALOGED
THE HARDCOVER EDITION AS FOLLOWS:
Kahn, Ashley.
A love supreme : the story of John
    Coltrane's signature album / Ashley
    Kahn.
p. cm.
Includes bibliographical references (p.)
    and index.
Discography: p.
ISBN 0-670-03136-4 (hc.)
ISBN 0 14 20.0352 2 (pbk.)
1. Coltrane, John, 1926–1967. Love
    supreme I. Title
ML419.C645 K3 2002
785'.34165—dc21   2002029623

Printed in the United States of America
Set in itc Century Light
Designed by Jaye Zimet

Acknowledgments

Belief begins with a leap of faith, at least a meeting. A sincere thanks to Ravi Coltrane for taking both. I could not and would not have imagined this enterprise without the willing support of the extended JOWCOL family. To them, my enduring gratitude: Alice Coltrane, Marilyn McLeod, Michelle Coltrane Carbonell, Kelly Ferguson, Bill Kaplan, and keeping the Philadelphia flame burning—Cousin Mary Alexander.

Without their particular gifts, no *A Love Supreme*; without their participation, no book. Deep bows to McCoy Tyner (and Paul Hoffer), Elvin Jones (Keiko Jones), and Rudy Van Gelder (Maureen Sickler).

A writer could not hope for a more dedicated editorial team: Neil Belton in London, Rick "Crash Master" Kot, Brett Kelly, and my agent and friend, Dave Dunton, whose daily cheer was the WD-40 when wheels stopped turning. At Viking Penguin: Paul Slovak, Jaye Zimet, Paul Buckley, Jesse Reyes, Kate Griggs, and Susan Petersen Kennedy. At Granta: Gail Lynch, Louise Campbell, and Sarah Wasley. For research, transcribing, and translating: Aaron Prado, Robert Warren, Jonathan Matz, Maria Alford, Adelheid Kuchling, Wivi-Ann Wells—et un vrai frère: Laurent Masson.

At Verve Music Group—my musical HQ—I found unbridled enthusiasm. Thanks to: Ron Goldstein, Bryan Koniarz, Hollis King, Regina Joskow, Lauren Fox, Kevin Reeves, Michael Kauffman, Lynn Kerman, Erick Labson, and Randy Aronson. For riding shotgun the entire way, special thanks to Ken Druker.

For their generosity in providing information, tapes, images, and energy, I am eternally grateful to an international cadre: Michel Delorme, Yasuhiro Fujioka, Lewis Porter, Hal Miller, and Carlos Santana.

For lending an informed musical perspective: Bob Belden, Archie Shepp, Dr. Art Davis, Curtis Fuller, Wayne Shorter, Frank Lowe, Branford Marsalis, Joshua Redman, Zane Massey, Cecil Payne, Yusef Lateef, Tommy Flanagan, and Ravi Coltrane.

■ For taking the time out of crazy schedules to share their impressions: Raviji Shankar, Patti Smith, Maurice White, Bono, Michael Brecker, Kenny Garrett, Bootsy Collins, Maurice White, Phil Lesh, and Dave Liebman.

■ For hooking me up with and/or hipping me to interviews, recordings, and other hidden treasures: Carl Woideck, Toby Gleason, Ed Michel, Bob Golden, David Peterkin, Frank Tiberi, Phil Coady, Steve Rathe, Toby Byron, Chip Stern, Chris DeVito, Bert Vuijsje, Bob Clark, Jim Cogan, and Dan Skea.

■ For holding the key to important archives and libraries: Dan Morgenstern, Vincent Pelote, Ed Berger, and Joe Peterson (Institute of Jazz Studies); Thurston Briscoe, Josh Jackson, Gary Walker, Dorthaan Kirk, and Cephas Bowles (WBGO-FM); George Boziwick (New York Public Library, Music Division); Monk Rowe (Hamilton College Jazz Archive); Michael Buening (Museum of Television & Radio); WKCR (Phil Schaap, Brian Linde); and James Briggs Murray (Schomburg Center of the New York Public Library).

■ For inspiration by example: Nat Hentoff, Ralph J. Gleason, Val Wilmer, A. B. Spellman, Amiri Baraka, Martin Williams, Francis Davis, and Bob Belden.

■ For helping to ensure the French leg of this adventure was a fruitful, friendly effort, merci à: Henri Renaud, André Francis, Frank Tenot, François Postif, Philippe Baudoin, Isabelle Marquis, Xavier Prevost, Valerie Lerot, Eve Boulan, Jean-François et Marie-France Tealdi, Pierre Lapijover, Christophe Deghelt, Yves Builly, Christiane Lemire, Veronique Jolivet, Daniel Richard, Daniel Berger, Dominique Bernard, Vivienne Sicnasi, and Nicole Colomb.

■ For helping to ensure that this book looks as good as it does, a spotlight on: Jean-Pierre Leloir, Chuck Stewart, Dale Parent, George Alper, Burt Goldblatt, Lee Tanner, Frank Driggs, Val Wilmer, Esmond Edwards, Herb Snitzer, Don Schlitten, Wivi-Ann Wells, Sy Johnson, Zane Massey, Marc Styron, Bonnie Kofsky, Louise Campbell, Kate and Rebecca Kalin, Vicki Gohl of Florentine Films, Fred and Mike at Jazz Record Center, Peter Max and Christine Kenner, Fraenkel Gallery, and Prophet Jennings.

■ For delivering what was needed with speed and a smile: Terri Hinte, Tara Lochen (Fantasy Records); Cathy Williams (Rhino Records); Harry Weinger, Sujata Murthy (UME); Chris Wheat, Jennifer Levy (Verve); Randy Haecker, Tom Cording, Seth Rothstein (Sony/Legacy); Tina Pelikan (ECM); Debbie Ferraro (Nonesuch); Colin Schofield (Zildjian); Lori Hagopian (Hal Leonard Publishing); Sue Hurring (*Modern Drummer*); Sara Lourie (Mosaic); Bob Golden (Carlin Music); Kathey Marsella, Wayne Sharp (Wilkins Management, Inc.); Sandy Sawotnick, Alan Leeds, Eric Leeds, Adam Kaplan, and George Gilbert.

■ For filling the sails with constant encouragement—thank you: Howard "Prez" Mandel, Michael Cuscuna, Herb Nolan, Alyn Shipton, Richard Mattingly, Chris Porter, and Lee Mergner. That DAT man: Jim Luce. In the wings: Dave Brendel and Paul Hall. Aides d'accès: Michael Shrieve, Cecilia Foster, and Adam Mansbach. Editorial bounceback: Andrew Caploe, Michael Hein, Lewis Porter, Michael Cuscuna, Ken Druker, and Peter Kahn. Migraine control: Dr. Heidi Kuchling.

■ I dedicate this book to a man whose distinctive sound resonates beyond category and time: John William Coltrane.

Contents

Partners in time: Elvin Jones and
John Coltrane, Kongresshalle,
Frankfurt, Germany.
October 31, 1963

Foreword
"Always a Spiritual Experience"

"Finally!"

That's what I thought when I heard about this project—finally, someone's going to do a serious study on one of John Coltrane's greatest achievements. There are so many things to say about *A Love Supreme*, you could write volumes just on that one album. It's worth it. How it was made, where it was made, why it's so important, how it reached such a broad audience. For me, when I listen to it today, it still brings up so many memories I don't know where to begin.

Now it's all here, in one book.

I can't say enough about how proud I am to have been part of the quartet that recorded *A Love Supreme,* part of a group that played and grew together. It was a band that gave me the freedom to explore the music, that invited innovation. We weren't playing by any rules—they weren't there.

Everything we were trying to do, everything we were about—McCoy, Jimmy, myself, and of course John—came together on that one album. Four individuals who gravitated together from different parts of the country, different backgrounds, all focusing around the personality of one man—John Coltrane.

John deserves all the recognition—all the credit—for what *A Love*

Supreme became. It was his music, his technique, his philosophy of sound, his liner notes. He should get the Nobel Prize for those notes! He seemed to catch the essence of exactly what it was we were thinking in 1964—the band, even the country in general—and put it into words. He was certainly the leader and the master. What the rest of us contributed was because of his leadership and example and stature as an artist. He created that impulse to excel.

If you want to know who John Coltrane was, you have to know *A Love Supreme.* It is like a culmination of one man's life, the whole story of his entire life. When a person wants to become an American citizen, he or she has to say the pledge of allegiance in front of God. *A Love Supreme* is John's pledge of allegiance.

We didn't know how *A Love Supreme* was going to be received beforehand, but I'm not surprised it has reached so many people, and that it has become his best-known album. It's unique. In a sense, it's not even jazz. It broadened the concept of what music was. It's totally spiritual: old people can appreciate it, little kids who haven't been indoctrinated into music in any way can appreciate it. Every time someone hears it, that music touches them somehow, even people who are churchgoers and have always thought that popular music or jazz was influenced by the devil.

We're all human beings. Our spirituality can express itself any way and anywhere; you can get religion in a bar or jazz club as much as you can in a church. *A Love Supreme* is always a spiritual experience, wherever you hear it.

The quartet never really talked about the spiritual aspect. It wasn't contrived; things just happened. We had all been brought up in families that were hardworking and churchgoing, and the music was a continuation of our upbringing. When I was a child in Pontiac, my mother and father would take all us kids to church on Sunday and we'd be there all day. We'd start off in Sunday school in the morning and would stay until evening services. All the people who belonged to that church would bring pies and cakes and all kinds of food, it was just one big family, and strangers could come off the street if they wanted to. My mother and my sisters all sang in the choir, and I loved to hear those gospel songs. When I listen to *A Love Supreme* it reminds me of those days. The spirit of God is in all of us, and when we started to play, that's what came out.

When Ashley Kahn first told me of his plans to write this book, I told him that if you're going to write about the music, it should take the readers and point them *back* to the music. If a writer can put enthusiasm into his expression of what he has heard, he can excite a great many people to listen. After reading this book, I am both pleased and excited to report that Ashley's done that. He's been true to the music and to the readers—he's talked to everyone involved and researched and listened *a lot*. I think this book reaches a pinnacle of what jazz and music writing stand for, and I hope that it will be a catalyst—that it will bring more people to listen to *A Love Supreme* and to John Coltrane.

—ELVIN JONES,
February 2002

Well, I haven't had much leisure time in the last fifteen years, and when I get any,

I'm usually so tired I just go somewhere and lay around, you know, for two weeks.

If I can get two weeks. And most of the time my mind is still on music.

—JOHN COLTRANE,
JAPAN, 1966

Introduction "The First Time I Have Everything Ready"

The directions were easy enough, even for an East Coaster. From Santa Monica, go east on I-10 to the 405, then north to the Ventura Freeway, a busy five-lane ribbon snaking westward through tree-flecked canyons. Take the Woodland Hills exit to an infinite stretch of Ventura Boulevard, where addresses require five digits and a succession of strip malls, supermarkets, and gas stations extend as far as the sun-protected eye can see.

There, in a nondescript, two-room office nestled between a Ralph's and a Von's ("if you pass the bagel shop, you've gone too far"), I waited to meet Alice Coltrane, widow of the legendary jazz saxophonist John Coltrane. A classically trained pianist born in Detroit and drawn to jazz at an early age, she first met Coltrane in 1963, eventually bore three of his children, played in his last groups until his death in 1967, and then led her own celebrated career well into the eighties. From this unlikely location, she now oversees the affairs of his estate in the office of JOWCOL Music (as in "JOhn W. COLtrane"), balancing those duties with the running of an ashram dedicated to the study of Eastern religions. Semiretired and spotlight-shy, she has modestly placed her performing years behind her—save for annual tributes to her late husband—and rarely accedes to interviews.

The sixty-four-year-old bowed slightly when we met, bringing her

hands together in prayer, up to her forehead. She was wrapped in a brightly colored punjabi dress and wore sandals, and her slender mien reflected both her age and her vegetarian regime. Across a desk, she spoke softly in sing-song cadences. I leaned forward at first to follow her words. But soon, with increasing vigor, she summoned the memory of a day more than thirty-five years earlier when she witnessed the conception of a timeless musical recording.

The caption:
The proud father at home: A still from a home movie shows Coltrane posing with John Jr. outside his Long Island home a few weeks before recording *A Love Supreme*

The tight focus of Mrs. Coltrane's recollection eclipsed all sense of historical context. It wasn't difficult to understand her tunnel view; millions who listened to and loved the music she described did so without any knowledge of its birth. But I was hoping for details *and* a broader perspective: the summer of 1964, after all, had been a season of consequence.

It was the tail end of a hot, portentous few months. LBJ was still settling into his newly inherited job as president, Vietnam was still a far-off series of skirmishes, and Malcolm X was still alive. A peacetime economy flourished as racial conflict loomed. The civil rights movement, which had crested a year before as 200,000 marched on Washington, seemed to stall. Riots flared in Harlem and other ghettos in New York and New Jersey.

The World's Fair was in New York City, and the most popular music of the day came from Liverpool and Detroit. While the Beatles and Motown ruled the charts, Bob Dylan delivered his timely third LP, *The Times They Are A-Changin'*. Within months, soul crooner Sam Cooke would respond by writing his own confident prediction: "A Change *Is* Gonna Come."

On the jazz front, a funky cousin of fifties hard bop was packing them in; groups led by Cannonball Adderley, Ramsey Lewis, and Chico Hamilton were at the crest of the "soul jazz" wave. The legends—Duke, the Count, Louis (whose freak hit "Hello, Dolly" had recently topped the pop charts)— were keeping veteran fans happy. The torch of "free" jazz, sparked only a few years earlier by Ornette Coleman, Charles Mingus, and Cecil Taylor, was now brandished by a new avant-garde. To many, their fierce, tradition-defying music blew with the politically charged anger of the time. The fraternity of the "New Thing"—Albert and Donald Ayler, Archie Shepp, Bill Dixon, and others—claimed a leader, a saxophonist whose aggressive style informed their own sound and exploratory spirit: John Coltrane.

"I don't think people are necessarily copying me," Coltrane stated at the end of that summer. To him, it was a matter of timing. "In any art, there may be certain things in the air at certain times . . . a number of people [may] reach the same end by making a similar discovery at the same time." What Coltrane did not know was that he was about to produce a singular musical statement that would hand him a far greater renown than ever before, transcending his category and his time.

For Coltrane, 1964 had been a period of nonstop work. His booking agency, Shaw Artists, had him crisscrossing the country for most of the summer in a station wagon with his quartet. Philadelphia, Chicago, New York, San Francisco. Back to New York. He needed a few weeks off, and he had the perfect excuse. On August 26, his first son was born. John and Alice brought John Jr. home to their recently purchased two-story house in Dix Hills, a quiet section of Long Island, New York. For Coltrane, it was a rare opportunity to put his horn down, his feet up, and just be with his family.

But Coltrane's obsessive nature would not let him rest. For five days he had secluded himself upstairs with pen, paper, and saxophone. "It was late summer, or early fall, because the weather was nice at the time in New York," recalls Alice. "There was an unoccupied area up there where we hardly ever went, sometimes a family member would visit [and] would stay there. John would go up there, take little portions of food every now and then, spending his time pondering over the music he heard within himself."

Alice remained busy with John Jr. and Michelle, her four-year-old by her first marriage. When he finally reappeared, she noticed that Coltrane—normally deep in thought—was unusually serene.

> It was like Moses coming down from the mountain, it was so beautiful. He walked down and there was that joy, that peace in his face, tranquility. So I said, "Tell me everything, we didn't see you really for four or five days . . ." He said, "This is the first time that I have received all of the music for what I want to record, in a suite. This is the first time I have everything, everything ready."

Three months later, Coltrane stepped into a recording studio to shape the results of his meditations into an album layered with music and meaning, like nothing he had ever produced. *A Love Supreme* was the title he had already chosen for his ambitious project.

■ *A Love Supreme* is the four-part jazz suite John Coltrane recorded over the course of one evening with pianist McCoy Tyner, bassist Jimmy Garrison, and drummer Elvin Jones. It caught Coltrane at a pivotal point in his creative trajectory: the crystallizing of his three years with this renowned quartet, moments before his turn toward the final, most debated phase of his career.

After hitting retail shelves and radio airwaves in February 1965, less than two months after its recording, *A Love Supreme* became a best-seller in jazz circles, and was heard in college dorms and ghetto apartments, on Harlem and Haight-Ashbury street corners: a unifying album boosted by good timing. "*A Love Supreme* reached out and influenced those people who were into peace," recalled Miles Davis. "Hippies and people like that."

Arriving at the midpoint of the sixties, *A Love Supreme* distilled the decade's theme of universal love and spiritual consciousness. "In the 1960s, we were in the age of Eastern religions, new spirituality and Hare Krishna, and that was Trane's matrix—he fit right in," remarks saxophonist Archie Shepp.

Yet *A Love Supreme* has never become dated, and through changing decades, from blue-skied optimism to jaded acerbity, the relevance of the music and its message has remained constant. "I know there are so many people who do not even want to hear music from five, ten years ago," comments Alice Coltrane. "But *A Love Supreme* has its own renewing spirit . . . it's timeless, ageless."

Today it keeps rarefied company as one of a very few jazz recordings adhered to by a cross-generational mix of rockers and ragers, hip-hoppers and headbangers. "*A Love Supreme* is probably one of the most beautiful and sublime recordings of the twentieth century," announced techno deejay Moby on a recent televised rock awards show. At the 2001 Grammy Awards Carlos Santana and Joni Mitchell jointly declared Coltrane's album Record of the Year (and then opened the envelope and awarded rock group U2).

Elements of the album—from the cover photograph of the pensive saxophonist to its distinctive mantralike bass line—regularly pop up in movies, magazines, and other musical recordings. Coltrane's resonant chanting of the album's title—the first time he allowed his voice to be heard on any recording—is its most-remembered, oft-quoted trademark. The very title, with its poetic inversion, is ingrained in our collective phraseology; publicists freely borrow it to signify a passion of perfection—spiritual, sensual, or product-selling.

Coltrane created *A Love Supreme* as a gift to the Divine. Years before rock stars honored their respective gurus on their albums, decades before hip-hop CDs listed the now obligatory shout-out to the Almighty, Coltrane unabashedly dedicated the recording, in his own words, as "a humble offering to Him."

Coltrane's two-part liner notes on the album—a "Dear Listener" letter and a poem addressed to God—are the sole examples of his own writing gracing an album. His words effected a public disrobing, an open admission of divine devotion. Many listeners of the day, more attuned to the cool, guarded aesthetic of the jazz scene, found the album's unblinking message of reawakened spirituality uncommonly discomfiting.

Resonating above all other elements is the impassioned sound of *A Love Supreme:* a cohesive balance of composition and improvisation, of form and energy, like no other title in Coltrane's collected works. It constructed, broke down, and re-erected a series of deceptively simple, minor-key blues structures. The melodies—briefly expressed but memorable—opened doors through which the quartet rode a roller coaster of precisely timed dynamics. The interplay of their distinctive styles was a powerful one: Tyner's tension-inducing chords; Jones's ecstatic drumming; Garrison's flowing bass lines. Coltrane's own tireless solos spiraled from meditative whispers to fierce, half-choked cries with the practiced rhythm of a Sunday preacher.

A Love Supreme blended it all into a mix that exposed the quartet's roots and influences: The propulsive, elevating effect of African polyrhythms. The lugubrious tempos of modal jazz. The wistful keening of Far Eastern folk music. The urgency of free jazz. The agitation of bebop. The familiar feel of the blues. The orgasmic release of gospel.

The jazzerati of the day never settled on a term for Coltrane's sonic menagerie; "spiritual jazz" is still the best they can muster. But like the most singular of artistic gestures—on canvas, paper, or vinyl—any category limits rather than delineates, and seems far too specific. "*A Love Supreme* wasn't a jazz record," maintains Ravi Coltrane, John's son. "They were just trying to make a musical statement."

"Music," Elvin Jones states. "That's what I call it."

■ "Music shouldn't be easy to understand," claimed John Coltrane in 1963. By that point, he was intimately accustomed to both acclaim and derision.

Controversy had become a familiar companion through a career of numerous recordings as leader and as sideman. He had learned to rise above his reviews. It was music that determined his path. At the apex of his collaboration with Miles Davis, he added emotive solos to the trumpeter's modal masterpiece *Kind of Blue,* and could have stayed that proven, subdued course. Instead, he took what he needed from the improvisational lessons of that association, experimented further, and forged his own hypnotic, exultant mid-sixties sound.

At first, Coltrane's album and Davis's best-seller may seem akin. But *A Love Supreme* is not *Kind of Blue,* neither in style nor in effect. The former suggests the in-the-moment intensity of live performance; the latter, renowned for its cool burn and Zen-like stillness, seems to draw its energy from a relaxed studio atmosphere.

Kind of Blue is celebrated for the way it so effortlessly slipped (and continues to ease) into the musical consciousness of generations. *A Love Supreme* is not so easy a sell; as a result, its climb to lasting popular stature is all the more impressive. To ears unaccustomed to modern improvised music, it contains too many new sounds and strange, extended structures. Even to the jazz-friendly, the raw emotion of Coltrane's cadences and the explosive barrage of Jones's percussion can initially be off-putting.

Frank Lowe, who filled the tenor sax chair in Alice Coltrane's group of the early seventies, admits it took a while to work on him: "I just remember the cumulative effect it had on me when I realized I had been listening to it." "To be honest, I didn't get any of it on the first listening," guitarist John McLaughlin recalls. "I actually couldn't even understand what he was playing musically, or what he was feeling emotionally."

Carlos Santana was a rock guitarist focused mostly on electric blues when a friend played him the album:

> **The first time I heard *A Love Supreme*, it really was an assault. It could've been from Mars as far as I was concerned, or another galaxy. I remember the album cover and name, but the music didn't fit into the patterns of my brain at that point. It was like someone trying to tell a monkey about spirituality or computers, you know, it just didn't compute.**

Today Lowe, McLaughlin, and Santana all have recorded sections of *A Love Supreme.* They are among the millions who faced the challenge of Coltrane's music, found a way into it, and count themselves among the album's faithful. "You have to come to the music yourself, gradually," Coltrane maintained. "Not everything must be received with open arms."

"We *should* challenge ourselves," Alice Coltrane enthused suddenly, while speaking of her late husband. "It makes us stronger, gives us clearer insight—better perception." If any jazz artist tested that maxim—and his listeners and himself—it was John Coltrane.

■ Today, Coltrane's brittle, vibratoless tone and restless phrasing is one of the most pervasive, recognizable sounds in modern jazz; in other musical vocabularies—R&B, soul, and rock—contemporary saxophonists seem unable to touch their instrument without quoting from his distinctive, vocal-like slurs, shrieks, and rapid-fire runs. The fact that so many of today's tenor saxists double on soprano is solely to Coltrane's credit. To many, his music defined the last great innovative leap in jazz. "It often seems the book was closed on jazz around the time of Coltrane's death," complained one writer recently.

All that furthers Coltrane's canonization—his sound, his legend, his wake of influence—continues to elevate *A Love Supreme.* The album is to Coltrane what a speech on the Washington Mall was to Martin Luther King Jr., what a mountaintop sermon was to Jesus Christ.

It's difficult to write of Coltrane and not sound heavy-handed. As enticing as the inevitable Trane/train metaphors may be, so are the Christ-like parallels. The saxophonist's life of self-sacrifice, message of universal love, death at an early age—even his initials—amplify the temptation.

Many who came in direct contact with Coltrane rely on the language of religion to express their feelings for the man and the album. "John Coltrane: John the Baptist, John the spiritualist, John the creator," remarks trombonist Curtis Fuller. "John was all of those things, the all-seeing eye, the Pied Piper. In *A Love Supreme* each one of those Johns showed up." Insists bassist Reggie Workman, "You will get the message [of *A Love Supreme*], if you're ready for it, as Hindu philosophy teaches us. If you're not ready for it, you've got to go back and prepare and come that way again. OK?"

"In your spirituality, you have the gurus who start you with a mantra initiation," notes Alice Coltrane, equating the giving of *A Love Supreme* with such an induction, and her husband as a spiritual guide:

The guru has given us a good and great work. Then he could say, "I don't really wish that you consider that this is going to serve the full purpose of your spiritual goal." Now John's gone on to other lands or

plateaus and still there are going to be higher tests, higher trials that we have to face. We require something that we can hold on to, that serves to build strength up for the next step in our journey. That is *A Love Supreme.*

Some have even come to worship the man and the album on a weekly, institutionalized basis. Every Sunday, San Francisco's St. John Coltrane African Orthodox Church draws an unusually mixed congregation, local regulars and young, T-shirted visitors, to praise God, behold Coltrane as a saint, and play and sing along to the music of *A Love Supreme.*

The irony of course is that a man who distrusted the idea of one single religious path—"When I saw there were so many religions, [one] kind of opposed to the next . . . I just couldn't believe that one guy could be right, and . . . somebody else has to be wrong"—left behind what has become a blueprint for organized ritual. "I don't really know what a listener feels when he hears music," Coltrane commented in 1961. Less than a year before his death, he emphasized, "I believe in all religions."

Writing on any music is a challenge: so much comes down to subjectivity, to personal reaction. When the subject is Coltrane, the bar is raised higher. He forced commentators to invent terminology to describe groundbreaking techniques and style. "Sheets of sound," one critic wrote of his sonic flurries in 1958. "Anti-jazz," wrote another a few years later.

A Love Supreme takes the bar and launches it skyward. The album's undeniable spirituality—another area of study that strains available vocabulary—opens the door to a realm where examination of specific details risks seeming desultory, where discussion of the spiritual might become a routine, insincere effort. Yet as I listened to the album again and again, I felt impelled to address Coltrane's impassioned spirituality. Though I consider • myself a dedicated agnostic and diehard rationalist, I am ready to admit that there is much that can seem the handiwork of some eternal force under spiritual direction: the seasons, gravity, mathematics, romantic love. "God breathes through us so completely," Coltrane wrote on *A Love Supreme,* "so gently we hardly feel it."

With a qualifying "if," I am one with Coltrane's sentiment. And I don't think I could put it any better than he did. I've therefore opted to curb the lion's share of my commentary to the how, why, where, and when of the album, to leave explanations that speak of religious import and transcendent power to the words of Coltrane and others, and to grant airtime to those who—while appreciative of the album's deep spirituality—prefer man, music, and album on a more immediate plane. Like Nat Hentoff:

> By the time *A Love Supreme* hit, Trane struck such a spiritual chord in so many listeners that people started to think of him as being beyond human. I think that's unfair. He was just a human being like you and me—but he was willing to practice more, to do all the things that somebody has to do to excel. The real value in what John Coltrane did was that what he accomplished, he did as a human.

■ *A Love Supreme* has never been the subject of intense focus, despite its entrenched reputation. A few Coltrane biographies of varying depth and description cover it in passing; Lewis Porter devotes a chapter to a strict musical analysis of it in *John Coltrane: His Life and Music*. But the album remains unstudied territory on many levels. From the outset, my marching orders were clear: pursue fresh research, rethink old perspectives, raise new questions.

As a subject of research, *A Love Supreme* not only bore book-length scrutiny but proved a writer's dream, branching into stories of historical and personal import, and unfolding myriad anecdotes.

With perseverance and luck, I uncovered rare items that added depth and context to my understanding of the album: A tape reel preserving Coltrane's only full public performance of *A Love Supreme.* A requisition form revealing musician payments for December 9, 1964. A handwritten poem that formed the structure of "Psalm." A smiling photograph of Coltrane relaxing at home with his newborn first son.

I was fortunate that three of the six original participants in the recording of *A Love Supreme* were still alive and generously gave their memories and insight—drummer Elvin Jones, pianist McCoy Tyner, and engineer Rudy Van Gelder. I also tracked down three who were involved with the more mysterious, second day of recording, and were equally willing to share their stories—bassist Art Davis, saxophonist Archie Shepp, and photographer Chuck Stewart.

Other conversations helped map the matrix of its influence: from generation to generation, as veteran pianist and former Coltrane sideman Tommy Flanagan opined: "I highly recommend it—it really has more to say than any of his other recorded music, as a statement, a collective." From musician to musician, as saxophonist Branford Marsalis remembers: "This trombone player I was playing with in Clark Terry's big band—Conrad Herwig—was the first cat I heard talk about *A Love Supreme.* I heard that and told Wynton to go out and get this shit." From father to son, as Zane Massey—progeny of Calvin, one of Coltrane's oldest jazz-making buddies from Philadelphia—relates.

> **I was just beginning to play saxophone, so we used to get together early in the evening before dinner for my daily lesson, doing long tones. I remember him playing *A Love Supreme* and explaining: "John isn't just playing anything. These are very thought-out ideas that he worked on for a long time." At the time I didn't really understand, but now I do.**

Testimonials from unlikely sources formed a capstone of the album's legacy. REM guitarist Peter Buck credits a high school teacher for turning him on to "a blast from another planet for me . . . There are lots of pictures of America in that thing, without [Coltrane] making any kind of conscious political statement." Proto-rapper and protest singer Gil Scott-Heron recalls, "it was 1968, I was nineteen years old [and] some of the guys I hung with at college played jazz every night in their room . . . one night [they] played *A Love Supreme.* Its impact on me was immediate."

U2's lead singer, Bono, offered a personal story that reached for a contemporary explanation of Coltrane's—and the album's—universal appeal:

> **I was at the top of the Grand Hotel in Chicago [on tour in 1987] listening to *A Love Supreme* and learning the lesson of a lifetime. Earlier I had been watching televangelists remake God in their own image: tiny, petty, and greedy. Religion has become the enemy of God, I was thinking . . . religion was what happened when God, like Elvis, has left the building. I knew from my earliest memories that the world was winding in a direction away from love and I too was caught in its drag. There is so much wickedness in this world but beauty is our consolation prize . . . the beauty of John Coltrane's reedy voice, its whispers, its knowingness, its sly sexuality, its praise of creation. And so Coltrane began to make sense to me. I left the music on repeat and I stayed awake listening to a man facing God with the gift of his music.**

I myself vividly remember a scene in Cincinnati, 1976. A record store clerk insisted I part with an additional $2.25 and add a used copy of *A Love Supreme* to my rock selections (I recall Mott the Hoople's *All the Young Dudes* in the same bag). I acquiesced, listened to it once, and then let it sit unplayed for close to three years. In college, I returned to it. Before I graduated, it was my favorite Sunday morning album.

In the years since, I have returned to it now and again, each listen an event unto itself, knowing that it asks for both time and uninterrupted attention: an old, spirit-stilling friend with a familiar story to tell. I have mentioned it or passed copies to companions and friends.

Ravi Shankar, whose deeply spiritual music profoundly influenced Coltrane, was the most recent recipient. When I asked to speak with him for this book, he informed me that he was unfamiliar with *A Love Supreme*. I knew that the last time he met with Coltrane in late 1964, he had asked the saxophonist, "Why is it that I hear this terrible inner turmoil in those shrieks? It really disturbed me." A few days after overnighting the CD, I heard back:

A $2.25 investment

> **I have been so moved by this record. I have heard it already three or four times, and played it for musicians who are with me now. It's beautiful, especially the climax in the third movement, then the resolution of the whole last piece ["Psalm"]. Then, reading the sleeve notes, I was so surprised by his total surrendering and believing and his love for God. I thank you so much for sending me this.**

When he passed away in July 1967, Coltrane had been planning to travel to Los Angeles to study with Shankar. I only wish it could have been Coltrane himself who first placed *A Love Supreme* before the master sitarist, and heard his reaction.

■ As I packed my equipment to drive off from my Woodland Hills meeting, Alice Coltrane stopped me. "The only thing I ask—I would just like to see an honesty in what you try to convey." I can think of no other way.

A Love Supreme

Live at L'Olympia, March 21,
1960: Coltrane in mid-flight . . .

Q: [Did Miles Davis have] a major stranglehold on you, or you got a chance to play like you do? **Coltrane:** Well, I've been free here [to do] almost anything that I want to try. I have the freedom to do it, so the freedom has helped me. **Q:** I heard you were splitting [from] the Miles group here, and trying something on your own. **Coltrane:** Yeah, I am.

—STOCKHOLM, SWEDEN, 1960

Miles Ahead, Miles Behind

March 21, 1960: John Coltrane stood, irritable, jet-lagged, still in his sideman role with Miles Davis, waiting to go onstage at L'Olympia music hall in Paris. It was the first night of a monthlong tour through Europe arranged by jazz impresario Norman Granz. It was also to be his premiere performance before a European audience, but Coltrane, customarily calm and even-keeled, was not in a good mood.

Drummer Jimmy Cobb, then nearing two years with the Davis group, remembers:

> **It seemed like it was a last-minute kind of a situation, because Coltrane [came to Europe] with the one blue suit he wore, a white shirt, one other white shirt, an airline bag, and some rum-flavored Life Savers that he liked. That's all he had. Miles probably talked him into doing it for the last time.**

In fact, on the phone Davis had grown insistent. Coltrane had only reluctantly agreed to remain with the group that had lifted him from obscurity five years before. But doing so required that he put his own plans on hold; he canceled a series of late-March dates as leader in New York's Five Spot

. . . Coltrane, Kelly, and Cobb . . .

nightclub. "He grumbled and complained and sat by himself all the time we were over there," the trumpeter still recalled years later.

Davis might have been dismayed by his star saxophonist's lack of enthusiasm, but he was not surprised. Coltrane's foot had been pointed toward the door for well over a year. His desire to leave the Davis group had even made headlines the summer before. While on tour out West, Miles had opened the *Oakland Tribune* to read an interview in which Coltrane spoke of his imminent departure. The trumpeter had, typically, exploded. "This made me real mad . . . I told him I treated him like my brother and here he was doing this kind of shit to me and telling a white boy all about my business."

Since joining Miles in 1955, Coltrane had grown accustomed to patiently dealing with Davis's short temper and his long, frosty stare. The two had developed a relationship that accommodated their respective quirks and habits, respecting personality differences rather than succumbing to conflict. "As much as I liked Trane we didn't hang out much once we left the bandstand because we had different styles," Miles later wrote. "[He] didn't hardly ever hang out, he would go back to his hotel room to practice . . . it was almost like he was on a mission."

For Coltrane, it had always been about the music, whatever the abuse or personal slights he endured. Normally, that was just water off his back. But now his frustration was mounting. Davis, in trying to placate his restless sideman, had only intensified the situation with a push-pull plan that deferred the inevitable:

> **It was hard for [Coltrane] to bring up that he wanted to leave . . . but he did bring it up finally and we made a compromise: I turned him on to [my manager] Harold Lovett . . . to handle his financial affairs. And then Harold got him a recording contract [and] set up a publishing company for Trane . . . To keep Trane in the band longer, I asked Jack Whittemore, my agent, to get bookings for Trane's group whenever we weren't playing, and he did.**

. . . Miles and Trane

Despite his assistance, Davis did not hesitate to pull on the apron strings one last time that March. For Miles it was the final tour he would enjoy with Coltrane by his side. For Coltrane, that evening in Paris served to introduce him to an audience that took their music very seriously: French jazz fans.

Miles chose a familiar songlist— "'Round Midnight," "So What," "Green Dolphin Street"—meant to satisfy fans both new and diehard. When the quintet—Miles, Coltrane, drummer Cobb, bassist Paul Chambers, and pianist Wynton Kelly—walked onstage, the welcome was enthusiastic and expectant.

Coltrane was mid-solo on the first number, "All of You," when the whistling and catcalls began. He was alone

JEAN-PIERRE LELOIR

3

with the rhythm section, Davis having soloed first and then left the stage. A breathless flurry cascaded forth. Coltrane built up steam, leaping between registers, finding sounds that tested ears attuned to more mellow tones. Frank Tenot, the legendary Parisian impresario who produced the 1949 festival that first brought Miles to France, recalls the evening with a smile:

> **I remember very well this show—it was Oscar Peterson, Stan Getz, and the second part of the evening was Miles Davis, all on the same night. I was on the left side in the audience, near the doorway to the backstage. I had to go see what was happening with the recording of the concert, to hear the sound. When John was playing, Miles would go backstage, you see. He didn't stay on the stage. And John was alone, and the people was very surprised why there was no John Coltrane like on _Kind of Blue_ and the session before with Miles [_Milestones_], and for Coltrane, it was a new step. So, part of the audience thinks that Coltrane doesn't play well, that he was playing the wrong notes involuntary. Too much drugs or alcohol or something like this. So they started to whistle.**

On the recording made that evening, one can easily hear the crowd growing restless during the saxophonist's solos; whistling and arguments erupt as Coltrane's improvisations continue. Tenot points out that Miles's modal masterwork _Kind of Blue_ had only just been released in France. It had entranced the French with its relaxed, late-night tempos; on it, Coltrane's solos fit hand in glove with the subdued lyricism of the rest of the band. But that night, each tune came off as if it was being played by three different bands, depending on the soloist of the moment: Miles, Coltrane, or Kelly.

For the first time, most Parisians were witnessing the raw, boundless intensity that would guide the rest of Coltrane's career; what had been a tentative, experimental breeze when he first upped with Miles was becoming a full-force gale. The trumpeter's modal experiments had proved the launching pad that propelled the saxophonist to another musical plane. If that was not clear from the audience's perspective, onstage it was impossible to miss. "That's the way he played every night, you know?" notes Cobb. "By that time he was through playing Miles's stuff. He had outgrown everybody's band except his own."

Parisian propensity for vocal dissatisfaction notwithstanding, Tenot is quick to add that "the audience was completely with him when he returned

JEAN-PIERRE LELOIR

Coltrane and Frank Tenot,
November 18, 1961

[to France in 1961], the year of 'My Favorite Things.' He had a big success."

But in 1960, Coltrane's live sound was still testing French waters. Following Miles's habitual set-closer, "The Theme," Tenot rushed backstage:

> **So after the show, I said to John, "You're too new for the people, they don't hear much [of what] they liked in the past. You go too far." And he had always a little smile on the face. He said, "I don't go far enough."**

"For all their theoretical sense of freedom, jazz musicians have a tendency to be surprisingly hidebound," wrote *New York Times* critic John S. Wilson in 1967. "As a rule, they find their mode of expression early in their careers. After that . . . basically the adventure is over." A "strong and influential" exception to the rule, Wilson quickly noted, was Coltrane's "process of constant development."

In 1960 Coltrane was thirty-three, an age when most of his contemporaries sought career stability. Yet his most adventurous work—including the creative apogee of *A Love Supreme*—was still to come. To better understand the course ahead, it is best to turn back and measure the path he had made for himself.

■ John Coltrane was born in 1926—the same year as Miles Davis—in the small North Carolina town of Hamlet. His family moved soon after, and Coltrane grew up in the larger High Point, surrounded by relatives, though an only child himself. His cousin Mary Lyerly—for whom he would compose the tune "Cousin Mary," and who now goes by her married name, Alexander—was the one family member close to his age, and they became constant companions.

Coltrane was a sensitive child with a quiet air of curiosity about him. Neither well-off nor poor—his father was a tailor, his mother a domestic and a seamstress—he was exposed to a rich mix of education, religion, and music from a young age. His mother, Alice, had attended college, and sang and played piano; his father, John, dabbled on various stringed instruments. Both parents were the children of Methodist ministers. Besides the parlor music his parents would play, the sounds of Coltrane's youth blended the hymns he sang in church, country blues from street musicians, swing numbers played by the touring orchestras that blew through town, and the jazz-inflected pop tunes heard on the radio at home.

But it was his father's musical habits that most influenced the youngster, as Mary recalls:

> **His father played violin and guitar in his room . . . I don't think I ever saw him outside the room, but he was always playing—as soon as he came home, before dinner he would relax. The same thing that John did in later years practicing . . . the very same thing. John's mother played piano, but I think he got a lot of that music from his father.**

Coltrane's musical awakening coincided with his first steps along a strict religious path. As the scion of two lines of preachers, the boy seemed to have little choice. But there was another reason. As he told it, his mother's father, the Reverend William Blair, held the most sway over the family:

> **In my early years, we went to church every Sunday and stuff like that. We were under the influence of my grandfather, he was the dominant cat in the family. He was most well-versed, active politically . . . pretty militant . . . I grew up in that [and] I guess I just accepted it.**

By all reports, Blair was a hard man to resist. As a community leader, he was persuasive and outspoken; as a preacher, he was more an academician than a pulpit-pounder. In fact, as Mary recollects, he was responsible for his grandchildren's education, and that of many other children as well:

> **My grandfather was instrumental in opening one of the first black schools in High Point where we were raised—the elementary school that we attended. He always fought for us. Christmas time we always got books . . . we had Langston Hughes, Paul Laurence Dunbar, [all] sorts of black books.**

The reverend's influence on the impressionable Coltrane was to last a lifetime.

"He used to buy books and then he'd let me have them," recalls saxophonist Pharoah Sanders of his mid-sixties stint with Coltrane's group. "They weren't about any one specific religion, but there were a whole lot of books around." "I remember him reading the Bhagavad Gita, or the Torah," echoes trombonist Curtis Fuller. "He'd say, 'Hey, Curtis, check this out.' Or the autobiography of guru Yogananda."

By the time Coltrane entered high school, he was familiar with the pervasive racism of American society. He had to look no further than the torn schoolbooks he used or ratty football uniforms he wore—hand-me-downs from nearby white schools—to remind him of his secondary status. "Those things John didn't like at all," his cousin noted, "that just got to him." Though proud of his family, he came to associate such separate-but-equal indignities with the small-town South, and after reaching adulthood, he would never return to High Point.

In 1939, when his school formed a band, he found himself with a clarinet in hand, learning the fundamentals and playing simple marches. In short order—as his ears grew attuned to swing-era hits like "Tuxedo Junction" and swing-era heroes like Count Basie's smooth-toned saxophone soloist Lester Young—Coltrane was hooked. He dropped the clarinet, took up the alto saxophone, and a lifetime of practicing began. "He kept that saxophone with him," recalled a classmate. "You could hear him all the time, from any other part of the [school] building, back in the music room practicing by himself."

Music—or more accurately, music-making—arrived at a turbulent time in Coltrane's life. A few months after picking up the saxophone, while he was still a young thirteen years of age, his father, maternal grandparents, and uncle (Cousin Mary's father) all passed away. The foundations of the Coltrane-Blair clan collapsed; emotionally and economically, his world changed forever. Before 1940 ended, with no adult men to support the family, his mother had to fill newly empty rooms with boarders, and she and her sister took on extra jobs. Coltrane became withdrawn; his school performance suffered drastically.

Instead, he turned to music for company, solace, and strength. What had been an enthusiasm became a means of survival; his saxophone, a spiritual lifeline. "The loss of his father at the beginning of his teen years was critical," notes biographer Lewis Porter. "In a sense, music became his father substitute." A high school friend summed it up: "for a while, I don't think he had anything but that horn."

As tragedy and grief forced his thoughts inward, Coltrane remained true to his probing nature and sought answers where others relied solely on faith. Over the next few years, as he matured physically and intellectually, he began to pull at the proverbial loose thread, unraveling all he had been taught.

"In my late teens, I started breaking away, you know, I was growing up and so I questioned what I thought about everything . . . I can tell you, it started with religion . . . the first questions of religion, that brought on everything." Coltrane began to structure his world, to interrelate aspects of his life—family, friends, and God; church, school, and now music—in a way that would satisfy his restless curiosity and nurture his growing sense of self. Out of the fire of family crisis rose a personal philosophy.

Whether it is labeled as sacred versus profane, gospel versus blues, God's work versus the devil's music, the classic (and still pervasive) African-American paradigm that holds church matters and popular culture in diametric opposition, that separates true spirituality from such music as jazz, held no sway in Coltrane's self-erected system. How could it, when he had found salvation through a saxophone? With the clarity of youth, he divined a common source—and common goal—to both pursuits.

In 1958, Coltrane described his unifying precept:

I think that the majority of musicians are interested in truth. They've got to be, because saying a musical thing is a truth. If you play a musical statement and if it's a valid statement, that's a truth right there in itself, you know. If you play something phony, well, you know that's something phony [laughs]. All musicians are striving for as near certain perfection they can get, and that's truth there, you know. So, in order to play those kinds of things, to play truths, you've got to live as much truth as you possibly can . . . and if a guy is religious and if he's searching for good and he wants to live a good life—[he] might call himself religious or he might not.

By adolescence, Coltrane had laid the foundation of a philosophy that would guide his life's work: playing right meant, and required, living right. Whether churchgoing or not, a dedicated musician could achieve the same level of spirituality as any other pious soul. At times Coltrane would lose sight of his guiding principle (as he later confessed in the liner notes to *A Love Supreme*); nonetheless, it would help steer his career during the long years of obscurity and gig-by-gig hardships.

■ Coltrane graduated high school in 1943 and immediately departed High Point to join his mother Alice, aunt Bettie, and cousin Mary in Philadelphia, where they had moved a year previously to pursue more promising wartime opportunities. He hopped between various jobs and residences before finally settling into a position at the local Campbell Soup factory and an apartment with his family. His mother, who worked as domestic during the week and only saw her son on the weekends, introduced him to the storefront church around the corner and marked his urgent need to continue his music. While in North Carolina, Coltrane had practiced and performed on school instruments; noting he had arrived with little beyond his clothes, his mother scrounged a few dollars and bought him a used alto.

For a young African-American man arriving from the rural South in 1944, Philadelphia offered a thriving black urban community, one of the largest of its day, a hotbed of activity and opportunity. There were jobs aplenty generated by the war effort and countless bars in which to spend one's paycheck. Theaters presented locally and nationally known entertainers.

With World War II drawing to a close, a variety of old and new sounds swirled about, offering excitement and inspiration to a young musician just starting out. Swing was developing a harder blues-based edge; bandleaders like Lionel Hampton and Louis Jordan were forging a hybrid that would become the soundtrack of black America in the fifties: rhythm and blues, or simply R&B.

Meanwhile, summits of musical sophistication were being scaled by alto saxophonist Charlie Parker and trumpeter Dizzy Gillespie, two alumni of singer Billy Eckstine's popular big band. "Bird" and "Diz" bent rhythmic convention with their jaw-dropping technique, daringly maneuvering through old song structures to create hip new melodies. Critics labeled this new music "bebop": frenetic, unpredictable, and demanding close attention rather than politely fading into the background like other popular musical styles.

Bebop would help usher jazz into small nightclubs and away from its more profitable role as the chosen social music of America, and many musicians were drawn to it. "A big break with the dancing tradition of jazz came in the forties with Diz and Bird," recalled Coltrane. "You got broken rhythms, complicated harmonic devices. There [was] so much beauty . . . in this music." To young black musicians it also carried an important social implication: the fathers of bebop, and almost all its practitioners, were "brothers." For the moment at least, it was *their* music.

Coltrane was mesmerized by it all. He had grown to idolize Johnny Hodges, the alto-playing star of Duke Ellington's orchestra. He modeled his sound on Hodges's, looking at photographs of the saxophonist, then studying himself in the mirror to ensure he held his instrument like "Rabbit." ("The confidence with which Rabbit plays! I wish I could play with the confidence he does," admitted Coltrane.) He also channeled a wider range of styles: to his love of Hodges and Lester Young, he added an affinity for Parker and the mellower tenor sound of a new arrival from the West Coast, Dexter Gordon.

Coltrane's eventual decision to become a professional musician seemed not so much a matter of choice as a fait accompli. His work ethic chimed with the growing demands of the music: he could be found woodshedding continuously, working on his technique. He took classes at the Ornstein School, a local music institute. After a year in the Naval Reserve that began in August 1945 and stationed him in Honolulu, he was inspired to use his GI benefits to pay for more advanced lessons at Philadelphia's Granoff Studios, where Dennis Sandole taught harmony and other subjects. "He would have achieved his objective with me or without me. I just sort of accelerated his progress," Sandole recalls of Coltrane's early determination, pronouncing him a "perfect student . . . in the conservatory he'd walk around with the horn all day long, playing."

Coltrane immediately became an anonymous journeyman, a role that would last a full nine years, from late 1946 to 1955. He lived in a tight community of like-minded jazzmen who shared his passions: saxophonists Jimmy Heath, Bill Barron, Jimmy Oliver, Jimmy Stewart, and Benny Golson; trumpeters Johnnie Splawn, Johnny Coles, and Calvin Massey; pianist Red Garland; bassist Percy Heath; drummers "Philly" Joe Jones and Charles "Specs" Wright.

"We were like second-string beboppers," commented Jimmy Heath. Heath spoke of the group's "camaraderie," recalling that it "was very important to the musicians to get together and have jam sessions . . . at the Heath house and Johnny Coles' residence . . . to learn this new language that had come about."

Together they formed a brotherhood that, in effect, became Coltrane's surrogate family; it was a circle with which Coltrane never lost contact, and to which he frequently returned for assistance and inspiration.

The intensity of Coltrane's musical focus initially set him apart from his colleagues. "Wherein some people would lay back on what they had already learned to play," Jimmy Heath commented, "if there was a specific problem that bothered him Coltrane would zoom in on that problem until he solved it":

Heath and Coltrane became especially close, visiting the "Philadelphia Library together [to] listen to Stravinsky and Western classical music . . . We weren't trying to play the scores per se. We were extracting the cadenzas and turning them around to fit our own groove." Heath formed a short-lived big band with Coltrane as one of his chosen soloists, and recalled certain untutored qualities in his colleague's sound at the time:

> **When Coltrane played in my band and took solos, he didn't know all the changes, but there was one thing that was noticeable to me— regardless of the tempo, his rhythm would always be good . . . his rhythm was similar to Parker and the bebop style, but wasn't playing Parker's clichés. He had that eruptive feeling that Parker had—of exploding into chords . . . he had that before he really learned all the right notes to play.**

While "avoiding clichés" would be a simple but accurate description of Coltrane's mature sound, Heath's observation reveals that Coltrane already was concerned with moving away from entrenched jazz habits, such as soloists' proclivity for quoting—with smooth sophistication or a sly wink— recognizable melodies or other well-known patterns.

The late forties found Coltrane balancing a dedication to the craft of jazz while taking on work playing the more popular R&B hits of the day. In some informal contexts—pickup gigs with jazz brethren in local watering holes like the Elate Ballroom, the Caravan Republican Club, and, not far from his apartment, the Woodbine Club—the freedom to blend the two styles occurred naturally. But in other cases, such as well-advertised dance shows with the city's more successful groups, the genres were segregated by the demands of the audience. "One had to earn a living and one would play whatever was necessary," Heath pointed out, noting that Coltrane soon discovered the value of low-end honking, bar-walking, and other R&B trappings of the day:

> **Trane worked in some of those kinds of bands to get out on the road and make some money. You know, when you're working those kind of bands and when the most famous saxophonists were Arnett Cobb and Illinois Jacquet and they do a little hooting and booting, so you learn how to do a little bit of that to satisfy the public.**

Philadelphia's legions of musicians proved a veritable farm team for traveling R&B bandleaders. Coltrane was recruited for the first time in 1947, leading him to join a colorful string of road bands over the next five years:

> **[What] I usually call my first professional job was a band from Indianapolis led by Joe Webb. This was in '47. Big Maybelle was in this band, you know, the blues singer . . . I don't know what the heck we were—rhythm & blues or everything [laughs].**

Writer Joe Goldberg translated this phase of Coltrane's career for his mostly white readership in 1965:

> **Coltrane's early experience, which for the most part could be dismissed superficially as local rhythm-and-blues work, all points in one direction . . . this music has been given different names [but] it is simply Negro popular music; the equivalent, in a sense, of Lawrence Welk, Les Brown or Doris Day.**

What was "simply popular music" to Goldberg was no less than the bluesy, fertile loam from which Coltrane's personal style would develop, according to many of today's leading jazz musicians. "The blues, black clubs, R&B—that is where Coltrane comes from," stresses saxophonist Dave Liebman. "The thing about Coltrane's later Impulse work is, if you do not have a very good understanding of the blues, you cannot play those pieces," asserts Branford Marsalis. "And I don't mean the twelve-bar blues, I mean the representation of what the blues is, all of this stuff that goes into growing up and living in a black neighborhood." "Anything blues is good," saxophonist David Murray echoes. "The better a blues player you are, the better a jazz musician you're going to be. It's not a racial point, it's about the experience."

It was an education that served Coltrane through the rest of his career and informed his music as well. He mastered the art of accompanying vocalists. He learned to juggle his time on the road with a life at home. He developed an innate vocabulary of horn arrangements, blues riffs, and effects that would—decades hence—seem revolutionary, as music journalist Robert Palmer wrote:

> **A lot that was perceived as new when . . . Coltrane did it in a new context—overblowing the horn to get a distorted tone, biting down on the reed in order to produce shrill squeals, playing lengthy solos that grew hotter and hotter until until they verged on hysteria—came directly from the R&B saxophone tradition.**

While playing with saxophonist Eddie "Cleanhead" Vinson, Coltrane had shifted to the instrument that became his mainstay: tenor saxophone. Coltrane had already been dabbling on the deeper, more resonant brother to the alto when, as Benny Golson recounted to Lewis Porter, an errant tenor player during the Philadelphia audition gave Coltrane the chance to prove his mettle on the bigger horn:

> **They played a song that had this tenor solo in it, so Eddie told John, "Pick up the tenor, play the tenor solo." John was a little hesitant about it, and Eddie insisted, "Pick up the horn!" He picked it up and he sounded like Dexter Gordon . . . it sounded so good it was grooving.**

He was stretching his musical horizons. "Before I switched from alto . . . it had been strictly a Bird thing for me," Coltrane admitted. "When I bought a tenor to go with Eddie Vinson's band, a wider area of listening opened up for me." As he had earlier with Lester Young's lyrical simplicity and Charlie Parker's harmonic dexterity, he began to interpret elements of his newer idols on his tenor. His later spectacular scalar runs owed much to what he began to extract from such challenging, aggressive players as tenor saxist

Coltrane during his brief tenure
with Dizzy Gillespie, 1951

Coleman Hawkins ("I was fascinated by his arpeggios") and fleet-fingered pianist Art Tatum ("One night I happened to run into him in Cleveland . . . I've never heard so much music").

Coltrane listened, studied, and grew. As the decade drew to a close, as both his abilities and the division between popular music and bebop-based jazz increased, he felt more and more stretched between the poles of art and commerce. He yearned to stretch his creative wings, to play with—and learn from—his betters.

In September 1949, through the efforts of Jimmy Heath, Coltrane's fortunes seemed to change. A week shy of his twenty-third birthday, he was drafted, along with Heath, into Dizzy Gillespie's big band. Together, the two young players had achieved one of the highest honors and most sought-after opportunities in music of the day: playing with one of the masters of modern jazz, with the promise of steady pay, critical attention, and musical challenges.

For Coltrane, the forties ended with a high-flying gig and—sadly and fatefully—a growing narcotics habit. Like many who followed in the footsteps of Charlie Parker, he had joined the brotherhood of users. First snorting, then shooting heroin, he found it softened the pressures of traveling, dulled the toothaches resulting from his appetite for candy and other sweets, and even seemed to improve his ability to concentrate on his music. But, as with so many other gifted jazz artists of his generation, heroin became an addiction that ultimately damaged his health and almost derailed his career. Until he went cold turkey in 1957, Coltrane's substance abuse kept him far from the assured, spiritually oriented goal of his youth.

■ Coltrane played with Dizzy Gillespie for eighteen months, from the end of 1949 through March 1951. The gig proved neither groundbreaking nor an instant career catapult. Coltrane looked upon the experience mostly with disappointment. "There were two frustrations," Porter notes. "He was playing lead alto [saxophone], which meant mostly reading and little improvisation . . . the other thing [was] that Gillespie was trying hard to make his big band economically viable by featuring commercial material." The self-deprecating saxophonist also remained convinced that his musicianship was subpar:

> **What I didn't know with Diz was that what I had to do was really express myself. I was playing clichés and trying to learn tunes that were hip, so I could play with the guys who played with them.**

Despite Coltrane's somewhat harsh self-judgment, Gillespie thought enough of his budding talent to keep him after replacing his large band with a smaller septet that returned Coltrane to the tenor chair. But it was still a temp job; by April 1951, Coltrane returned to Philadelphia. "I stayed in obscurity for a long time," he would later state. "I saw so many guys get themselves fired from a band because they tried to be innovative that I got a little discouraged from trying anything different."

The next three years were, in many respects, a seesaw cycle for Coltrane: from jazz to R&B to jazz; from junk to booze and back to junk. He toured and recorded with Gay Crosse, then found freelance work in Philadelphia. He toured and recorded with R&B sensation Earl Bostic, whom Coltrane praised for his "fabulous technical facilities . . . he showed me a lot of things on my horn," then freelanced back home.

Then I worked with one of my first loves, Johnny Hodges. I really enjoyed that job. I liked every tune in the book. Nothing was superficial. It all had meaning and it all swung.

It was one of his most fulfilling sideman roles to date, his first prolonged exposure to a top-tier jazz traditionalist, one unswayed by the R&B styles of the day. "It was my education to the older generation," he remarked with satisfaction. But again Coltrane's drug habit was found inconsistent with the band's priorities and he was let go.

By the midpoint of the fifties, the winds of cultural change were blowing hard. In black communities, the sound of rhythm and blues seemed less related to jazz than ever. Doo-wop harmony groups like the Orioles and the Cadillacs, piano-led boogie bands like Fats Domino and Little Richard, and blues-infused guitarists like Chuck Berry and Bo Diddley crowded the airwaves and jukeboxes. The R&B crossover to white rock 'n' roll audiences, and the arrival of Elvis Presley, were just around the corner. Big bands—save for a few perennial favorites like Count Basie and Duke Ellington—were becoming musical dinosaurs. Instrumental jazz, as performed by the small, post-bop groups in which Coltrane found himself most often, had always been a somewhat marginal pursuit. With the explosive growth of other genres, it now appeared even more so.

In Philadelphia, a new jazz generation, small but dedicated, was coming up, a fresh pool of talent to maintain the city's reputation as a producer of first-class players: trumpeters Ted Curson and Lee Morgan; saxophonists Odean Pope and Archie Shepp; pianists Ray Bryant, McCoy Tyner, and

Bobby Timmons; organist Jimmy Smith; bassists Jimmy Garrison, Reggie Workman, and Henry Grimes; drummer Albert "Tootie" Heath. To some of them, Coltrane became a model of focus and determination. To others, like Tyner, he filled a more personal role:

> **He was more than just a guy I knew who was great—he was like a big brother to me. I met him when I was seventeen and we both loved music, so we got close real quick. I used to go sit on his mom's porch and we would talk. That's one thing I did like about growing up there, the fact that it was such a great community sort of feeling.**

Had chance and circumstance been different, Coltrane might have remained a relatively large figure in the small pond of Philadelphia. Given his penchant for sharing his craft, he might have found his way to teaching at one of the local music schools. Midway through 1955, Coltrane was twenty-nine and had been off the road for almost a full year. His life seemed to be

With R&B legend Earl Bostic (on alto), 1952

easing into a more stable existence. With the benefits from his GI status, he had helped purchase a house for his mother, Cousin Mary, and himself. He appeared ready to settle down with a woman named Naima Austin (who had changed her name from Juanita when she converted to Islam) and her daughter, Syeeda (née Antonia). He had just agreed to fill the tenor seat in Jimmy Smith's quartet for a week at the small club Spider Kelly's.

Asked a few years later whether he believed in predetermination, Coltrane paused and pondered:

> **I believe you could say you make almost what you want, in a way you do, but *when*, that seems the part that you don't have much to do with . . . You gotta set your course, but when you arrive . . . it doesn't always happen like you planned.**

There was no planning for the life-changing event that came next: a phone call from a drummer friend in New York City.

Weeks after joining Miles: Jazz City, Los Angeles, January 1956 ■ Miles Davis was desperate. He was in the midst of preparing for his first national tour arranged by a high-powered booking agent, and Columbia Records—the most prestigious and financially generous record company around—was looking over his shoulder,

checking on him. "If you can get and keep a group together, I will record that group," George Avakian, Columbia's top jazz man, had promised. To Miles, an alumnus of Charlie Parker's groundbreaking bebop quintet, "group" still meant a rhythm trio plus two horn players, but he still had only one: himself.

The summer of 1955 had been good for the trumpeter. He was clean and strong, six months after kicking a narcotics habit he described as a "four year horror show." His popular comeback had been hailed when, unannounced, he had walked onto the Newport Jazz Festival stage in July and wowed a coterie of America's top critics with a laconic, muted solo on " 'Round Midnight." And he already had the foundation of his dream quintet firmly in place: Texas-born Red Garland on piano, young Paul Chambers from Detroit on bass, and the explosive Philly Joe Jones on drums.

But Sonny Rollins had disappeared. Miles's chosen tenorman—blessed with a free-flowing horn style and dexterous rhythm—had long been threatening to leave town. Rollins, it later turned out, had checked himself into a barred-window facility in Kentucky to kick his own drug addiction. Davis had to find a replacement—and soon.

A number of possibilities topped the list: Julian "Cannonball" Adderley, the new alto sensation from Tampa, was one. Sun Ra's accomplished tenorman John Gilmore was another. But the former had to return to Florida to complete a teaching contract, and the latter simply "didn't fit in," as Miles remembered. "His sound wasn't what I heard for the band." With time running out, he turned to his drummer and recruiting specialist, Philly Joe, who mentioned his home buddy John Coltrane.

Coltrane was not unknown to Davis. As early as 1946, Miles had been impressed by an acetate of an impromptu bebop session recorded during the saxophonist's Naval Reserve tour of duty. They had met a year later, according to Coltrane. His subsequent tenure in Dizzy Gillespie's big band led the two to their first appearance together in New York. In his autobiography, Davis recalled with glee a memorable matchup he orchestrated in 1952. "I used Sonny Rollins and Coltrane on tenors at a gig I had at the Audobon Ballroom . . . Sonny was awesome that night, scared the shit out of Trane."

Coltrane agreed to audition with the group and came to New York. Miles was not expecting much, but the saxophonist surprised him. "I could hear how Trane had gotten a whole lot better than he was on that night Sonny set his ears and ass on fire," Davis recalled.

Miles heard a sound that, though still developing, was singular and uncommon. Almost all tenor players at that point in time blew under the spell of one of two massively influential pioneers: the brash, highly rhythmic Coleman Hawkins, or the breathy, understated Lester Young. Even the much-heralded playing of Dexter Gordon—Coltrane's early model—vacillated between those two stylistic poles. But Coltrane was searching for something original, and that quest had become part of his sound. He repeated phrases as if wringing every possibility out of note combinations. He was determined to avoid predictable melodic lines; instead, unusual flourishes and rhythmic fanfares cut through the structure of the tune.

Despite his positive appraisal of the saxophonist, Miles kept his initial impression to himself. Coltrane, accustomed to a sideman role and an open dialogue with his bandleaders, requested direction ("I just played what the others expected from me," the saxophonist confessed). In his typical manner, Davis left him to his own devices, unnerved that a self-professed jazz player required spoken instruction. "My silence and evil looks probably turned him off," he admitted later, though unapologetic for his behavior:

Trane liked to ask all these motherfucking questions back then about what he should or shouldn't play. Man, fuck that shit; to me he was a professional musician and I have always wanted whoever played with me to find their own place in the music.

Coltrane packed his horn and returned home disgruntled, ready to rejoin Jimmy Smith. But at that point, whether or not the saxophonist was hip or original enough was suddenly less important than Miles's immediate need. "Trane was the only one who knew all the tunes," Miles noted. "I couldn't risk have nobody who didn't know the tunes." He instructed Philly Joe to call Coltrane back.

■ The Miles Davis Quintet was unlike anything Coltrane had experienced. It was neither a jazz outfit offering standard repertoire nor an R&B revue with stock arrangements, but more a traveling workshop, perfecting and developing a group sound. The quintet quickly became a study in contrasts—urbane yet funky, swinging hard but with an effortless, lyrical ease.

Offstage, Coltrane was quiet, self-effacing, Davis cocksure, demanding. But on the bandstand and on record, they reversed roles. Coltrane, with saxophone in hand, became the unbridled, garrulous one. When Davis raised his trumpet, he played the introvert, blowing brief, hushed tones, exuding vulnerability. Miles realized he had found a perfect counterpoint to his own subdued sound. "After we started playing together for awhile," he later revealed, employing his pet term of endearment, "I knew that this guy was a bad motherfucker who was just the voice I needed on tenor to set off my voice."

A gnawing hunger to hone their craft overrode the differences in their personalities. Coltrane solemnly and ceaselessly studied music exercise books; Miles would write out chord sequences on matchbooks, ruminating for hours on one musical puzzle. The pair fell into a student/teacher relationship.

We used to talk a lot about music at rehearsals and on the way to gigs I'd say, "Trane here are some chords but don't play them like they are all the time, you know? Start in the middle sometimes and don't forget you can play them up in thirds. So that means you got 18, 19 different things to play in two bars." He would sit there, eyes wide open, soaking up everything.

One immediate fan who agreed with the Miles's assessment of Coltrane was Bob Weinstock, chief of Prestige Records, Miles's label at the time. He witnessed their interaction during the new quintet's first session:

In November of 1955, Miles brought his quintet into the studio and that's when I first heard Coltrane. Bird had just died a few months earlier, but when I heard Coltrane, even though he played tenor, I couldn't help but think, "Here's the new Bird."

The first windfall of Coltrane's hookup with Miles took place then and there. Reported Weinstock, "I approached him at that session to sign a contract. When he signed, I figured the usual three or four LPs a year." As it turned out, Coltrane would not deem himself ready to record an album under his own name until May 1957, halfway into his three-year contract. But in the next year and a half, he became an integral part of the Prestige family, blowing on an ample number of sessions led by others, including bassist Paul Chambers; pianists Mal Waldron, Elmo Hope, and Tadd Dameron; saxophonists Johnny Griffin, Hank Mobley, Al Cohn, and Zoot Sims; and a rare one-track meeting with the man who had once set his knees knocking: Sonny Rollins.

Coltrane soon became, in the words of pianist Tommy Flanagan, one of the "one-take masters . . . tenor players [like] Sonny [Rollins], Coleman Hawkins or Gene Ammons [who] seemed to know what they were going to do when they walked into a studio."

"Trane's Blues," an overlooked example of Coltrane's compositional talent from the quintet's second recording session for Prestige Records in May of 1956, reveals the side-by-side effect of the group's two horns. Serene and poised, Miles phrases his solo like an offhand chat, playing off the light swing of the tune, pausing, breathing in between the notes. A slight drum roll introduces Coltrane. More textured in tone, he answers Davis, building a rougher, more urgent reply, finding loose, melodic lines to lead him to longer statements that conclude tentatively.

Their contrasting approach was even more pronounced during performances, and less balanced. Often, Coltrane would take three, four, even five times as much time for his improvisations as did Davis. Their own words revealed their respective philosophies: Miles listened to "what I can leave out"; for Coltrane, "it took that long to get it all in."

Coltrane soon jumped from fading anonymity into the spotlight of national jazz attention, a glare that could be as harsh as it was inviting. Many writers puzzled over—and some directly denounced—Coltrane's new, "exposed" style. "As a soloist, Coltrane appears to have the equipment but indulges too often in extended double-time flurries that are notable for their lack of direction," read a typical review of that period. Why were his solos so long? Was he practicing or performing? Was that harsh rasp intentional, or just a loose mouthpiece? Critics wanted what they were familiar with—polish, not process.

Public opinion was just as mixed and extreme as that of the jazz writers. Bassist Art Davis, who would mature into one of Coltrane's musical sparring partners, recalls offering him support the first time he heard the quintet, "because some people couldn't understand [Coltrane] and were hostile. Not everybody, but there were some people talking and booing, even though that was his hometown in Philly":

> **He just played. He paid no attention to it—no reaction. He was playing with Miles in Philadelphia in 1956 at the Showboat Club and I had an experience like I had when I first heard Bird. It seemed like there was a puzzle, and all the pieces just fit in your mind, even though they were not together, you could put them together. That's what I heard with John, everything that he played made sense. He was playing a blues I remember, and I think he played the proverbial "Bye Bye**

Blackbird." I remember he soloed long and it was just beautiful. During the intermission, I went up to him and thanked him. I remember he smiled and said, "Thank you."

Though it would persist throughout his career, Coltrane quickly became inured to negative reception. He came to look upon it philosophically, as proof of connection: any heartfelt response was better than none. Ironically, the toughest critic Coltrane faced in his first year with Miles was himself. "Why Miles picked me, I don't know," he told a British jazz magazine. "Maybe he saw something in my playing he hoped would grow." But of all Coltrane's efforts onstage or in the studio, it was the recordings that made him wince—even years later. "I am quite ashamed of those early records I made with Miles."

Coltrane had joined Miles during the period of Davis's unusual contractual overlap between Prestige and Columbia Records. Between 1955 and '57, the former label stockpiled recordings for current and future release, while the latter had begun work on the trumpeter's debut album for the label, to be shipped when his Prestige contract expired. In just under a year (October '55–September '56), Coltrane participated in sessions that ultimately yielded six albums for Prestige and one for Columbia.

If nothing else, Coltrane became schooled in the ins and outs of recording improvised music, and gained an appreciation of the delicate balance of knowing when to re-record, and when to respect first-take spontaneity. When Columbia released Davis's more meticulously crafted album 'Round About Midnight on March 18, 1957, the power of Coltrane's potential blew straight out of the grooves.

"Coltrane's what you hear on *that* record," stated Cecil Taylor of his first hearing of the disc. An entire wall of resistance—including some fans still hoping for the return of Sonny Rollins—fell away. Coltrane's solos now sparkled with a sense of assurance. His improvisation on the title track earned him unqualified praise; writer Martin Williams hailed it as his "most provocative solo from this period."

But with unfortunate timing, just as the world was given notice of Coltrane's confident arrival, Davis—like Dizzy and Hodges before him—served him his walking papers.

The situation had been building for a while. Coltrane's pernicious drug problem had been getting the better of him. In his autobiography, Miles reported his star saxophonist as showing up at gigs in rumpled clothing, picking his nose distractedly and nodding out onstage, and drinking heavily at the bar when he could not score. Miles initially resisted judgment, knowing personally of the suffering Coltrane was experiencing. "I just tell them if they work for me to regulate their habit," Miles once said. "You can't *talk* a man out of a habit until he really *wants* to stop."

In October 1956, however, Davis exploded at a date at New York's Café Bohemia, berating Coltrane for his slovenly appearance and tardiness. According to Davis, the saxophonist was too much in a stupor to respond with anything but silence. Exasperated, the diminutive trumpeter slapped his taller sideman in the head, and slugged him in the stomach. Coltrane still offered no resistance. A nonplussed Thelonious Monk, who had witnessed the one-sided argument, stepped in and urged the saxophonist to quit and join his band.

A man with higher self-regard might have struck back or at least walked away for good, but Coltrane was an extremely humble, nonviolent individual. And with a young family (he had married Naima shortly after joining Miles) recently transplanted to New York and a growing habit to support, he needed the pay. Despite the assault, he intermittently returned to Davis over the next few months. But the trumpeter's pique was only followed by further disappointment. In April 1957, he ran out of patience and fired both Coltrane and Jones for "their junkie shit," replacing the two with Sonny Rollins and Art Taylor.

■ Coltrane had tripped and fallen before, but never from the height he had reached with Miles. The tumble was long and hit him harder than any well-aimed punch or previous firing could. With his meal ticket gone and his self-respect running low, he retreated home to Philadelphia. But even among family and friends, something was painfully, spiritually wrong. Sometime in early May, Coltrane made a life-changing (and -affirming) choice:

> About that time I made a decision . . . that's when I stopped drinking and all that. I was able to play better right then . . . that helped me in all kinds of ways when I stopped drinking. I could play better and think better and everything.

A divine offer: junk for jazz. That's the popular understanding of Coltrane's resolve in kicking his addiction. His own liner notes on *A Love Supreme* imply such an arrangement:

> During the year 1957, I experienced by the grace of God, a spiritual awakening which was to lead me to a richer, fuller, more productive

life. At that time, in gratitude, I humbly asked to be given the means
and privilege to make others happy through music.

But other comments made by Coltrane argue against so narrow an interpretation. As he told French writer Michel Delorme in 1965:

A few years ago I recovered faith. I had already lost and regained this faith. I was brought up in a religious family, I had the seed of it inside me, and, at certain times, I recover my faith. All this relates to the life one leads.

It would seem Coltrane's decision to go cold turkey was only part of a more holistic plan, one needed to renew a spiritual vow he had made a long time before. Coltrane was doubtless referring to his spiritual and physical recovery in 1957—and how his music, health, and life's mission interrelated—when he said to writer Ralph Gleason in 1962:

There was a time when I went through a personal crisis, you know, and I came out of it . . . I felt so fortunate to have come through it successfully that all I wanted to do if I could, would be to play music that would make people happy.

What had been the seed of a "live right, do right, play right" philosophy in his adolescence appears to have taken mature form with his withdrawal from narcotics dependency. Whatever role his coming clean played in his spiritual reaffirmation will never be known for sure; it seems Coltrane's struggle was intensely private. "I'm sure that there was some sort of revelation or something that had come to him that he had to change his life," says Cousin Mary. "But if he talked to people about those things, he didn't talk about it with me."

What is certain is that he was strong enough to detox himself sometime in May 1957 even while performing nightly, though the ordeal was not easy on those closest to him. "Naima was with him all the time through the thick and thin of all of that," recalls Cousin Mary, adding:

John was playing a club [the Red Rooster] and Naima called here at night and said, "Mary, I think maybe you should come out here. John is acting very strange, playing like he's six years old, like he's never seen the horn before." So he was beginning to change then, to go into that thing. I never did go to the club, but [trumpeter] Johnny Coles came back with him and stayed here all night. And John went into his room upstairs where he stayed, and he kicked that habit right here in this house. Cold turkey.

As fate would have it, Coltrane's accompaniment for the Red Rooster engagement included two of the three sidemen who would constitute his famous quartet and eventually record *A Love Supreme*—bassist Jimmy Garrison and pianist McCoy Tyner. To Tyner, that week was "definitely a turning point" for Coltrane:

It was the first time I played with him, at the Red Rooster. He didn't have a band, and he used Cal [Massey]'s rhythm section with myself, Jimmy and [drummer] Tootie Heath. It's funny, I remember [bassist] Reggie Workman had come in to hear us and said, "Wow, I think maybe John that night wasn't feeling well"—he expected a little bit more, and so did I. But I witnessed the transition, watched him come out of that thing, and he did it pretty quickly. I remember that it didn't take him long to get himself together because I think he really was determined.

Tyner credits the women in Coltrane's life for providing the support he needed to get clean. "He had people around him that loved him, especially Naima, she was crazy about him. He had a support system there. It wasn't like he was strung out, hanging around the street."

As they grew closer, the now clean Coltrane told Tyner of a nighttime visitation he experienced. "I remember he told me he had a dream about Charlie Parker, and Bird told him that he was on the right track." Tyner was unsure whether the spirit of Parker was referring to music or drugs, but "after the change, Trane's playing just took on another character—it began to blossom."

Nat Hentoff offers a captivating before-and-after double portrait (specifically, 1954 versus early sixties):

I kind of remember . . . it was before he joined Miles. I think it was after he left Johnny Hodges. I saw Trane, he had a pint bottle of some kind of whiskey. He was all strung out, and he looked so forlorn. Then, not so long afterwards, there was Trane with his band, with Elvin Jones, and standing like some kind of spiritual force. It was . . . stunning, I just couldn't move. He didn't just think abstractly about the changes that could happen in somebody if that person found his spiritual way. He knew it as essentially as you could know it.

Coltrane's musical partners marked the change as well. "I remember I looked at him and I said, 'Damn, boy, what happened to you?'" says Jimmy Cobb. "He said, 'Well, I just stopped doing everything. Have been—did' [laughs]." Marvels Tyner, "It was almost like he had something he had to get done. You know? He had a lot of work to do."

■ Coltrane threw himself back like a man "on a musical mission," according to Tyner. He returned to New York and, finally fullfilling his contract with Prestige Records, strolled into his first session as a leader, clean and reinvigorated, with a band featuring members of his Philadelphia family: Cal Massey, Johnnie Splawn, Red Garland, Tootie Heath. *First Trane* was the result. The cover photograph, a portrait of the saxophonist taken the same day as the session, showed him serious and collected: akin to the portrait that would look out from *A Love Supreme.*

Esmond Edwards, who was a photographer working for Prestige chief Bob Weinstock at the time, recalls:

> I took the picture of him resting on a table in Rudy [Van Gelder]'s backyard, the parking lot, with his horn . . . I had been about a year going to the sessions with Bob. We had a deal with Rudy—I think Alfred Lion [of Blue Note] had Wednesdays, and we had Fridays. So every Friday, we had to do a session. One day Bob said, "Look, I've got enough to do in the office, you go do the date." I was totally unprepared for it—it was the very first John Coltrane album.

First Trane was a mix of originals ("Bakai" by Cal Massey; "Chronic Blues" and the all too appropriately titled "Straight Street" by Coltrane) and rather unusual covers ("Violets for Your Furs," "Time Was," "While My Lady Sleeps"). As Weinstock recalls, an almost encyclopedic retention of song structures was a rare talent, peculiar to Coltrane and few others:

> There were certain musicians who knew every song ever written, almost: Stan Getz, Red Garland, Al Haig, and John Coltrane. You could name any song from any stinking movie of the twenties, thirties, or forties, and they knew it. Those four people were incredible and I worked with all of them.

While the album is replete with earnest solos throughout, one of its stand-out moments occurs in the introduction to "While My Lady Sleeps": a moody, hypnotic motif is established by bass and piano alone, a minimal outline of the melody of the tune. Coltrane had learned well from Miles's example; he would return to such trancelike, reductive approaches to melodic construction repeatedly in the years ahead.

Another revelatory moment takes place at the very end of the same tune, as Coltrane blows breathily, sounding a

A nightly workshop: Coltrane with Monk, Ahmed Abdul-Malik (bass), and Shadow Wilson (drums), late summer 1957

note that seems to sit between two others. It's a startling example (and evocative use) of "multiphonics"—reaching for more than one tone at a time—and reveals how his intrepid spirit had led him to probe the very nature of his saxophone, ostensibly a single-note instrument. Coltrane credited one of his Philadelphia circle for sharing the technique:

> **John Glenn . . . showed me how to do this. He can play a triad [a three-note chord] and move notes inside it—like passing tones! It's done by false fingering and adjusting your lip.**

In addition to expanding the vocabulary of his horn, Coltrane's woodshedding became a study in personal endurance. His wife reported him working for twenty-four hours a day and falling asleep with horn in hand. Jimmy Heath quotes Naima as calling him "ninety percent saxophone." With religious conviction he worked on musical exercises and scales in various practice books, as keyboardist Joe Zawinul remembers. "A lot of the scalar material Coltrane was playing was Nicolas Slonimsky's *Thesaurus of*

Scales and Patterns. Most of the reed and trumpet players played out of different violin books, and also scale books like [Carl] Czerny."

The effect of the next six months on Coltrane's sound cannot be understated; a creative gate was flung open. The pace alone at which his playing

developed is a marvel, the most immediate evidence of his re-dedication. In a nonstop series of recordings and performances, he explored harmonic pathways at will, applying the ingrained scalar patterns he had been studying incessantly. His solos became bursts of virtuosity, slaloming through chord changes. He began to layer notes together in clusters in an effort to pronounce full chords. His sound became

so distinctive that critic Ira Gitler coined a new name to describe it—"sheets of sound"—a term he was never able to shake. Yet for all his drive and self-directed research, Coltrane could not have done it alone. If his experience with Gillespie, Hodges, and Davis is considered musical training on an undergraduate level, his restless, autodidactic searching made clear that he was eager for an advanced degree. All he needed was someone to provide the proper instruction and sponsorship, and in pianist Thelonious Monk, he found his professor.

Monk's hands-on guidance was a far cry from Miles's tight-lipped tutelage. Whereas the trumpeter had been one to feel his way into music in an almost anti-intellectual manner, to "hit it and quit it," Coltrane found in Monk "a musical architect of the highest order," a fellow theoretician who shared his compulsive, analytical approach. "Monk is exactly the opposite of Miles," the saxophonist commented. "He talks about music all the time . . . if, by chance, you ask him something, he'll spend hours if necessary to explain it to you." Monk even added to Coltrane's desire to blow chords on his saxophone:

> **Monk . . . showed me how to make two or three notes at one time on tenor . . . [he] just looked at my horn and "felt" the mechanics of what had to be done to get this effect.**

Class was in session whenever the two would get together: in the studio when recording for Riverside Records, during an extended engagement at Manhattan's Five Spot, at the piano in Monk's apartment where lengthy, intense discourse took place. Coltrane described their one-to-one routine:

> **I'd go by his apartment, and get him out of bed [laughs]—he'd wake up and roll over to the piano and start playing . . . I'd get my horn and start trying to find what he was playing . . . he'd tend to play it over and over and over and over . . . he would stop and show me some parts that were pretty difficult, and if I had a *lot* of trouble, well, he'd get his portfolio out show me the music . . . he's got all of it written and I'd read it and learn it . . . when I almost had the tune down, then he would leave me to practice it . . . [When] I had it pretty well, then I'd call him and we'd play it down together. And sometimes, we'd get just one tune a day, maybe.**

Monk's patience certainly helped Coltrane grasp the material they began to play together. The music Davis had favored had been familiar to Coltrane before he joined the trumpeter—blues, ballads, and bebop workhorses. Monk's songbook of his own originals—"Epistrophy," "Ruby, My Dear," "Trinkle, Tinkle"—was riddled with strange melodic leaps and rhythmic shifts.

"Monk's music had been played already before Trane with different saxophonists," remarked Tommy Flanagan. "But I think Trane was more precise . . . he was more careful about learning things exactly like the writer meant, especially with Monk." "With Monk's music," wrote Martin Williams, "one has to know the melodies and their harmonies, and understand how they fit together in order to improvise well, and Coltrane understood this."

Monk was not simply a rule-breaker. Just as Coltrane's playing reflected a love of musical logic—building solos by taking patterns through an ordered path of permutations—so the pianist's compositions revealed a passion for internal structure. Coltrane was intellectually intrigued, yet, even after their practice sessions, slightly unprepared for their live debut, as writer Amiri Baraka noted:

> **The scene that stands in my mind is the night he opened with Monk and he was botching the heads [arrangements] of those tunes . . . Trane would be stumbling and trying to get the tune together.**

Not that Coltrane had much choice; he was the only melody instrument on the bandstand. But being the lone horn player afforded the saxophonist the chance to extend his solos further than ever before. And—most importantly to the path that would lead to *A Love Supreme*—the experience provided him the uncommon opportunity to hear himself within a quartet-in-progress, as soprano saxist Steve Lacy witnessed:

> **When he played with Monk I was there every night I think . . . it started out—very clumsy, very obscure, very maladroit, and then each night it got a little more relaxed . . . and then it got into a kind of security and then it took off from there into a freedom and into a wild abandon . . . to watch that unfold was a revelation . . . in those days, the gigs lasted long enough so that something could really happen like that.**

The creative explosion of 1957 was not limited to Monk's orbit. While appearing at the Five Spot, Coltrane found time to participate in no fewer than ten studio sessions, seven as sideman and three as leader, including his most enduring album of that period, *Blue Train*, the best evidence to date of his growing capabilities as a composer.

Blue Train was recorded by special arrangement for Blue Note Records, with permission from Prestige, who owned Coltrane's contract. Though both labels hired many of the same musicians and employed the same studio and engineer, there was one significant difference between the two. " 'Blowing session'—that was the common term used for those [Prestige] sessions, where there was very little preparation as far as rehearsal," stated guitarist Kenny Burrell, who co-led a session with Coltrane in 1958:

> **You were called to come to the date, maybe bring one or two original compositions, expected to learn and record compositions by other musicians, create stuff on the spot, and have a good time.**

"Most recordings were just loosely organized jam sessions," Bob Weinstock, head of Prestige, echoes. Coltrane knew well of Prestige's one-take approach from his experience with Miles; Blue Note, on the other hand, had a reputation for crafting its output, providing latitude for more in-studio rehearsal and alternate takes. "To me [*Blue Train*] was well-schemed and well thought out," trombonist Curtis Fuller remembers. "Every one of those songs had its own quality, would stand alone on its own merits."

Fuller was one of a young team of hard boppers Coltrane assembled for the album, which also featured trumpeter Lee Morgan, pianist Kenny Drew, and his fellow sidemen from Miles's quintet, Paul Chambers and Philly Joe Jones. *Blue Train* was Coltrane's first true outing as composer and album conceptualizer, crafts he would fine-tune over the next few years. He took a sheaf of original, blues-based melodies, arranged them for three-horn front line, and left his sidemen with the impression that they had participated in an important event. "We came out of that *Blue Train* date saying, 'Man, did you hear that stuff Trane was playing?' " says Fuller. "Trane had that ability to play beautifully even on extreme tempos, and the ballads— he had a way, his playing just touched you. But that date was just different . . . and you knew it, it had a spiritual quality."

■ As Christmas 1957 approached, Miles returned from a three-week stay in Paris where, in a brief, impromptu session, he had recorded the music for a film noir soundtrack. Whatever the inspiration—the melancholy ambience of director Louis Malle's *Ascenseur pour l'échafaud,* or the sea change of visiting France—the trumpeter had set aside the standard jazz songbook and loosely improvised over a simple set of scales. He liked the result, and saw the approach working in the context of his band.

He could also hear Coltrane back by his side. Miles had spent the year working with a series of replacement saxophonists, eventually luring Cannonball Adderley into the band. But now he wanted to add to, not subtract from, his lineup: "I had this idea in my head of expanding the group from a quintet to a sextet, with Trane and Cannonball on saxophones." As it happened, 1957 had been busy enough for Monk; the pianist's decision to take a hiatus freed Coltrane to consider Davis's offer to rejoin.

He did not take long; by Christmas the new sextet was performing in Chicago. The result was a creative pressure cooker—less solo time onstage, more lyrical ideas in the air—in which the tenorman's blues roots and recent experiments in harmonic flexibility dovetailed perfectly with the challenge of an expanded lineup. The Adderley-Coltrane pairing particularly drew attention. Miles hailed the novelty of "Cannonball's blues-rooted alto sax up against Trane's harmonic, chordal way of playing, his more free-form approach," while Adderley marked their similarity:

> **That was interesting especially because Trane had an extremely light, fluid sound and my alto sound has always been influenced by the tenor so it was heavy . . . sometimes it was difficult to tell when one instrument stopped and the other started.**

But as Coltrane himself wrote, the most significant change he discovered with Miles was a new musical path called "modal jazz":

> **I found Miles in the midst of another stage of his musical development . . . in his past he [was] devoted to multichorded structures. He was interested in chords for their own sake. But now it seemed that he was moving in the opposite direction to the use of fewer and fewer chord changes in songs. He used tunes with free-flowing lines . . . due to the direct and free-flowing lines in his music, I found it easy to apply harmonic ideas that I had.**

Though the concept of modal jazz might warrant further explanation to the layman, suffice it to say that it provided a desired freshness for which both Miles and Coltrane—as well as other notable jazz players of the day—were searching. Many felt tired of performing a repertoire littered with musical clichés and leftover bebop formulas that fell under the heading of "chord changes." As a result, and inspired in part by his successful soundtrack experiment in Paris, Davis's music began to rely on scales rather than established chord patterns. The group's normally blistering tempos were slowed, as the harmonic movement was stilled. They began experimenting with time signatures other than straight-ahead 4/4 time, such as waltzlike 3/4 and 6/8 meters. The sextet first put the idea to practice on *Milestones* in February 1958, of which Miles wrote:

> **This was the first record where I really started to write in the modal form and on . . . the title track, I really used that form . . . when you play this way, go in this direction, you can go on forever . . . the challenge here, when you work in the modal way, is to see how inventive you can become melodically.**

Not surprisingly, the already verbose Coltrane found comfort in the more expansive framework of modal structures. "Miles's music gave me plenty of freedom," he enthused. "It's a beautiful approach."

(Just how beautiful—and successful—it could be was not fully realized until almost a year later when Miles reunited his sextet of 1958—Coltrane, Adderley, Chambers, drummer Jimmy Cobb [who had replaced Jones], and, most importantly, pianist Bill Evans [Red Garland's successor]. With Evans's ethereal style and compositional input as well as pianist Wynton Kelly's help on one track, Davis created what many consider a once-in-a-lifetime jazz masterpiece: *Kind of Blue*. But that's another book.)

One other chapter of the modal jazz story bears mentioning. As their music fell more into scalar forms, Coltrane, and many of his colleagues, shared a fascination with tonic patterns other than the usual major and minor scales. Some found what they needed in books, such as Slonimsky's scalar exercises. Others studied classical compositions that used exotic folk scales, or leaned toward foreign sources, listening to flamenco and Indian records. Coltrane, as would become increasingly evident in his recordings, was not satisfied with anything save all:

> **I want to cover as many forms of music as I can put into a jazz context and play on my instruments. I like Eastern music . . . Spanish content, as well as other exotic-flavored music. In these approaches there's something I can draw on.**

From 1958 through '59, whenever Coltrane and Miles performed and the tapes were rolling, the full promise of their collaborative magic was finally fulfilled. Even their impromptu live recordings merited focused listening. As a result, Coltrane became, as Adderley saw it, "not so much commercially successful, as commercially acceptable."

In a year-and-a-half flash since his spiritual resurgence, Coltrane had shifted his career into high gear, and as his three-year contract with Prestige was running out at the end of 1958, his manager jumped at the chance to shop for a more lucrative deal. Discussions ensued with producer Orrin Keepnews at Riverside Records and Nesuhi Ertegun at Atlantic.

■ In 1958, Atlantic Records was a leading independent label, best known for its success in the R&B market with doo-wop groups (the Chords, the Clovers), girl singers (Ruth Brown, LaVern Baker), and blues shouters (Big Joe Turner). With recent hits by Ray Charles, Chuck Willis, and the Coasters, the rock 'n' roll explosion was also smiling on the label, to the delight of its chiefs: brothers Ahmet and Nesuhi Ertegun, Jerry Wexler, and Miriam Abramson (now Bienstock).

"This company was started by jazz lovers," says Ahmet Ertegun. "But we didn't start it to make jazz records. We started Atlantic Records to make rhythm and blues records—to make general-selling records. We were hoping to build a label that could support itself." Atlantic's jazz interests were left wholly to Nesuhi Ertegun, with little attention or involvement from the more profitable end of the company.

Atlantic's jazz roster in 1958 reflected Ertegun's varied and highbrow

taste: a one-time recording by Thelonious Monk with Art Blakey pushed the label into musical territory close to Coltrane. When the saxophonist became available, as Miriam Bienstock relates, "Coltrane was a project that Nesuhi brought in to the company and really nurtured." Setting aside other offers, Coltrane's manager Harold Lovett accepted Ertegun's: $7,000 for a one-year contract with an option to extend the deal, plus a Lincoln Continental.

As 1959 commenced, Atlantic wasted no time getting Coltrane into the studio. On January 15, the label paired him with Modern Jazz Quartet vibraphonist Milt Jackson for a set made up mostly of standards and released under the name *Bags & Trane,* a title that relegated Atlantic's new star to a less-than-headlining premiere. Coltrane did notice that Atlantic could offer something Prestige could not.

Multiple takes and ample recording time were perquisites that came with being signed to a label with its own studio (as Atlantic had) and in-house engineer (Tom Dowd). As he had with *Blue Train,* Coltrane began to prepare the music for his first solo album on Atlantic.

It's no coincidence that Coltrane recorded *Giant Steps* only two weeks after he finished *Kind of Blue*. The same emotional depth and self-assurance powers his work on both. (Incidentally, both albums also share bassist and drummer Paul Chambers and Jimmy Cobb, while pianist Wynton Kelly appears on one track on each.) But while the latter's modal framework points to a future path of jazz expression, the former serves as a masterful farewell to the world bebop created, a world of labyrinthine harmonies and chord changes, a world Coltrane had aspired to and in the past three years had finally mastered.

The majority of the tunes were outgrowths of Coltrane's at-home exercises, as he explained in the album's liner notes. "I sit there and run over chord progressions and sequences, and eventually, I usually get a song—or songs—out of each little musical problem."

Pianist Tommy Flanagan, Coltrane's neighbor at the time, performed on six out of the album's seven tracks. Flanagan notes that although *Giant Steps* took time to master, "that whole date was challenging, so one tune prepared you for the next one." The pianist adds: "[The songs] didn't really resolve the way you would expect most progressions to, even though it was logical. It was logical but it was different for the time."

The rest of the selections presented an impressive display of his ability to artfully connect structure, sensitivity, and sincere acknowledgement. As Miles had begun to name songs after friends and acquaintances—"Lazy Susan," "Freddie Free-loader"—so Coltrane created a series of tunes dedicated to his own circle. Says Mary Alexander, "*Giant Steps*—we sort of called it a family album [laughs]. It had 'Naima' on it, 'Syeeda's Song Flute,' 'Cousin Mary,' and 'Mr. P.C.'" (The last was Coltrane's tribute to Paul Chambers.)

If there is one album that can be deemed Coltrane's declaration of creative independence, it is *Giant Steps*. "That date was different from [his] earlier record dates," opined Flanagan. "It seemed to be the only one that he knew that he was onto something. We all knew it."

Though it would not be released until 1960, the album signaled the saxophonist's arrival as a fully matured triple threat: soloist, bandleader, and composer. But, by Coltrane's own estimate, the record also felt like a creative dead end. He had taken the road of chord changes—the harmonic highway first laid out by bebop's pioneers—as far as it would go:

I didn't know where I was going to go next, I don't know whether I would've just thought of abandoning the chord[al approach] . . . and he came along doing it, and I heard it and I said, "Well, that must be the answer."

"He" was a new jazz arrival named Ornette Coleman, "it" a style of playing that felt like a breath of fresh air to Coltrane.

Keeping Miles happy: toward the end of a four-year stint with the trumpeter, St. Nicholas Arena, New York, November 27, 1959

■ If there is one constant to the forward momentum of jazz, it is that the rate of change is inconsistent. A few years of rapid progress can be followed by a longer period of stylistic entrenchment. Bebop went from fringe to fashion between 1945 and '47; the popular sounds working from bop's chordal complexity and rhythmic invention—cool, hard bop, Third Wave— evolved at a slower pace through the fifties.

As 1959 ended and a new decade began, jazz shifted again to the fast lane. The year had already been a banner one for timeless and influential recordings, Coltrane's *Giant Steps* and Miles Davis's *Kind of Blue* being joined by other singular statements combining compositional richness and improvised energy—Charles Mingus's *Mingus Ah Um,* Duke Ellington's *Anatomy of a Murder*—when Ornette Coleman's quartet blew into town and took up residency at the Five Spot in November.

Coleman introduced a novel approach that was fresh, different, and very divisive; the standing-room-only crowds at the small Lower East Side bar, which was filled with all the top players of the day, found themselves moved or repulsed by the nightly freedoms the Texas-born alto saxist took with the rules of jazz structure. In earning the epithet of "free jazz," Coleman's style stood out from other innovations. Where modal jazz and exotic scales had opened up the music on one path, Coleman had not relinquished the idea of following a pre-composed structure or specific scale. His chosen route was liberation through collective improvisation: allowing all members of the group to play as if they were front-line soloists, a strategy that required a level of interaction relying heavily on an emotional connection between all musicians and the music itself.

If there was one element of this new style on which all agreed, it was the force of the emotion it conveyed: Coleman's music, with its system of sighs, yelps, moans, could sound playful and irreverent, doleful and severe, fierce and frenzied. One of Coleman's staunchest defenders—Modern Jazz Quartet pianist John Lewis—spoke to his label head, Nesuhi Ertegun; in short order Atlantic signed Coleman and released his New York debut, *The Shape of Jazz to Come,* with its liner-note prediction that "what Ornette Coleman is playing will affect the whole character of jazz music profoundly and pervasively."

Coltrane was mesmerized by the melody-driven music of his new label-mate. While Miles and Cannonball would take a few years to embrace Coleman's innovations, Coltrane was an immediate convert. It's impossible to gauge Coleman's specific influence on Coltrane; the latter was already well on his melodic way by the end of 1959. But a feeling of personal gratitude pervaded his praise over the next few years. "I feel indebted to him," Coltrane admitted.

When busy schedules permitted, Coltrane sat in with Coleman, visited his apartment, and even received instruction. "He was interested in non-chordal playing and I had cut my teeth on that stuff," Coleman mentioned years afterward. "He later sent me a letter which included thirty dollars for each lesson." Coltrane recorded with Coleman sidemen Don Cherry and Charlie Haden, and eventually inherited his bassist Jimmy Garrison, whose experience at Coleman's side helped shape Coltrane's future sound.

■ But even with the striking musical progress he was making, Coltrane remained mainly a hired hand, straining to leave Miles behind, his own group a dream waiting to be realized. His calendar for early 1960 shows him hopping in and out of Miles's group, playing with pickup bands in a variety of venues, including the New House of Jazz in Philadelphia and Town Hall in New York. In March, Miles cajoled him into the European tour; Coltrane made it clear it would be his last as a sideman.

When the group returned to New York's Idlewild (now JFK) Airport in early April, save for a few impromptu jams and one last studio session, the Coltrane-Davis coalition had reached its end. Coltrane stepped out alone, prepared to take charge, pointed toward a future that would build to a series of creative and commercial peaks, culminating in *A Love Supreme.*

Among the items in Coltrane's luggage was a hand-me-down gift from Miles, an instrument that would have a profound—and almost immediate—effect on his career. One writer summed up the four-and-a-half-year collaboration: "Davis did Coltrane three great favors. He hired him, he fired him and he gave him his first soprano saxophone."

The quartet at their height:
Teatro dell'Arte, Milan, Italy,
December 2, 1962

If you want a photographic reproduction, don't buy Picasso. If you want a popular song, don't listen to Coltrane.

—RALPH J. GLEASON, 1960

The Classic Quartet

Leave it to the mainstream press to latch on to the most obvious elements. In 1964, around the time John Coltrane was composing *A Love Supreme*, *Time* magazine first approached the Bob Dylan story by way of his harmonica. When *Newsweek* tackled Coltrane in 1961, its focus was the strange, straight horn he had single-handedly restored to prominence.

Though Miles would often take credit for introducing him to the soprano saxophone, Coltrane divulged an earlier encounter to the weekly magazine. It was "late in 1959," he said, when he returned to New York from an engagement in Washington, D.C., leaving behind a fellow musician but retaining his horn. "I opened the case and found a soprano sax. I started fooling around with it and was fascinated."

The instrument's nasal timbre and ability to emit Eastern sonorities fit Coltrane's interest in foreign music and scales. And it allowed him a greater fluidity than he had enjoyed before. "You can play lighter things with it—things that have a more subtle pulse. After the heaviness of the tenor, it's a relief to shift to soprano."

It's rare that a musician embraces a new instrument mid-career, and even rarer that, within a year of such a decision, it propels his career to another level of renown and artistry. But such was Coltrane's drive and determination in searching out new sounds, and such was his luck in finding the right song for the soprano.

■ By late 1960, Coltrane had been with Atlantic for almost two years. Over a variety of sessions, with a variety of sidemen, he had come to know both the label and the studio well, and for good reason—they occupied the same building, the offices being downstairs, the studio on the top floor of the brownstone at 157 West 57th Street. Therein, Nesuhi Ertegun took a hands-on approach to all jazz projects, dealing with the artists both professionally and personally, and scheduling all sessions with Tom Dowd. Dowd was one of the extravagances Atlantic had allowed itself in its early years, hiring him part-time in 1952. Being a veteran jazz fan and performer ("I played in university bands, all the bass instruments: tuba, sousaphone, arco bass"), Dowd took a special interest in Nesuhi's signings, and welcomed the chance to record jazz in the studio he had personally constructed. By 1960, he was working around the clock for Atlantic and had come to regard a Coltrane session as out of the ordinary:

Live on soprano: Jazz Gallery, New York, May 6, 1960

Nesuhi would call me and say, "We're going to do Coltrane at two o'clock today," and I knew I'd have four or five pieces, I'd have the place set up. I'd go about my business editing or mastering or something, and I'd hear the elevator door open and close and I'd look around and there was John. I'd wave to him, and he'd go into the studio and stay there in the corner, and he'd run arpeggios for like ten or fifteen minutes, and then he'd put the instrument down, change mouthpieces, change reeds, you know what I'm saying? I mean, he went through four or five permutations, just standing there doing nothing but running scales, playing to himself. He was serious, just like it was a classical recital.

On October 21, Coltrane arrived early as usual, with both of his horns. He had only been performing publicly on the soprano since May and had first played it on a recording four weeks later, on the tune "The Blessing," during a session co-led by trumpeter Don Cherry (eventually released in 1966 on the album *The Avant-Garde*). By chance, Frank Tenot, the Parisian concert producer, was visiting New York, and had been invited by Ertegun to attend the session:

Atlantic Records studio, 1960

> The first time I saw Coltrane in New York was when he recorded "My Favorite Things" in Atlantic's studio. It was under the supervision of Nesuhi Ertegun, and for me, it was a great shock—I remember Coltrane at first tried to play tenor, and then for the second take he played soprano, and then there's a take, I don't know if it exists, where he's playing soprano *and* tenor.

Coltrane had recently begun performing the waltz-like number, and was ready to record it:

> Some times we have to live with a tune for quite a while, and other times we just fall into it. Now, "[My] Favorite Things," a fella said, "Why don't you try this tune?" I told him I wanted some music, and so I bought the song sheet and took it to rehearsal, and just like that, we fell right into it . . . we had the shape of it at the rehearsal, but it took us a little while to grow and get ex-

panded and recognize the different parts and know just how we were going to play it, but it was a very short period of time.

Coltrane had taken standard jazz practice—retooling tunes from recent Broadway shows or movie soundtracks in a hip, instrumental mold—and given it a new twist. Applying a few licenses learned from Miles, he streamlined the structure of the well-known song from *The Sound of Music,* inserting a section in the middle that suddenly abandoned the tune's familiar melody and became an open vamp over which Coltrane soloed, alternating between major and minor scales.

I try to pick . . . a song that sounds good and a song that might be familiar . . . and then I try to have parts in the song where we can play solo . . . in a modal perspective, more or less, you know? So therefore we end up playing a lot of vamps within a tune.

The idea of simplifying well-known songs, then opening up them up with modal sections, was a device Coltrane would use often over the next few years ("I don't know how long we're going to be in that, but that's the way it's been for the last eight months," he would say a year later). It was also an approach that would dovetail with his growing assurance on the soprano.

■ The "My Favorite Things" session was also significant for whom Coltrane chose to accompany him in the studio: it was his first recording date with his own working band.

Since drifting from Miles's orbit, Coltrane had had his eye on assembling a consistent, complementary group of musicians. At first, as his recordings in 1959 show, he borrowed rather than recruited. *Giant Steps* featured seasoned players with other gigs—pianist Flanagan led his own outfit; Paul Chambers was with Miles; only drummer Art Taylor was a free agent. Coltrane's support on the date generating most of *Coltrane Jazz* was Miles's famed hard-swinging troika: Kelly, Chambers, and Cobb.

By 1960, as Coltrane's musical approach had developed, so had his demands. He needed sidemen comfortable in chord-based as well as more exploratory, chord-free territory, musicians able to deal with his lengthy solos and who could match the intensity in his playing. "I have several men in mind," he told a Swedish deejay, admitting that a quartet was what he envisioned, "and maybe several weeks after I start I might add a fifth man."

The months following his departure from Miles were an ongoing audition process. A quartet featuring relatively young jazz arrivals—pianist

Steve Kuhn, Philadelphia bassist Steve Davis, and drummer Pete LaRoca—never quite gelled to Coltrane's satisfaction. That summer, he called on his young friend from Philadelphia, McCoy Tyner, who had been patiently awaiting his chance to join forces with the saxophonist:

> **I remember when he was writing "Giant Steps" and "Countdown." He was showing me what he was doing and I wanted to record with him, but he told me, "I know you can play, but you're too young."**

Nonetheless, Tyner was confident: "we had a sort of verbal understanding that if he ever got his own group, I would play piano." When the pianist became available after a stint with Benny Golson and trumpeter Art Farmer's group, the Jazztet, Coltrane replaced Kuhn with Tyner, who remarked, "John's group is where I belonged."

It's easy to hear why Coltrane felt an affinity for Tyner: he played what the saxophonist knew best. As a soloist, he was harmonically astute and cleanly stated, working along the lines of bebop's founding pianists, Bud Powell and Thelonious Monk ("Bud Monk" was Tyner's teenage nickname). As a sideman, Tyner had a percussive attack and sophistication that brought to mind Red Garland, and he was happy to submit to Coltrane's direction. ("When I began with John, I accepted the responsibility of being an accompanist.") And as an intrepid musician, Tyner had also begun to explore the fresh avenue of modal jazz—signposted by an album he had studied—while seeking a balance with preceding styles:

> **Kind of Blue was a major influence on the music, spearheading the modal playing. Everybody wanted to play those songs. I was into doing it all. You don't take away, you add on to it—playing the multiple changes and the modal thing, trying to incorporate what was historically in the music with what was going on at the time.**

As Miles had heard the latent talent in Coltrane, so too had the saxophonist divined a certain promise in Tyner's nascent style. "I was very young," Tyner admits. "Playing with John really gave me a chance to develop my style into what it became, because you can hear something, but it takes a while for it to manifest itself." And despite a twelve-year age gap, Tyner found that Coltrane treated him as an equal. "John was much older than me [but] it was a mutual, respectful type of relationship, and that's what made it work."

Coltrane and Tyner connected on a level that went deeper than common neighborhood roots or shared musical taste. "Our personalities complemented each other," Tyner recollected. Both were quietly intense and musically focused. Both were drawn to religious paths, the pianist becoming a Muslim, like Coltrane's wife, Naima. Tyner also spoke of music in the same spiritual terms as Coltrane:

> **When a man's faith is never tried, I don't think he'll ever learn anything. You have to have trial and tribulation, or what are you going to learn? There has to be some adversity for you to know that you have the right tools, if you are equipped to make it.**

"I've known him a long time and I've always felt I wanted to play with him," Coltrane summed up his decision. "Our ideas meet and blend. Working with McCoy is like wearing a nice fitting glove."

Even more changes were at hand. Coltrane discussed the band's line-up with his new pianist as LaRoca gave up the drum seat just prior to a West Coast tour. "We had to accept the fact that it just wasn't going to happen with that setup," Tyner states, noting that Coltrane's first inclination had been to hire the man who had been so instrumental in securing his job with Miles. "He loved Philly Joe a lot, but I think he was a little bit hurt about Philly Joe not being able to give him what he needed musically, because they kind of grew up together." Former Coleman sideman Billy Higgins was hired as a stopgap, while Coltrane set his sights on another, New York–based drummer. "John told me about Elvin Jones—'I think he'd be a great drummer,' he said—and I said, 'Yeah, I've heard of Elvin.' John had really enjoyed playing with him, but I didn't know that much about him."

Born in 1927, Jones was roughly the same age as Coltrane and, like his future bandleader, arrived in New York City in 1955 with the rudiments of a heavier, distinct style that set many ears atilt. Jones did not fit smoothly into the standard timekeeping role, as he took rhythmic liberties that drew uncommon attention to the drum kit. "It's hard for a young person when you feel what you're doing is correct, but you're not accepted," the drummer recalled of his first years in New York. "My telephone didn't ring as often as it could have."

The roots of Jones's busy, polyrhythmic style can be heard on Sonny Rollins's live album *A Night at the Village Vanguard* (1957), when, as Branford Marsalis notes, "There is nothing in his playing where you would say 'Oh my God!,' like when he played with Coltrane":

What you hear if you check out the Sonny Rollins record is, I think, the most important aspect of Elvin's playing: he came through the tradition of swing drumming—not at the expense of the tradition—and extended that concept.

Ravi Coltrane, who came to play in Jones's group in the mid-nineties, hears a promise of future greatness in the same recording:

> **I listened to *A Night at the Village Vanguard*, and Elvin's young there, but still, there's so much fire. In '57, his thing was kind of uncommon-sounding, because it's not yet refined and polished. Sonny and Elvin do some trading [alternating four-bar solo passages] on "What Is This Thing Called Love," and the fours that Elvin plays are not always fours. Sometimes they're three, sometimes three and a half . . . For me, that's the plus . . . Later, he refined it into being the standard.**

"When exchanging fours or eights, I was always thinking in terms of musical phrasing as far as the composition was concerned," Jones remarked on his performance with Rollins. "I think the phrasing should never be confined to a rigid pattern . . . [yet] you can't play that way all the time; it depends on the artist. But playing with more expression was certainly appropriate with an artist like Sonny Rollins."

Or with John Coltrane. The saxophonist had first played with Jones early in 1958 when the drummer—whom Miles Davis knew from an extended stay in Detroit in early 1954—substituted for Philly Joe Jones on a weeklong Philadelphia engagement. A looser, jamlike setting later that year, as saxophonist Wayne Shorter recalled, furthered the Jones-Coltrane relationship:

. . . and Elvin Jones.

One time John called me and asked if I wanted to do a—we called them "Monday Nights at Birdland"—with him. It was myself, that night we [had] two pianos, Cedar Walton and Tommy Flanagan, and a bass player, George Tucker. And we had someone playing on drums, and then in walked Elvin Jones. They took turns and he played a couple of sets with us. That was sort of a nucleus for the kind of rhythm section that Coltrane was looking for.

An air of inevitability pervades their coming together. As Jones revealed in later interviews, he and Coltrane shared the same focus and concerns. Coltrane's playing consciously avoided established patterns and phrasing. "You can get bogged down in clichés," Jones remarked on his own drum style. "Even if you have to play clichés all the time, there's enough variety to give you a good vocabulary and endless possibilities of variation." A melody player to the extreme, Coltrane admitted his need "to be more flexible where rhythm is concerned. I feel I have to study rhythm more." Jones held a complementary belief: "It isn't necessary to follow chord by chord, but [a drummer] should know the melody . . . that way the song can be played as a unit, not just two or three people carrying the whole thing and the drummer sitting back there just keeping time."

Even Coltrane's fixation on the intricacies of the saxophone—his exploring false notes and endless testing of reeds and mouthpieces—

matched Jones's near-scientific regard for his instrument. "Some people are more sensitive to rhythmic pulses," the drummer once stated:

> **The more sensitive you are, the more you can utilize the subtleties of timekeeping. Take for example, the subtleties of the cymbals; there are endless possibilities for changing the color and tone of the music through the cymbal tonal range . . . there are no two cymbals that sound alike.**

When Coltrane's tour reached Denver in September 1960, Coltrane flew in the newly available Elvin Jones, and the drummer's effect was immediate. "That first night Elvin was in the band, he was playing so strong and so loud you could hear him outside the club and down the block," remembered Steve Davis. "Trane wanted it that way. He wanted a drummer who could really kick." But Jones was not all thunder and bombast; his playing had a peculiar elasticity that the entire quartet enjoyed. Tyner recollects Jones's style and—with a laugh—his bold confidence as well:

> **That first night, Elvin said, "Relax, I got it!" And he did. I learned a lot about time playing with him because he had such an ability to flex the time, but always under control. You felt like in between beats there was twenty-four hours, he was just so flexible. That's one of the things I loved about the music in that band. It was like putty, you could do what you wanted with it: stretch it out, play with it.**

The group returned to New York City and, with little time to relax, headed straight for the studio. Coltrane had found the musical colleagues he desired—and was one man away from the lineup that would record *A Love Supreme.*

■ "My Favorite Things" was tackled by the new quartet on their very first day in the studio; it proved to be the first trickle of a four-session outpouring that took place at the Atlantic studios in a one-week period in late October. The dates eventually yielded three groundbreaking albums: *My Favorite Things, Coltrane Plays the Blues,* and *Coltrane's Sound.* With Tyner, Davis, and Jones at his side, Coltrane reworked standards, introduced originals, and exoticized the blues.

Coltrane closed an autobiographical sketch in *Down Beat* magazine around this time with hope for the state of jazz: "I feel that we have every reason to face the future optimistically." He may as well have been reading his own tea leaves. As 1961 unfolded—as JFK assumed office, the USA-USSR space race launched the first men into orbit, and the world, following Chubby Checker's lead, learned to twist—Coltrane's career shot to its highest altitude to date. He may have been unaffected personally by success, but the indicators were impossible to ignore.

"My Favorite Things" was a radio and retail hit that attracted listeners outside the jazz world with its trancelike sound and the unusual, reedy charm of the soprano saxophone. Atlantic, noting the tune's unexpected popular appeal, secured Coltrane's assent and edited the album version to fit onto the 45 rpm format to satisfy the singles market and gain jukebox play. But just as Nesuhi Ertegun was enjoying his greatest success with his new star, another producer was about to pull Coltrane away.

Within the offices of ABC-Paramount—a major record company best known for teen idols such as Paul Anka and Fabian—producer Creed Taylor had maneuvered the creation of a jazz label. Impulse Records had debuted in late 1959 with a set of releases showing an uncommon attention to creative detail, from the music within to the packaging without.

George Avakian, former head of Columbia Records's jazz efforts, recalls the impressive arrival of Impulse:

> **It was revolutionary in appearance—[the Impulse LPs] looked like a two-LP set, but the front flap was just the cover and when you opened it up, there were two "pages" of text and photos. The single disc was inside the back half of the package, and the back cover was a standard company design—three vertical stripes, black on the sides, and credits down the middle against white.**

Even before the full impact of "My Favorite Things" had been felt, ABC executives had bowed to Taylor's wishes, loosened the purse strings, and bought out Coltrane's contract. As Atlantic had done to Prestige, so a deep-pocketed label poached one of Atlantic's top jazz artists. The saxophonist now merited a $10,000 advance for one year, with two-year options that soon rose to a $20,000 annual advance.

By the start of summer, Coltrane was well aware of the requirements—and pressures—of his new status as the only musician exclusively signed to Impulse. When asked if he found enough time to practice, he complained,

> **Not too much now . . . because I got to make three records a year. I'm always walking around trying to keep my ear open for another "Favorite Things" or something . . . Commercial, man . . . I used to go**

into the woodshed and just stay in there all day and practice and that was all there was to it. I didn't have to worry about making a good record because that wasn't important.

If he was to spend more time recording, Coltrane informed Impulse of his desire to return to a familiar engineer in whom he held the most confidence. "I wasn't party to the conversation," recalls Rudy Van Gelder, "but when Creed Taylor brought him to Impulse, I've been told he said he wanted to record in my studio. I had also been working for Creed for many years, so it worked out just fine." By 1961, the engineer had moved from recording in his parents' living room in Hackensack, New Jersey, to a new location closer to Manhattan:

> During the time [Coltrane] was [signed to Atlantic], I was building the new studio in Englewood Cliffs, roughly late 1958, '59, and '60—very different from Hackensack: high ceiling, wooden beams angled upward and arches reaching toward the peak, with masonry walls. It created a feeling that seemed to fit the spiritual direction that his music was taking. He seemed the same person to me, but his music was dramatically different.

Coltrane's music had changed. What had been merely suggested in the titles of past Coltrane recordings ("The Believer" [1957], "The Blessing" [1960]) now surfaced in a more meditative aspect of his playing. The harmonic flurries, the "sheets of sound" Van Gelder had last witnessed in 1958, were tempered by freely lyrical solos, employing the trance-inducing scales of foreign influences, which the saxophonist referred to as "folk music." Dovetailing with his own inner-directed focus, Coltrane's search for new melodies, scales, and inspiration led to an investigation that plumbed deeper than mere musical research:

> Most recently I've been listening to folk tunes and been trying to find some meaning in that. I feel that basically the music should be dedicated to the goodness in people, the good things in life . . . folk tunes usually spring from these simple things . . . maybe I can work on this, listen to them and learn to combine what's done around the world with what I feel here.

"Coltrane was very interested in the international quality of scales," Lewis Porter states, but adds that "he was also interested in the power of folk

Impulse: Creed's Vision

In March 1959, *Billboard* magazine greeted music aficionados with an optimistic front-page report heralding an era in which jazz seemed to have reached a high-water mark of acceptance, prevalence, and profitability. Scanning further, readers of the trade weekly would have noticed that a rather broad definition of jazz was used in making its case: healthy sales of albums by Duke Ellington and Ahmad Jamal were lumped together with the breakout success of Henry Mancini's jazz-style "Peter Gunn" TV theme.

"Wait a minute! I don't call that jazz," counters Jerry Wexler, top partner at Atlantic Records during that period. "'Peter Gunn' was a freak, an accidental cross-over. It happened because of the television [exposure]." With a hate-to-burst-the-bubble sigh ("Every few years, there's a hubbub: 'Oh, looky here! Jazz is coming! Jazz is selling!'"), he adds:

You know the old saying—as the tide comes in all the boats rise. When you have good years, there's a general escalation of sales and jazz sales may come up with it somewhat. The only time jazz ever was a popular medium was back when pop was jazz—the big-band era.

Nonetheless, the common perception in 1959 was one of jazz renewal, enough to produce buoyant headlines and find executives willing to give the nod to jazz-related efforts. On December 5, 1960, *Billboard* printed the birth announcement for a project that had been gestating for more than a year: "ABC-Paramount Bows Jazz Label—Impulse."

Impulse was conceived by a corporate couple forced together in the early fifties when federal antitrust decisions rocked the entertainment industry, severing theater chains from film studios (like Paramount Pictures), and smaller TV broadcasters (like the Blue Network) from larger sister networks (like NBC.) Blue was reborn as the Amer-

The late '50s—rather than the '20s—may yet go down in musical history as the real "Jazz Age." Jazz is moving into the pop market in every arena—records, TV, radio, TV films, singing commercials, etc.—and next Monday will even make the White House, via a "Jazz Jubilee" concert sponsored by Mrs. Dwight D. Eisenhower.

—*Billboard,* March 9, 1959

ican Broadcasting Company, linked with the orphaned Paramount Theaters chain, and immediately sought to establish itself as a cross-media force. ABC-Paramount had TV and theaters; what they wanted was a record label.

Sam Clark, a Boston record distributor, was recruited as the label's first president; Clark brought in Larry Newton, head of the R&B label Derby Records, as his number two. With deep corporate funding, Clark's mission was clear from the outset: ABC-Paramount was to affect the stance of a major label.

Newton recalls the playing field they entered:

In the fifties, there were mainly two levels of record companies. The big ones—Capitol, RCA/Victor, Columbia was big with [producer/artist] Mitch Miller, and Decca was still strong—that was it. The rest of the labels were indies [independents]. We were shooting to be a major.

To achieve the appropriate robustness—hit records, a full catalog—ABC-Paramount pursued a two-part plan: purchase or partner with smaller record companies, and hire in-house producers to develop new talent and projects. A successful deal with Philadelphia's Chancellor Records, yielding pop charters from teen idols Frankie Avalon and Fabian, was evidence of the former; ex-trumpeter Creed Taylor and pop-oriented arranger Sid Feller were examples of the latter.

Feller recalls ABC-Paramount's early trickle of hits. "We were in existence almost five months before we issued our first record in November 1955," he says. "Paul Anka came to us in our second year and we had a few million sellers with Lloyd Price, Steve Lawrence and Eydie Gormé. That kept us in the major leagues." But the hits came with a price:

We spent a lot of money, and sold very little. Columbia had a dozen artists selling at that same time—same with RCA and Capitol. We would have one or two [singles] selling but put out hundreds of other records which meant nothing. Was it a struggle? Yes, but we always had somebody who was selling.

In 1959, ABC-Paramount gambled, offering Ray Charles a generous advance with an unheard-of twist: they structured the deal as a partnership, allowing the star pianist/singer to maintain ownership of all his recordings. In short order, Charles was lured away from Atlantic Records. "After Ray came, everything went major from then on," says Feller, who arranged many of Charles's sixties hits. The wager paid off. With an unbroken series of best-selling singles and albums, Charles returned ABC's investment many times over, helping to fund other adventurous projects.

Meanwhile, Creed Taylor had been toiling away quietly, recording thematic albums for empty niches in an expanding music market:

I would go to the record bins across the street from the Paramount building and think about musical categories that were not represented. For instance, they didn't have any oriental music, so I did Hi-Fi in an Oriental Garden and it really sold quite well.

Taylor, formerly top jazz producer for the small Bethlehem label, had an agenda. Though his concept-driven titles proved satisfactory to ABC, "jazz was my mission [but] I didn't push it as a priority, I snuck it in." Taylor stealthily recorded multi-instrumentalist Don Elliott's *The Voices of Don Elliott*, pianist Billy Taylor's *My Fair Lady Loves Jazz*, and trumpeter Kenny Dorham's *Kenny Dorham and the Jazz Prophets*, of which the producer proudly notes, "It sold well for its time—about 10,000 copies." Trombonist Grachan Moncur III was working in ABC's sales department in 1956 when he witnessed an early signing effort:

Cannonball and Nat [Adderley] came through the office one day—they had just migrated into town. Creed was giving them a tour of ABC and they looked into my office and saw me sitting there with a desk. They were so surprised to see a black dude with a desk, you know what I mean? Cannonball was very impressed. He said, "Good to see you, my man."

In 1957, Taylor was approached by writer and singer Jon Hendricks with a bold concept: a vocal re-creation of Count Basie's biggest hits, with singers handling the horn arrangements and solos, plus a rhythm section. Utilizing the then-young studio technique of overdubbing—recording and re-recording different performances on the same reel of tape—the album was built around the trio of Hendricks and two bop-flavored singers, Dave Lambert and Annie Ross.

Sing a Song of Basie was a smash. "It just came out of nowhere, it made Lambert, Hendricks and Ross," Taylor notes, recalling the marked incongruity that resulted. "Here they were on the same label that had Paul Anka and Danny and the Juniors—the rock 'n' roll bands of the time."

By 1959, circumstances were ripe for a distinct, dedicated jazz label at ABC. When Taylor unveiled his proposal to his higher-ups, it was fully conceived: top jazz artists, high production standards, and elegant packaging. He already had a name in mind:

I first tried to clear "Pulse" [as a label name] because I had thought of the motto "Feeling the Pulse," but that wasn't available as a copyrightable word. So I put the "I-M" in front. The exclamation point was the designer's idea.

Taylor was given the green light. With his design team, Taylor chose an eye-catching orange-and-black color scheme for the label's logo and albums. An exclamation point was added to the label name for added punch. He decided to employ laminated foldout covers, normally used only for double albums, as a standard feature. "The gatefold was not being used except on very special albums, but all of the Impulse titles were to be gatefolds." Even the album titles merited close attention.

The Music ♪♪♪ REPORTER

Vol. IV No. 1—Nashville, Tennessee ● The Music Industry's Most Aggressive Weekly ● Monday, August 24, 1959—AMCR 25c

ABC-Paramount Success Saluted

A happy Sam Clarke in 1959

IT'S THE MOST!-

FOR YOUR MONEY

RCA CUSTO
SERVIC

I tried to juxtapose the visual on the album cover with the title itself, like Gil [Evans]'s Out of the Cool *or [jazz composer/arranger] Oliver Nelson's* Blues and the Abstract Truth. *They're all combinations of words that grab you. I mean, there's nothing really abstract about the blues but it's a truth.*

By mid-December 1960, Impulse catalog numbers A-1 through A-4—one title by composer/arranger Gil Evans, two from trombonist Kai Winding, and a Ray Charles big-band project—were ready to ship. Taylor describes the initial reaction to the label's first wave: "It was a landslide on all fronts! Radio airplay, distributors running out of stock. There was nothing else out there like that. Ray Charles's *Genius + Soul = Jazz* sold 150,000 LPs within a couple of months."

Others active in 1960 agree. *Billboard*'s West Coast bureau chief, Eliot Tiegel, states, "[Impulse] knocked me out. They took it one step beyond what Blue Note and smaller independents had done." How the fledgling label fit into the jazz hierarchy of the day is recalled by George Avakian, Columbia Records's former album sales and jazz chief:

Impulse was not major competition to Columbia, which remained the leader in jazz recording for years after I left [in 1958]. Atlantic was defi-

nitely number two. After that it was a mixed bag, including very different companies [such] as Impulse and the Norman Granz labels [like Verve]. Right behind were Pacific Jazz and Blue Note.

By mid-1961, Impulse had issued a total of six albums, the last being Coltrane's label debut, *Africa/Brass.* But as the label drew attention, so did its creator. Before the summer was over, the film studio Metro-Goldwyn-Mayer had recruited Taylor to take over Verve Records, purchased from jazz impresario Norman Granz the previous December. Taylor completed his final Impulse duties, including editing *Africa/Brass,* while sitting in MGM's New York offices. He left behind a label with an artfully honed identity and a promising future.

At first there was this "who in the heck is an Oliver Nelson and what is Blues and the Abstract Truth?" *kind of thing. Soon enough there was a thread of "What do you mean? It's on Impulse. It's good-looking, great-sounding stuff."*

Creed Taylor in the studio, early sixties

music," and describes the spiritual-musical link that foreign music had come to represent to Coltrane in 1961. "He thought that by using folk music, he could get closer to the elemental source of music."

Coltrane cast his net wide, using LPs to search globally, and applying what he found to his band. He told Ralph Gleason,

> **I have an African record at home—they're singing these rhythms, some of that native rhythm, so I took part of it and gave it to the bass and Elvin plays the part. McCoy managed to find some kind of chords . . . it's a little different from what I've been doing . . . I had to make the melody as I went along.**

"Africa" was the cornerstone of his first studio effort for Impulse, a big-band date that matched the core of his quartet (himself, Tyner, Jones) with a host of New York's top brass players (trumpeters Booker Little and Freddie Hubbard, French hornist Julius Watkins, and tuba player Bill Barber, among others), as well as a few of his more regular musical sparring partners, like multi-instrumentalist Eric Dolphy.

Coltrane had known Dolphy—who played alto saxophone, flute, and bass clarinet—since meeting him in Los Angeles in 1954. After Dolphy moved to New York in 1959, they renewed their friendship. Peas from the same analytic pod, they recognized many of the same driving qualities in each other: both were determined students of melody, harmony, and emotive expression; both relied on emotive effects in their playing. Their irregular practice sessions—Dolphy's distinctively bright, sharply stated voice set against Coltrane's darker, slurred phrasing—led to a yearlong relationship following the making of *Africa/Brass,* as Coltrane's first Impulse album was titled.

Africa/Brass was Coltrane's most ambitious recording effort to date, an album generated from two sessions at Rudy Van Gelder's. The compositions—originals by Coltrane ("Africa" and "Blues Minor") and Massey ("The Damned Don't Cry"), and adapted traditionals ("Greensleeves" and "Song of the Underground Railroad")—reflected the bandleader's increasing attraction to long-form work. "I like extended jazz works and written compositions," he commented that year. "I'm studying and learning about longer constructions."

Using aspects of "My Favorite Things"—the vamp-oriented middle section, the unusual 3/4 meter—as his model, Coltrane stretched the formula to allow more room for solos. "We play 'Greensleeves' . . . sort of like 'Favorite Things,' " he admitted. "It doesn't have as much contrast because

From left: Eric Dolphy, Coltrane,
Reggie Workman, and Art Davis
at the Village Gate, New York,
August 1961

we're not going from a major vamp to a minor, but it does have a good mood if it's in the right tempo."

Coltrane's experimental use of dual bassists was another ploy from his informal get-togethers that he formalized on *Africa/Brass,* one which had initially been inspired by the exotic music he listened to at home. "I've been listening more and more to Indian music—I've been trying to use some of their methods in some of the things we're doing," Coltrane told a Dutch reporter in 1961. "I wanted the band to have a drone [sound, so] we used two basses," he explained further on the liner notes to *Africa/Brass.* "Reggie [Workman] and Art [Davis] have worked together, and they know how to give and take."

By June, Coltrane had accomplished much: a busy series of sessions that mirrored the prolifigacy of the preceding October, the expansion of his working band to a quintet, and the acquisition of a new bassist in another young Philadelphian, Reggie Workman. This momentum continued through the remainder of 1961 with a successful tour of Europe, Coltrane's first as a leader.

Coltrane wanted to try it all, at least while in New York. "There are still quite a few avenues open for jazz and they're all going to be explored. I know that I'm going to try everything," Coltrane announced. But on tours outside of New York City, Coltrane focused on his quintet, featuring a program that tested the staid: Dolphy's improvisations included upper-register squeals, and Coltrane's own garrulous solos were peppered with harsh tones and register leaps, leading various reviewers to react in the extreme.

John Tynan, in his "Take 5" column in *Down Beat,* sounded off loudest. "A growing anti-jazz trend," "nihilistic exercises," "musical nonsense" were the terms he chose to describe the quintet's Los Angeles appearance. A few weeks later Leonard Feather, in his own column, concurred: "Tynan's comments on the 'anti-jazz' trend were acute as they were timely . . . too many of us have been too bashful in bringing forth publicly these truths." Even Coltrane's primary booster at the magazine, editor Don DeMicheal, penned a lukewarm review of the group at the Monterey Jazz Festival, praising special guest guitarist Wes Montgomery over Coltrane's "intonation trouble" and "animal sounds" and Dolphy's "trying to imitate birds" and solos that lacked "clear direction."

The following April, DeMicheal provided equal airtime in the form of an interview titled "John Coltrane and Eric Dolphy Answer the Jazz Critics." In more of a call for understanding than a defense, Coltrane—with no indication of either vitriol or humor—commented sincerely on how he determined the length of his improvisations ("I'll try to build things to the point [midsolo] where this inspiration is happening again, where things are spontaneous and not contrived . . . if it doesn't happen, I'll just quit, bow out"), on Dolphy's influence ("He's had a broadening effect on us . . . we're playing things that are freer than before"), on charges that his music did not swing ("Maybe it doesn't . . . every group of individuals assembled has a different feeling—a different swing"), and on his own heartfelt spiritual outlook:

> **It's just recently that I've tried to become even more aware of this other side—the life side of music. I feel I'm just beginning again . . . [music] is a reflection of the universe, like having life in miniature. You just take a situation in your life or an emotion you know and put it into music.**

To be sure, the "anti-jazz" issue was a contained conflagration, a small skirmish compared to the politically and racially charged firestorm that would engulf the general jazz scene in a few years. But never had such a high-profile established musician been dismissed so summarily by leading jazz writers. When Charlie Parker, Thelonious Monk, and Ornette Coleman had met resistance, it had been upon their respective arrivals. Mid-career controversy seemed solely Coltrane's lot.

Yet, to the many whose experience of Coltrane was limited to listening to studio recordings and reading reviews, the intensity and innovation of his onstage performances remained an unknown quantity. His next album would capture their controversy, and add to the legend.

■ Bob Thiele had a simple, straightforward idea that appealed to Coltrane. "For his second album, we decided to record live at the Village Vanguard." Thiele was a record producer whose love affair with swing-era jazz had led him to a successful career with more popular music styles. When Creed Taylor accepted an offer to run MGM's Verve Records, departing Impulse in mid-1961, ABC-Paramount approached Thiele. He jumped at the chance to return to jazz. Taylor had left him a label in mid-bloom; but with only nine albums released, Impulse already boasted the beginnings of a moneymaking catalog, a solid reputation in the jazz marketplace, and a contract with one of the stars of modern jazz—John Coltrane. Thiele had a reputation for being a wheeler-dealer and having many irons in the fire simultaneously. "He had a lot of *seichl*—good, common sense. Horse sense," says Dan Morgenstern, who helped Thiele launch *Jazz* magazine in 1961. He offers a thumbnail sketch of the man who would be swept along by Coltrane's rocketlike path during the sixties.

> **He was a veteran record producer, an old hand at dealing with the vagaries of the business. From the start, he was a rich man's son, had a little money to play with, had a few of his own labels but they never achieved any kind of commercial stability—they always went down the drain. But he was a good talent spotter. Creed Taylor brought Coltrane to Impulse, but Thiele was able to see that there was something there, and he established a rapport with Coltrane.**

Impulse catalog number A-10 was Thiele's debut project in his new position. "I was apprehensive, a little nervous about doing it," he confessed. "I had not known Coltrane before then":

> **In fact, my first meeting with Coltrane [was] at the Village Vanguard . . . I showed up to record for one night and wound up recording four nights . . . by the second or third night I was really becoming involved in what was happening and just listening.**

The eventual album distilled four nights of reels to three tracks. "Spiritual"—an evocative precursor to the deep, trancelike effect of *A Love Supreme*—and the standard "Softly, as in a Morning Sunrise" constituted the first side of the album. If the uninitiated wanted to hear what all the fuss was about, they needn't look further than the blues-based tenor improvisation that filled side B. "Chasin' the Trane" was the name Van Gelder concocted for this recording, which critics of the day derided as "a treadmill to the Kingdom of Boredom" and "one of the noblest failures on record."

To most ears "Chasin'" offered no familiar form and little recognizable melody. It was instead a sixteen-minute, stream-of-consciousness tour de force, and the closest Coltrane had yet come to his goal of learning to "start from nothing—no 'in' plan, no intro, no solo routines." He had tackled the impromptu exercise as a trio, moving Tyner out of the picture altogether, and taken the germ of a melodic idea and pursued it, hell-bent on pushing the limits of the blues shape. Its length and energy finally provided home listeners an accurate sampling of the unpolished unfolding of Coltrane's live statements.

"The melody not only wasn't written, it wasn't conceived before we played it," Coltrane stated in the liner notes. "We set the tempo, and in we went." "We," in this case, included Coltrane, Jones, and a new arrival: yet another bassist from Philadelphia who had impressed Coltrane and been invited to sit in at the Vanguard—Jimmy Garrison.

■ During his European tour Coltrane had spoken openly of his concerns with his current band. He was still shopping, and was willing to explain why:

> Though I don't particularly have any reason to complain about Reggie Workman, he hasn't reached that level of maturity [equal to Paul Chambers] yet. I've figured it out with Elvin though. What he needs is a bassist who's a real "force of nature" because he plays so hard that if you don't respond with the same authority, you're practically overtaken. With Elvin, you need a flexible bassist, because often he's ahead of the time: you have to follow him and lead him at the same time . . . I don't know an available bassist who can do it.

Jimmy Garrison had changed greatly since 1957, when he first accompanied Coltrane the week the saxophonist went cold turkey. With the help of home buddies like Philly Joe Jones, he made the transition to New York in 1958 and slipped in and out of bands led by Curtis Fuller, Lennie Tristano, and Bill Evans. After Garrison left Evans (but not before recommending his replacement, Scott LaFaro), a chance meeting led to his being introduced to recent arrival Ornette Coleman, who eventually recruited him to replace Charlie Haden. In 1961, as Garrison recalls,

Completing the quartet: Jimmy Garrison

> I was with Ornette Coleman, and Coltrane and Eric Dolphy came into the Five Spot one night and sat in. I had decided to leave Ornette for economic purposes, and no other reason than that . . . Coltrane asked me to come down to the Village Vanguard to play with him, and that's where we made "Chasin' the Trane." When we finished playing, Coltrane said, "Man, if you ever decide to leave Ornette, please come to me."

Garrison's musical abilities, already solid and assured, had progressed rapidly in his year with Coleman, where he was taught by the same instructor Coltrane had turned to the previous year:

> Being with Ornette, I had to really study his music. Most people thought it was just a lot of catch as catch can, but it's not like that at all. Just a very small part of his theory: knowing that any note can be a part of the whole spectrum of notes. If you train yourself to think like that, you can come up with melodies that you didn't even know existed. That's certainly why Ornette's music had such an impact, because they had broken out of the conventional way of getting melodic lines . . . Also, rather than my being just a backup bass player, when I was with Ornette I was part of the melodic front line, always in the front with them—right in between him and the trumpet player. It kind of changes you psychologically too, because you start thinking, "I'm a part of what's going on melodically, here."

Coltrane's approach was reminiscent of Coleman's, Garrison found, but with a significantly different charge:

> When I was with Ornette, it changed my way of thinking about music, my approach to the bass. When I joined Coltrane, I thought, "Certainly, I'll be able to utilize this" . . . Coltrane . . . had broken out of the conventional way of playing like Ornette, but it had to do more with the sheer energy of the band—I could say the spirituality of the band.

Coltrane marked the footing and flexibility he needed for his quartet in Garrison's bass work, as the bassist noted his own ability to match Jones's prowess on drums. "I'll tell you, if you're strong, and can do your thing, it's not difficult at all playing with Elvin. But I've heard bass players not quite as strong as they should be, and it was difficult for them."

As 1962 began, Coltrane replaced Workman with Garrison, and by that spring, he let Dolphy go—a move he had intimated to a British writer asking of his plans for the quintet: "I'm not sure, but it will probably revert back to a quartet. Most of our things were conceived for a quartet, and the group sounds more like a quartet-plus-one than a quintet."

Had Coltrane (for argument's sake) hung up his horn after 1961, had his efforts with Dolphy constituted the final phase of his progress, his enshrinement as one of the primary soloists in modern jazz would have been assured. Like Lester Young, Coleman Hawkins, Johnny Hodges, and his other heroes, he would have been mainly praised for his innovations on the saxophone, with his various compositions elevating him a head higher than most.

But in 1962, as leader of what would evolve into one of the most awe-inspiring lineups to emanate from the tradition, Coltrane joined the highest echelon of jazz musicians. Louis Armstrong had his Hot Five (and later All-Stars), Duke Ellington had his various big bands, and Miles had his first great quintet. Now Coltrane boasted a band that would catalyze his full creative potential, fit into his Chrysler station wagon—the group's principal

Murat Theater, Indianapolis, April 30, 1962

mode of transport—and eventually reach their creative summit on *A Love Supreme.*

In Tyner, Garrison, and Jones, Coltrane found what he had been looking for: sidemen whose individual prowess and musical flexibility assured that all could contribute equally to a collective whole—to, as he put it, make it "happen fortuitously, without being forced."

In the chronology of Coltrane's career, the years of the "Classic Quartet" stretch from 1962 through '65. During this period, they quickly evolved into an A-list act, able to headline major nightclubs or top the bill at jazz festivals. They reigned as one of the most recognizable and inimitable groups, conscious of their singular sound and status, as Tyner maintains:

> **I said, "John, I know a lot of guys around doing a lot of things, but I think we're doing something really unique." I didn't mean that in an arrogant way—I just meant that I loved what we were doing.**

The band developed a reputation for being one of the hardest-working outfits on the road, their nightly energetic output calculable by liquid measure.

"I remember Elvin used to get so wet playing with Coltrane he would go to the bathroom after the set, wring out his pant leg and sweat would pour out on the floor," remarks Jimmy Cobb. Jones credits the band's internal chemistry for his energy and enthusiasm:

> **Playing with these three, John Coltrane, McCoy Tyner, and Jimmy Garrison, to me it was almost the most important thing in my life. The only thing I could think about during that period of time . . . I couldn't wait to get to the bandstand and play with these guys every night.**

A growing fan base felt the same way. During tours in late 1962 and '63, Europe embraced the quartet as conquering heroes, and in annual reader polls in music magazines, Coltrane and his sidemen were consistently top vote-getters. As accolades poured down and album sales stayed up, however, Coltrane remained humble, musically centered, spiritually focused.

"I don't give these polls more than they deserve," he averred, "inasmuch as they are capable of giving you a rating . . . But if this [success] happened to me without achieving what I personally wanted, I wouldn't sacrifice my search for the satisfaction of my fans."

Cecilia Foster (née Jones), cousin to Elvin, tells of the saxophonist's reaction to his listeners' praise:

> Whenever I'd say to John—me trying to be hip—"Boy! John, you really burned on that last set!" he'd look at me for a long time and say, "What do you mean by that? What did you hear that was different? What was so impressive?" When I couldn't explain, he would say, "Don't be like so many people we know. If you can't explain what the difference was that you heard, what impressed you, just don't say anything." He was really quite a teacher as far as I was concerned. He taught me how to listen to jazz, what to listen for, how to be humble and not frontin' on the music.

Perhaps the most sincere and informed appreciation came from jazz veterans who began to pop up at Coltrane's gigs. At McKie's in Chicago, Jones recollects, "I came off the stage and there was Louis Armstrong sitting at the bar. 'Hey, Elvin!'—he was acting like he knew me—'You want a drink?' I said, 'No, I already ordered . . .' He just came in to listen to the music."

Tenor saxophonist Frank Foster recalls the mutual admiration of the day.

> When I was with the Count Basie orchestra, I was working in [New York's] Greenwich Village at the Jazz Gallery in 1962. In one of the intermissions, two of my cohorts and I rushed out of there to go hear Coltrane, who was playing somewhere else in the Village, probably the Half Note. We were in a big hurry to get there and half way to the club, we ran in to him—and I think Jimmy Garrison or McCoy Tyner—right there on the street. We greeted each other warmly. "Hey, how you doin'? What's happening?" We told them that we were going to the Half Note to hear him, and he said, "Oh man, we were coming to hear you!" So we were both frustrated [laughs].

Foster was one whose tenor began to show heavy traces of Coltrane's mature sound. "Coltrane brought a more intelligent, complicated, and then, spiritual, style—I understood all of that, and that's why I was very much in agreement, spiritually in line with what Coltrane was doing." Others who had come up through blues and bebop, immersed in chords and harmony—Cannonball Adderley, Wayne Shorter, Charles Lloyd—began to incorporate elements of Coltrane's multiphonics, hard-edged phrasing, and arpeggiated flights into their own playing by the mid-sixties.

Earning the respect of one's contemporaries was one thing; siring an entire generation of saxophonists was another. By decade's midpoint Coltrane was being credited with widespread influence similar to that of his own heroes: Lester Young and Johnny Hodges. "I never thought of myself as a leading tenor player," he stated.

A jazz underground had taken root, peopled by a growing number of players whose music bristled with the same abrasive emotion and fiery spirit that blew through Coltrane's music. "Horn players—especially saxophone players—gravitated to him, because they were learning from him," explains Tyner. "Like Pharoah [Sanders] was very much inspired by a certain aspect of John's playing. Archie [Shepp] was another guy."

"John was eleven years older than I am, and he was older than Wayne [Shorter] and all the other guys as well. So he was an elder figure—a big brother to us," says Shepp, who, like Sanders, was part of a growing list of saxophonists—Albert Ayler, Marion Brown, John Tchicai, Ken McIntyre, Roscoe Mitchell, Frank Lowe, and others—looking to Coltrane as both a musical and personal role model. "The things he expressed were appreciated by us all, because he lived that way, that's who he was."

Other standard-bearers had led the jazz avant-garde during, then out of the fifties: keyboardist/bandleader Sun Ra, bassist Charles Mingus, pianist Cecil Taylor, and of course Ornette Coleman. But to the younger wave of "energy" players (as they came to be known) Coltrane was walking point in the mid-sixties. Shepp notes:

> When we talk about the avant-garde, a lot of it was inspired by the work of John Coltrane, as far as I'm concerned. But giving credit where credit is due, Cecil was his own man long before he heard Trane, and so was Ornette. What I'm suggesting is that Trane gave these guys a sort of credibility by synthesizing their ideas, making it swing, and adding to it a spirituality. Coltrane was our leader—he remained so.

Such was the collective force of this youthful vanguard that critics who had comfortably employed terms like "avant-garde" for Mingus and "free" for

Coleman threw up their hands, abandoned old vocabulary, and chose a catch-all name for the controversial sounds that flooded in after Coltrane: the "New Thing." Despite a growing resentment among musicians who had come up through the ranks of bebop against the newcomers who had not, Coltrane found inspiration among the "energy" players, as Shepp relates:

> **At that time, he was listening to some of the younger players, I think, as a sort of catalyst for himself—because he had explored so many things by himself. For example, Albert Ayler was impressive to him, because he had a very strong religious background like Trane, and Albert was doing something with sound and the range of the horn that he found some affinity with.**

Coltrane caught gigs featuring Ayler and others, sometimes taping the performances to listen to while on tour. The purveyors of the "New Thing" returned the favor. To Shepp and others, attending Coltrane performances held as much importance—and spiritual weight—as Sunday services. "It was like being in church. Within that quartet, he created what became for me a new music. Like Bach and Mozart, Coltrane actually raised this music from the secular to an area of serious, *religious* world music."

In Coltrane's choice of venue, Shepp marked a strong link to the black community that would hold sway over many purveyors of the "New Thing":

> **In Chicago, he always played on the South Side at McKie's—he never went to Mr. Kelly's or the big joints. He'd be right in the community. He'd always play a joint in Watts [when] in L.A., and a joint in San Francisco [Jazz Gallery]. And in New York, he'd always play the Half Note.**

Shepp's recollection is largely on target. Pep's in Philadelphia, the Blue Cornet in Brooklyn, and the Royal Arms in Buffalo are a few more examples of small bars in black neighborhoods Coltrane frequented in the early sixties. But according to the saxophonist, it wasn't so much the location or clientele as the venue itself that held the appeal. "I like playing in smaller places, so I can see what people feel," he was quoted as saying. "I would like my music to be part of the surroundings, part of the gaiety of a club atmosphere."

Whatever the neighborhood, the more informal the venue, the more Coltrane could extend his performances and explore his repertoire. Nonetheless, as Shepp adds, the appearance of Coltrane's urban connection dovetailed with the freedoms he assumed:

There were nights that I would hear him at the Half Note, and ohhhh, he'd make any Black Panther proud. The law says they close at three, and at 2:30 one Saturday night the band was just coming on the bandstand, so they made an announcement that they were going to lock the door. They stopped serving drinks, those that wanted to leave could leave, and those that wanted to stay . . . nobody left. The place was packed. And man, they played until four o'clock in morning.

By 1963, the Half Note, a small bar–cum–Italian restaurant on Hudson Street just west of Manhattan's SoHo district, had become Coltrane's venue of choice when home. Despite the cramped quarters—the quartet performed on a small ledge above the bar to two adjacent rooms—Tyner recalls that he never seemed happier or more outspoken with the band than during those open-ended performances:

Playing on the edge: Coltrane at the Half Note, New York, 1964.

"It was so intense at the Half Note that it was almost unbearable at times. I found I had to go out of the club so I could breathe again. He would not stop playing a solo until he had explored every aspect of the tune—I'm tempted to call them devices—whether it was a certain scale or a set of intervals."

—SY JOHNSON

Many nights he would come off the bandstand and say, "Wow, I really enjoyed that, you guys!" He was very vocal about it if you were doing something that he really liked and if it really helped him if you conveyed something musically, he would tell you.

Coltrane gladly took weeklong engagements, using them in a workshop manner, trying out—or dropping—material as he chose:

One time we were at the Half Note, and we played one song I really liked. I asked him the next night, "What about that song we played last night?" He said, "Well . . ." Not that he didn't like it, but he was always moving ahead to the next thing. Some songs he would play—like "My Favorite Things," "Chim Chim Cheree," "Mr. P.C.," "I Want to Talk About You"—became regular pieces for the band, signature pieces. But if he felt that it wasn't happening, he would just discard the piece and move on. That's why he kept playing certain tunes, because they were good specimens for growth.

Coltrane chose his nightly set lists himself, bowing to no one's whim but his own, a whim that others had come to trust. There were quantifiable reasons to merit the confidence.

■ Despite the general recoiling of many jazz writers, Bob Thiele discovered that *Live at the Village Vanguard* was a healthy seller. It was the first lesson in a long course of study. He began to get a feel for the uncommon demands of Coltrane's music: "it requires some concentration on the part of the listener, and you know, a little bit of intellect. It's that kind of music." He learned to trust Coltrane's instincts, to follow his lead:

Leading with the label star: an Impulse ad from 1964

> **[Coltrane] explained everything to me, why he was playing the way he played, and how he felt music could go . . . he was really the first guy who took vamps, and played endlessly on three chords. He always felt restricted playing within the chord, staying within the chords of, say, a Cole Porter song.**

Restrictive or not, Thiele saw safety of a sort in old standards. To the veteran producer, the songs of Rodgers and Hart, Irving Berlin and Frank Loesser were a means of stilling the critical rumble that, despite his confidence in Coltrane's ability to steer his own course, his music biz sensibility could not ignore.

"I think that he was less affected by the reviews than I was," Thiele admitted. "After you've been in the record business for years and years, you're always concerned about the commercial aspects . . . how well the record will sell."

In 1962 and '63, Coltrane agreed to Thiele's plan to intersperse albums with accessible material among his more adventurous, abstract recordings. "Impulse was interested in having what they might call a balanced sort of thing—a diverse sort of catalog, and I find nothing wrong with this myself." In those years, while Coltrane continued to compose stark melodies with dronelike accompaniment ("Tunji," "Up 'Gainst the Wall"), he recorded three albums—one of jazz standards (*Ballads*) and two memorable encounters (with Duke Ellington and vocalist Johnny Hartman)—that had the desired commercial effect. Five-star reviews and solid sales followed.

Even the higher-ups at ABC, Impulse's parent company, took notice. "He was our leading jazz artist, far and away," recalls Larry Newton, head of ABC in the mid-sixties. "We had some good players, we had Max Roach, but no one like Trane." ABC's in-house counsel Bill Kaplan recalls a mid-sixties meeting that paints a telling portrait of the artist as label star, cognizant of his stature, and wise in his boardroom ways.

> **ABC was buying companies here and there. At one point I went to Chicago to buy a catalog of music that had some pretty good songs in it, and one of the songs was "Twilight Time." So anyway, we're sitting in Newton's office with John, and Larry is expounding, "John, you should do another *Ballads* album. That album was so good, it was so beautiful." John said, "Maybe," and then Larry said, "And if you do, we just got a beautiful song, we'd love you to do it—'Twilight Time.'" John said, "I don't know that." So I said, "Well, it goes like this"**

[sings]. "No, I don't know that." "Oh, sure, John" [sings again]. "No." I must've done it about three or four times, and then Bob Thiele walks in. Larry says, "We were just talking to John about doing 'Twilight Time' and he doesn't know the song." Bob, who always had a cigarette dangling from one corner of his mouth, started whistling. And John says, "Oh, that song! Yeah!" I said, "I've been had." Either Coltrane had a great sense of humor or I'm not as good as I thought I was.

From 1962 through '64, all of Coltrane's albums—including *Impressions* (featuring more live material from the Village Vanguard recordings), *Coltrane* (with another waltz-time soprano piece, "The Inchworm"), and *Live at Birdland* (another glimpse at his onstage ferocity via takes of Mongo Santamaria's "Afro Blue" and his own "The Promise")—did well for Impulse. In fact, he came to be their leading light; as the label experimented with a number of one-shot projects—Duke Ellington, Count Basie, Sonny Rollins—Coltrane was a thread of continuity.

Another factor promoting Coltrane's ascendancy was sheer market saturation. While Impulse recorded and issued his newest material, Prestige and Atlantic followed a clockwork routine of releasing albums from their respective troves. Top reviews of *Coltrane* (Impulse 21) certainly were more impressive next to high praise for *Coltrane Plays the Blues* (Atlantic 1382) and *Standard Coltrane* (Prestige 7243), but when all hit the market in the same two-month period at the end of 1962, confusion would seem inevitable.

Then again, Bob Weinstock maintains that most jazz consumers were familiar enough with the record labels to wade through the deluge. "See, Prestige had a following like Blue Note did, and the people that loved Prestige would buy all these titles regardless of who it was, because of the label. I saw no [sales] rise because he was with Atlantic or Impulse." Had the idea of strategizing with competing labels ever crossed his mind, Weinstock reports that no dialogue existed between himself, Thiele, and Atlantic's Nesuhi Ertegun:

> **I never considered those things, I never talked to anybody. I just did want I wanted to do. I always had a release schedule for two, three, four years in the future. Like Brother Jack McDuff every six months, then Miles, Coltrane . . .**

Thiele was gratified, if perplexed, by the success of his Coltrane releases. "I remember in the early days of recording Coltrane, it was impossible to hear a Coltrane record on the air and yet his records were selling." The question was, to whom?

> And we were always trying to figure out who was buying them. Then I went on a tour, with [big-band leader] Stan Kenton and some other people, as a judge of student bands. When I arrived on a campus and was with student musicians, all they wanted to talk about was John Coltrane. And they had all of his records.

The entire music industry had begun to notice a burgeoning market on campuses across the country, and started looking for ways to understand and exploit it. It was still a small market—largely white and privileged—but substantial enough to warrant in-depth coverage from the leading trade magazine. *Billboard*'s annual "Music on Campus" installment debuted in early 1964, placing Coltrane among its "Top Artists on Campus," alongside folk groups Peter, Paul & Mary and the Kingston Trio, comedians Dick Gregory and Bob Newhart, and fellow jazzmen Miles Davis and Duke Ellington. But the collegiate audience—and white America in general— told only part of the story. Singer Patti Smith offers evidence that in the early sixties, Coltrane was reaching an even younger—and cross-racial—set of fans:

> I attended a fully integrated high school in rural south New Jersey. When I was fifteen, in 1963, I was part of a loosely formed jazz club that would meet in a basement on Sunday afternoons. It consisted of friends, mostly black, between the ages of fifteen and twenty who were interested in the music of Roland Kirk, Nina Simone, Thelonious Monk, and most importantly, John Coltrane. The older kids would share their records and experiences, some of them actually having seen the musicians play live. I remember clearly when *My Favorite Things* was placed on the turntable in the humble basement of my friend, Billy Corsey. We all sat around and were transported. R&B music I loved because it spoke to my awkward teenage self, and I like to move and dance to it. But Coltrane spoke to my soul and my developing intelligence.

Coltrane spoke with particular force to black America, where politics and culture—the civil rights movement, R&B music, and jazz—were tightly enmeshed in a rising wave of racial pride. "The pervasiveness of jazz in the ghetto," writes one historian of the early sixties, can be seen "in those glorious jukeboxes where Jimmy Smith, Miles Davis and Cannonball Adderley

Live at the Newport Jazz
Festival, July 7, 1963

rubbed shoulders with Martha Reeves, the Impressions, Muddy Waters and Howlin' Wolf." "As of now, jazz is still quite colored," opined Cannonball Adderley in 1964. "You can certainly tell Stan Getz is white, as contrasted with, say, John Coltrane."

Jazz had already begun to reflect the increasingly confrontational stance of black America. Drummer Max Roach, saxophonist Sonny Rollins, and singers Abbey Lincoln and Oscar Brown Jr. pushed social commentary front and center with albums whose titles (and covers) bristled with their political message. Rollins's *Freedom Suite* (1958), Roach's *Freedom Now Suite* (1960), *It's Time* (1962), and *Speak, Brother, Speak* (1962), and Brown's *Tells It Like It Is* (1963) charted the progress of jazz-as-protest.

Though Coltrane's spiritual sensibility set him on a more pacifistic course, he allowed himself to be more outspoken in the titles of his songs. The dirgelike "Alabama," recorded in late 1963 after the infamous bombing of a black church in Birmingham that killed four schoolgirls, left little doubt as to the source of its inspiration. The title of "Up 'Gainst the Wall," a loose-limbed workout without piano, had a definite law-enforcement ring to black listeners of the period.

Whatever Coltrane's intentions, as Max Roach points out, it wasn't so much what the saxophonist made explicit as what could be inferred from his music: "I heard many things in what Trane was doing. I heard the cry and wail of the pain that this society imposes on people and especially black folks." But, as Sonny Rollins cautions,

John was much more than that era. A lot of guys try to identify John with just the sixties as if his playing meant "well, let's go and fight" or

something like that, in a narrow way. John should not be defined in my view in that narrow sense of that quote-unquote civil rights movement. The civil rights movement has always been going on. It's going on now, it was going on before the sixties.

Coltrane's relevance—both timely and timeless—secured his position among a politically aware segment of both the black and white communities, adding another significant stratum of support that stretched from jazz clubs to college campuses, ghetto apartments to suburban basements.

Bob Thiele never made any effort to identify the typical Coltrane consumer. Years after, he was content to intuit his audience through his own experience: "it would seem to me you're either affected immediately or never. Coltrane affected me, and I'm honest enough to say I don't know why."

By 1964, the Classic Quartet had become a genuine phenomenon, displaying nightly feats of stamina and endurance, a collective force unlike any group that had come out of the jazz tradition to that point, as saxophonist Joshua Redman explains:

> Jazz is built on this notion of tension and release, and I think that all the masters—Louis Armstrong, Charlie Parker—mastered it. Louis going for those high Cs, man, that stuff is part of the heart and soul, the lifeblood of jazz. But you don't have that same sense of build and sonic turbulence—and you definitely don't have that sense of ecstasy—with, say, Charlie Parker that you have in a Coltrane solo. Coltrane, with as much control and knowledge as he had, made it sound so uncontrolled, untempered and unbridled. As far as an entire group, I would have to say that Coltrane's quartet at that point represented the apex of that notion of tension and release.

"They were a real band," Ravi Coltrane avers. "These guys were really talking to each other, they knew how to finish each other's sentences." Dave Liebman concurs, meting out the credit among all four players, as well as the extended period they spent performing the same material. He recounts a conversation he had while touring in the drummer's group in the seventies:

> "Elvin, I got to ask you. How many times did you play 'My Favorite Things'?" He said, "We played it every night for five years. You tell

me." I said, "About 1200 to 1500 times?" "Man, we played it every night like there would be no tomorrow. Like it would be the last time we played it." And I said, "I can tell you that's the truth because I heard you play it every night and I tell you man, it [the song] never fell asleep on my watch." I think it was also the time of history for jazz. They worked a lot—forty-five weeks a year, six nights a week, three sets, sometimes even four sets on the weekend. You're talking about getting the blade sharp as can be.

What then distinguished them from other groups of the day? Redman suggests a point of comparison:

If you listen to Miles's group at that time, you hear something that was much more conscious—they're much more explicit about the way they're subdividing the beat, superimposing one rhythmic feel over another. With Coltrane's group, there's this feeling of freedom and turbulence—whether they're playing off triple feels or duple feels— but in a completely flowing and organic way. It's so implicit.

In 1964, as spring gave way to summer, the quartet was well into its third straight year of an ever-inspiring run. Coltrane himself had survived a personally unsettled period; he and Naima had separated in 1962. "That was a funny period in my life," he remarked. "I went through quite a few changes, like home life . . . it was a hell of a test for me."

Coltrane was now deeply in love, living with Alice McLeod, the young pianist whom he had met and pursued the year before. They were expecting their first child within a few months, and had plans to purchase a house. In the past few months, Coltrane had begun to write poems, leaving notes in verse for Alice to find. They read sincerely and simply, and could be interpreted equally as declarations of personal adoration or as expressions of spiritual love:

How kind you are to me—to give—the universe revealed I see / Yes now I'll go to sleep—it's right, sweet—I rest in peace / At night—

Coltrane began to think of his poetry as a compositional tool, finding melodic ideas in the cadences of language. He had experimented with the idea before; "Alabama," recorded the previous November, derived from a written source, as Tyner explains:

1-6-64

Good morning my Dear

Another new Day. Another New chance to share in God's great story. {To Be To Give} Don't forget to be kind — (To Be) Forgiving — (To Be) Helpful — To be strong + just + To Be fair. Pray + Give Thanks. You are Born again. Work + ... I Love] You are Born Anew.

JC's

The song "Alabama" came from a speech. John said there was a Martin Luther King speech about the four girls getting killed in Alabama. It was in the newspaper—a printed medium. And so John took the rhythmic patterns of his speech and came up with "Alabama."

In late April and in June of 1964, he returned to the studio to record his first album of completely original material since his days with Atlantic. The compositions were mostly built on the lyrical flow of his own poems. "Sometimes I go at it that way because it's a good approach for musical composition," Coltrane divulged. "Some of the pieces on the album *Crescent* are likewise poems, like 'Wise One,' 'Lonnie's Lament,' 'The Drum Thing.' "

Released in late 1964, *Crescent* was a clear departure from his previous Impulse output. Save for his thematic efforts—*Ballads, Johnny Hartman*—it came across as more of a complete statement than anything he had recorded before. It was hailed for its distinctive unity of mood—introspective, wistful—and for its overall construction, which allowed generous solo space for all four members of the quartet to shine.

After years of musical searching—of tireless, cyclonic energy—Coltrane seemed to have found a stylistic resting point. The underlying intensity was in no way diminished, but there was a notable lack of explicit struggle in the sound. Critic Martin Williams, dipping into a new vocabulary to replace the usual terms "frenetic" or "restless," wrote of *Crescent*'s "moments of contemplation, relative serenity and perhaps resolution [in] the remarkable progression of pieces on the 'A' side . . . the title piece followed by the 'Wise One' and 'Bessie's Blues.' "

Among Coltrane's expanding audience, many saw a refinement—even a culmination—of the quartet's possibilities. "I think *Crescent* is one of that

quartet's most under-rated albums, one of their most perfect albums," comments Frank Lowe:

I can't say Trane's playing is not as free as it was before—the search is there but he's more contained in a way. It's like he's painting these portraits, and they're already finished. The whole thing seems a summation of his previous stuff, brought into neat little packages and made accessible.

Dave Liebman agrees:

I think *Crescent*, which is my favorite of all Coltrane recordings, is a summary of one aspect of the Coltrane Band: chord changes, real swinging, 4/4 jazz time. Especially "Crescent" and "Wise One," and "Lonnie's Lament" to a lesser degree, are pretty contained, not so wild as "Resolution" or "Pursuance." But those two records—*Crescent* and *A Love Supreme*—sum up that four- to five-year period of the quartet which is probably the most exciting band ever to play jazz.

In many ways, *Crescent* plays as a sketchbook to *A Love Supreme*'s fully conceived canvas. The warm, restrained reverence of "Wise One" is a template for "Acknowledgement"; the unrushed, 4/4 swing of "Bessie's Blues" a model for "Resolution"; the piano and bass solos on "Lonnie's Lament" a precursor to "Pursuance"; the lullaby-lilt of Coltrane's horn plus the sensitivity of Jones's mallet-play on "The Drum Thing" a foreshadowing of "Psalm."

But for some, like jazz producer Michael Cuscuna, *Crescent* upstaged Coltrane's masterwork-to-come. "I was still so much under its spell that I could digest *A Love Supreme* for what it was, but it never etched its way into my soul the way *Crescent* did." Nevertheless, the love of one album led the teenager to get an early report on the next:

I was at Birdland one night, the quartet was playing and I finally got up courage enough to go up and talk to one of them, because Elvin Jones was sitting just two tables away. I told him how much I loved their music, and he said, "Oh, we just finished an album called *A Love Supreme,* and I think you'll really like it."

Coltrane at ease on the stairs
connecting Van Gelder's
studio and home

John used to tell me how to listen to the music, so that I could get the most out of it. He would say things to me like, "You listen to a song, five times, Cecilia. Listen to it instrument by instrument. Play that song and listen to the bass all the way through. Listen to it again, and listen to the saxophone. Don't just listen to it once and then attempt to give it a critique."

—CECILIA FOSTER
(ELVIN JONES'S COUSIN AND FRANK FOSTER'S WIFE)

Chapter 3

December 9, 1964: Creating A Love Supreme

Like many one-man operations, Rudy Van Gelder's studio was run in a way only he could decipher. That certainly held true for the pages of the engineer's pocket-size planner, which reveals a nonstop flow of work in late 1964.

"The week of December 7, 1964, was a busy one for me," Van Gelder reports. "I was doing two sessions a day, Monday through Friday." Sure enough, his schedule book shows Creed Taylor blocking the studio on Monday morning, two appointments to master albums for the classical Vox label on Wednesday and Thursday, and a slot reserved for Blue Note Records on Friday night that brought forth Sam Rivers's *Fuchsia Swing Song*.

Impulse had also commandeered Van Gelder for almost half that week. McCoy Tyner led evening sessions on Monday and Tuesday with Garrison, Jones, and two Latin percussionists that yielded his album *Plays Duke Ellington*. The following Wednesday and Thursday nights were set aside for Bob Thiele and Coltrane, according to Van Gelder's cryptic scribble: "BT" and "Trane."

Alice Coltrane remembers her husband departing in the late afternoon of December 9 for the studio in his Chrysler station wagon, as he had many times before. Tyner and Jones recall Coltrane phoning them earlier that week to arrange the date, then traveling the familiar route up through Manhattan, across the George Washington Bridge over to New Jersey to meet the rest of the band. Impulse requisitions show the label ordering payment to Garrison and Jones for hauling their own equipment to the studio, as well as the charge for transporting an unusual instrument for a jazz session—a tympani. Total cartage fee: $6.

Each session could run up to four hours. As Van Gelder recalls, what occurred that Wednesday evening was somewhat of a departure from Coltrane's typical modus operandi:

> **This is the way it worked for most of the sessions he did. He would call me directly and say, "I would like to come in Wednesday at 7 P.M. and work for two or three hours." I would say "OK." They would arrive— always on time, I might add. I would have the session set up. Sometimes the producer wouldn't even be there. John would show the band what he wanted and they would do one piece and that would be the end of the session (two hours maybe). John would do that for as many sessions as it took to make enough music for an album.**

"However," Van Gelder adds, "*A Love Supreme* was not made that way . . . they did the whole suite in one session."

ABC-Paramount's payroll records—contract #107679—reveal the engineer charging Impulse for a four-hour recording session—#1092, running from 8 P.M. until midnight. Thiele inherited much from Creed Taylor when he took over at Impulse; unfortunately, Taylor's independence was not part of the package. Thiele's expenditures—artist advances, studio costs—were subject to scrutiny. But there were ways, as he revealed, of flying under the fiscal radar:

> **I was always over-budget with Coltrane and the executives were never happy, because they weren't interested in music, they were interested in sales. So I used to record Coltrane at night, rather than having to announce during the day what I was doing. Then I could go**

in the next morning and say what a wonderful Coltrane at Van Gelder's,
session we'd recorded the night before. December 10, 1964

Sadly, Thiele did not schedule a photographer to shoot the session that produced *A Love Supreme,* nor did he bring a camera. (He did call photographer Chuck Stewart to shoot the next day, however; many of the shots from
December 10 grace this chapter.) But Thiele was there, ever-present cigarette dangling from his lips. His star artist had not recorded music for
release, live or in the studio, in over six months—the longest gap while with
Impulse. By past pattern and contract, Coltrane was almost overdue.

Thiele certainly would have wanted to be there, if only to bear witness,
for by 1964, there was little else for him to do. Never one to take more of a
role than to suggest general ideas, Thiele had ceded all primary A&R
duties—selecting material, choosing sidemen, even scheduling the sessions—to Coltrane himself. It was a rare privilege the saxophonist had
earned, according to Van Gelder:

That fact that [Coltrane] had the influence with the record company
[and] was in such control of his own music that he could decide

> when he wanted to come in . . . leave and come back another time
> when he was ready to do another one . . . that's unique, that doesn't
> happen now.

Thiele agreed: "There can only be a handful that can conceivably record on the same basis as Coltrane." Coltrane in charge meant that Thiele—already "a very laid-back kind of producer" per Van Gelder—affected an even more backseat stance. "I believe he had one way of doing jazz dates and another way of doing pop dates. He would produce Coltrane in a certain way, letting John develop the whole thing."

Thiele offered his own take on his in-studio task:

> "Encouragement" is the word, because there were many nights that
> we recorded when I felt that he was really into something and there
> was a subtle situation where I had to get him to continue . . . having
> him continue when maybe he didn't want to or maybe some of the
> musicians didn't want to.

Tyner agrees that Thiele was more on hand than underfoot:

> Bob was there, but he was never like, "Guys, OK, how about doing
> this?" If he had anything to discuss, he'd discuss it with John, in a cor-
> ner or something. He'd sit on the stairs listening. Bob was never the
> audacious type of guy out there trying to show how great a producer
> he was.

Thiele biographer Bob Golden puts it succinctly: "His job basically was, as decreed by Coltrane, 'just make sure the lights are on and the tape is running.' "

In the case of *A Love Supreme,* he even yielded responsibility for the lights, as Tyner relates. "I remember something very unique about that recording session—Rudy turned the lights down. They were on, but they were low, and I guess he wanted to set a mood, but I never saw him do that."

"Yes, I did turn the lights down in the studio," confirms Van Gelder, but adds that he did that "quite often on sessions to alter the atmosphere a little. I still do it once in a while." He had started the practice in his Hackensack studio; the late-night ambience he affected in 1954 on Miles Davis's "Blue Haze" recording was one instance of note. To the engineer, establishing an appropriate and comfortable environment was simply part of the job, extending beyond the control room to the entire studio:

> **Everything I do is related to creating the perfect mood for the musician—the location, the room, the sound of the room, the way I approach him on an individual basis, the results that I think the producer wants. Everything is related to mood. For example, at one point on this project [Joe Henderson's 1991 album *Lush Life*], I turned out all the lights in the studio—I mean all of them, in the control room and in the studio. All anybody could hear was Joe playing, I believe it was on "Lush Life." That's about as mood-oriented as you can get.**

Van Gelder's penchant for detail was legendary. Bob Weinstock recalls that the engineer's meticulous reputation engendered a habitual greeting at jazz sessions:

> **There was a joke among the musicians—they'd come in the door, and they'd say, "Ready, Rudy?" And of course, he was *always* ready, you know? I'd just tell him who was coming, and he knew what to do with the sound and all that. I never worried about the sound, the musicians never worried about the sound. They'd just say, "Ready, Rudy?"**

On December 9, the priority was clearly comfort as well as custom: the evening hour, dim lighting, and the engineer's readiness all replicated the environment of a well-run nightclub gig. "When we got into the studio, we liked to capture the live effect, just like we were playing live somewhere," recalls Tyner. Even the positioning of the quartet suggests relaxed, onstage intimacy. Photographs of similar Coltrane dates show the members of the group situated within a few feet of one another in a semicircle, facing toward the control booth, despite the studio's generous dimensions. Interestingly, in photos from the December 10 *Love Supreme* session, Van Gelder bucks common studio practice and places Jones's drum kit, easily the loudest instrument, not far from Coltrane.

Jones's positioning certainly attests to Van Gelder's ability to control the sound levels from musician to musician. Most engineers would have simply sequestered the drum kit away from the band and behind baffles, the movable dividers that prevent audio leakage from one microphone to another. As Jones revealed in the mid-seventies, unlike his experience with Coltrane, his later recording practice had become one of struggling

Rudy Van Gelder

To a music enthusiast and fledgling sound engineer growing up in the fifties, the key to unlocking the magic on his favorite LPs lay on the back cover. "In those days, everybody read everything on the back of every record," says Phil Ramone, who discovered one name common to the jazz albums he loved the most. "I used to buy a lot of records made at Van Gelder's—tons":

> So I absolutely knew what the importance of the engineering was, even then when there was a naiveté in me that made me just jam forward to know everything. I knew that some of the stuff that was on RCA and other labels were different in attitude and I think a little bit more conservative. Rudy's work was more aggressive.

At the same time, young piano student Donald Fagen was living with his parents, spending his allowance on jazz albums and studying them just as intently. By the seventies, he would help define a standard-setting studio sound with his own jazz-infused rock group, Steely Dan. "One of the things we were looking for was clarity. And not too much reverberation or echo to cloud or muddy up the actual sound of the instruments":

> If there's any model, I would say [it would be] a lot of jazz records Rudy Van Gelder recorded in the late '50s. They have a very dry but live sound . . . natural, but studio natural.

Beyond a distinctive, recognizable sound—"crisp" and "robust" are descriptions others use—a cloak of mystery obscured most details beyond the name. Who was Rudy Van Gelder? How did he do what he did? Stories circulated from musicians and producers to a curious public telling of an exacting, bespectacled gent who was an optometrist by day, an engineer by night; who purposefully removed the brand names from his recording equipment to shield his process from others; who did not allow food or drink in his studio or smoking in his control room; who wore gloves

He had been in other studios, so he must have felt that I could help him be heard the way he wanted to be heard. The fact that he was here said it all.

—Rudy Van Gelder
on John Coltrane, 2001

while handling microphones.

In the contemporary jazz community, Rudy Van Gelder's name has grown to mythic proportions. He is one of the few nonmusicians whose contributions over a half-century match those of most performers. As the music's greatest freelancer, he intuitively defined the sound of not just one, but a number of important labels. ("Those great Blue Note, Prestige, and then Impulse records were all Rudy," says producer Joel Dorn.) Single-handedly, Van Gelder erected and ran one of the genre's most important studios, placing staid Englewood Cliffs, New Jersey, on the jazz map. He was John Coltrane's engineer of choice, earning a personal thank-you on *A Love Supreme*, an album owing much of its surviving vibrancy to the man who did his best to "meet the demands of the client—the musicians, the producer—to give them what they would expect."

"When you were with Rudy, you knew that you were home," says McCoy Tyner. "He dealt with us like we were family."

And the fabled fastidiousness, secrecy, daytime job . . . the gloves? All true.

In 1957, Rudy Van Gelder was experiencing growing pains. For close to ten years, he had watched his hobby evolve into a second profession. He had studied to be an optometrist, ran a full-time practice, yet found himself more and more often in his parents' living room in Hackensack, New Jersey, placing microphones and turning knobs. "I was examining eyes one day, and Wednesday, I'd be recording Miles Davis!"

Through the jazz grapevine, word had spread. "I had some friends who were musicians, they would come over the house to jam, and I would record them. It just happened to be that that was a living room, and that happened to be where the musicians were playing, That's how it started."

As the popularity—and profusion—of the records he made with the giants of modern jazz (Thelonious Monk, Sonny Rollins, J. J. Johnson, John Coltrane) mounted, Van Gelder's living room earned an international reputation. Mid-session photographs taken by Francis Wolff, Blue Note Records's art director, made floor lamps and window blinds seem natural accoutrements to any jazz date.

But, as Van Gelder recalls, the comfortable confines were proving limited in size and availability. "The pressure was on me to record into the evening, then into the late evening, more days per week, and of course, my parents were living there. There was also pressure on me to record larger groups . . . that was getting to be too much. So I had to get out of there."

Locating a lot in Englewood Cliffs—a quick fifteen-minute drive from Hackensack, and only twenty from downtown Manhattan—Van Gelder had plans drawn up to his specifications for a house with a connecting studio. The building's exterior would have a faintly Nordic aspect, with its most distinctive feature a large, low-hanging roof on the building's northern end, reaching almost fifty feet high, embracing the recording room underneath. Upon entering the studio directly from the driveway, visitors were greeted to a surprise: a stunningly reverberant, atriumlike space, defined by two huge wooden arches intersecting far overhead. The pyramidal, ribbed ceiling—wooden slats neatly connecting the arches—leant the appearance of an inverted hull. Impressed musicians and producers would remark on how—with its vaulted effect and exposed masonry block walls (the blocks custom-made)—the studio radiated the feel of a small, modern-style church.

Relative to the living room in Hackensack, the resulting performance space was voluminous, defining an irregular diamond that could hold groups from small bands to full orchestras. It had a smooth cement floor, and generous headroom above. On the southern side Van Gelder set the control room, enclosing enough space behind large glass panels for a full bank of recording equipment. To enhance a comfortable ambience, he chose lighting fixtures that projected a warm glow,

ran a bench along one wall, and often placed rugs and plants around the area where the band would perform.

In 1959, he moved his recording operations and his wife into the new facilities. Unhindered by past limitations, he now stepped up his work pace, recording from morning through evening, every day except Sunday.

Coltrane's introduction to Van Gelder had come in 1955, during his second record date with Miles Davis, which led to three years of commuting to Hackensack. While contracted to Atlantic Records from 1959 to '61, Coltrane recorded almost exclusively with engineer Tom Dowd at the label's studio (the 1961 *Olé Coltrane* date being the sole exception, it was placed in the

hands of Phil Ramone at his A&R Studio). After signing to Impulse in the spring of 1961, Coltrane reunited with Van Gelder, bringing his first big-band project into the engineer's two-year-old studio—an effort that would have easily overflowed a suburban living room.

Creed Taylor, informed by Coltrane of his desire to work with Van Gelder, notes that the relationship between the two was tighter than most. Van Gelder, who maintains a consistently professional manner with all musicians and clients—and expects the same in return—warms to the subject of the saxophonist. "The reason he came back here is because Coltrane liked the way I recorded and he said so," relates the engineer with a hint of pride.

Perhaps the two recognized a bit

Stanley Turrentine and the Three Sounds at Van Gelder's studio in its first year of operation, December 16, 1960

of themselves in each other. Terms that describe one's personality and approach to his respective craft—"precise," "prepared," "preoccupied," "private"—accurately define both. Plus they worked well together: "He was just a very pleasant person to deal with," says Van Gelder. They certainly shared a reverence for the music they were creating—and were happy with the results. "There was definitely a mutual admiration there," adds Taylor.

Through Coltrane, Van Gelder met a new generation of jazz players, among them two whose talents would shape *A Love Supreme*. Each carries distinct impressions of their experience in his studio. Tyner was most impressed by the engineer's strict focus:

We all loved him, even though he was very firm about some things he wouldn't tolerate, like bringing supper into the control room itself: food, drinks, none of that. John smoked cigars and pipes, but I don't think he smoked in the control room—maybe out in the studio. He would fraternize with us on a limited basis—once you got to know Rudy, and got to talk to him like when the session was over, he'd comment on the session, sometimes he'd laugh. But he was there to make sure everything was set up, and during breaks he would check everything. He had things to do.

Jones recalls the studio itself—and the gloves:

Well, that room was perfect, there were perfect acoustics

in there. Rudy was a meticulous guy—he built that place himself. It was like he was doing an eye operation or something [laughs]. He was wearing gloves when he was handling the microphones, "Don't touch the microphone!" We used to laugh about that.

As fastidious as Van Gelder appeared to some, others marked a deliberate sense of professional privacy. "I made a record there and never saw the tape machine," Joel Dorn recollects. "It was behind a small wall and you didn't go behind the wall. Rudy sat there like a chemist." He and I collaborated on a few Modern Jazz Quartet albums," recalls Tom Dowd. "He was secretive. You couldn't ask him, 'Hey,

Rudy, what mike did you use there?' or 'What echo chamber?' No comment. But that's his personality. Rudy is professionally trained."

But Van Gelder follows no hard rule concerning discussion of his equipment preferences; he has occasionally been quite forthcoming. In a review of a 1957 Thad Jones album in *Audio* magazine, he openly described his four Ampex tape recorders and the Altec Lansing monitor speakers in Hackensack. As recently as 1995, for a special multimedia edition of *Blue Train*, he spoke at length of the Scully lathe (on which he created lacquer masters for client labels in the LP era), and divulged an almost career-long affection for the Telefunken U-47 microphone (an early fifties arrival which he continues to employ).

Tracking *Blue Train* in Hackensack, September 15, 1957: (left to right) Coltrane, Curtis Fuller, and Lee Morgan

Van Gelder at the door to the Engelwood Cliffs studio, early sixties.

Part of the reason for Van Gelder's tight-lipped response to technical inquiries is the concern of being misconstrued, as he implied in 1957:

There is no universal microphone, and I wouldn't want to describe one of my set-ups as it might seem to commit me to one particular technique . . .

of course the Telefunkens are likely to appear in a photograph of a date, but that reminds me of the story of the company which recorded with one make of microphone and then brought out another make for the pictures. [Van Gelder today identifies that company as RCA.]

Van Gelder went on to reveal an economic approach to miking ("when one mic will do the job, I never use two"), a restrained use of reverberation ("I have an echo chamber and use it when necessary . . . [but] I try to avoid anything that seems artificial"), and a flexibility among performances ("I may also vary my set-up from track to track, not treating rhythm numbers and ballads the same way").

To some, the secret to Van Gelder's sound lay in a delicate balance of music and room sound ("he had a very unique way of getting presence . . . nobody had that sound," Tyner says); others credit the studio itself. "Even though Columbia [Records]'s 30th Street Studio had the church reverberation, it had more of a pop sound," insists Ramone. "Van Gelder's rooms all had a live edge to them. I think you can spot it a mile away."

Contemporary engineers continue to speak highly of his work, singling out his ability to remain true to the musicians' own sound. Ramone remains impressed by his handling of the particularly eruptive sound of Coltrane's Classic Quartet without limiting their performance:

In my estimation, one of the things that Van Gelder did— certainly people like Tommy Dowd did too—was to allow the explosion of the rhythm section or the whole quartet, allowing them to become more musical, rather than say, "Look, guys, you've got to step back from the mic," or, "That's too loud."

Whatever the microphone or its placement, the proof of Van Gelder's contributions to jazz lies in the lasting vibrancy of his recordings: *A Love Supreme* a stellar, enduring example. Like Coltrane, he was driven to ceaselessly explore his craft assiduously and scientifically, forging a distinct sound. "It is my wish not to become set or sterile in my approach, though I seem to have formed a style of my own . . . so some of the words of my critics would lead me to believe," he admitted in 1957. More than forty years later, Van Gelder insists on sharing the credit: "I really don't like to think of it as being 'my sound.' I feel each producer has his own recognizable stamp either by artist or the nature of the music." He adds:

What it is, is my feeling and my approach to the musicians I'm recording at a particular session. What I'm doing really is trying to let the musicians be heard the way they want to be heard. What it really is, is the musicians' sound.

against being isolated: "When I walk into the studio and engineers always say 'OK, drum over here. They've already got a little corner picked out where they always place the drummer . . . but I'm sort of doubting whether it's right. I know I'd feel more comfortable if I weren't in the same corner all the time."

Coltrane's studio manner revealed him as a graduate of the Miles Davis school of session preparation: the fewer words and the fewer run-throughs, the better. By 1964, as his sidemen report, he sought an effective balance of minimum instruction and maximum spontaneity. Tyner:

John said very little about what he wanted. If he had certain specifics that he wanted to add to the music or how he wanted it played, he would say it. I think this is so important, because it was an on-the-spot improvisation, honestly approached music, with nothing pretentious about it at all. In the case of *A Love Supreme*, it was actually songs, but the structure itself was very limited. A simple melody line,

The production trio: Coltrane, Van Gelder, and Thiele

and not too stretched out. I remember he worked out a bass line with Jimmy, and told Elvin, "This is what I'd like," and basically, that's the way it went.

For Tyner, Coltrane offered a little more, but not much:

He'd write down the symbols to a set of very basic chords—B-flat, B-natural, E, just regular chords—and you could hear the relationship of the chords, how they were fitting with each other. But it wasn't like he said, "I want you to play this, I want you to play that." We'd been playing together for so long at that point that the band had a sound, so it wasn't like we were stuck in a situation where we were tied down to these chords. In other words, you could do what you wanted, keeping the form in mind. That's what *A Love Supreme* was about.

Jones actually recalls even less instruction. For him it was just another quartet date: "That first day, he didn't have any extra people around [as they would the next day]. We didn't have any written music, he'd have some notes that he'd refer to, but as far as the rest of us were concerned, we'd just follow what he did." Jones, blessed with a quick ear for melody, was not worried about structure. His concern was timing:

> **In those sessions, I would always wonder what the duration of a piece was going to be. I tried to think in terms of how the dynamics were going to flow, whether a piece was going to be ten minutes or half an hour. Nobody had to tell me, it was something I had to pick up on. On** *A Love Supreme,* **there were interludes, and we'd stop and go from one theme to the next.**

Garrison, Coltrane, and perhaps some very sparse musical instructions

An instinctive language between the band members clued the drummer when to build—or dissipate—his intensity. "Once the form had been stated, it would be as though we'd been playing it for years." In fact, the material itself had a familiar ring. "We had been together three or four years when we made this recording," remarks Jones, "and throughout that period of time I had certainly heard some of these phrases." Not only phrases, but full tunes, as Tyner points out:

> **On *A Love Supreme*, actually we had played some of the music in the clubs before we recorded it. By the time we got into the studio, we didn't know exactly what was going to happen but we were very familiar with what we felt we had to do. I think that's why John liked to play the songs for a while, open them up. The more familiar you get with it, the more interesting places you can go with the song.**

The most distinctive feature of the music, according to Tyner, was its overall structure. "It was definitely a kind of a suite. It was beautiful, because the movements were connected." With a practiced understanding of song construction and recording techniques, Coltrane had carefully thought through the evening in advance.

Cognizant of the time restrictions of the LP format, he decided that two out of the suite's four movements would be on side A, the remaining two on side B. ("The long-playing record has certainly been a great asset to us," Elvin Jones once said. "If you have an idea, you've got a chance to complete it.") He would record the suite in the order it would appear on the album. Parts three and four—clocking in at almost twenty minutes—would be tackled as a unit, one after the other.

Before the evening was over, Coltrane would have enough material for a full album. That in itself was a surprise to Van Gelder. "An unusual thing that I recall about the *Love Supreme* session is that because he had preplanned all the music he did the full suite in one session":

> **This was one reason I enjoyed working with John. He would usually record only one or two titles per session—that's the way he worked at the time. In contrast, other jazz labels would usually try to do one whole album in one session.**

Van Gelder recollects, "I usually ask them ahead of time what is going to happen, so they did tell me the general format of the piece." In his mind they were to record only three tracks. "I never knew it was supposed to be in four parts, however, until I read John's notes for the album." All the need-to-know aspects of the suite's sections—key choice, how each would link to the next, when he would chant during the opening portion—were to be discussed that evening in the studio.

What Van Gelder recorded that evening was set in stone. How each instrument sounded relative to the others, how each was heard within the audio environment created by the room and by Van Gelder's volume levels, could never be altered:

> **All of them were two-track recordings, which eliminated any possibility of mixing later. The advantages of doing one or two tunes at a time in a direct-to-two-track mode allowed me to concentrate more on the balance, mix and overall sound. Yes, we could edit between takes, but we couldn't change the balance.**

In 1964, Van Gelder recorded in stereo; a reel-to-reel machine moving at 15 ips (inches per second) recorded the master copies for later editing and then mastering (the creation of the acetate platter that creates stamps for manufacturing vinyl albums). In the interest of maintaining some degree of isolation between the instruments on the master recording, the engineer opted to separate saxophone and drums as much as possible. A close listen to the surviving copies of the master tapes reveals Coltrane at "hard left"—positioned all the way on the left channel—Jones "hard right," Tyner's piano centered between the two, and Garrison's bass at right-center.

"I am certain there was no mixing involved—that is, mixing from a multitrack tape after the original sessions were recorded," notes Kevin Reeves, a mastering engineer at Universal Music with hands-on familiarity with most of the Impulse tape library, having mastered dozens of tapes for reissue. "One could accurately say that *A Love Supreme* was a 'live to two-track' recording." Reeves points out that such separation, though minimal by today's standards, enabled Van Gelder "to maximize the effectiveness of any enhancement—EQ [equalization, the balancing of different frequency ranges], or processing—that would take place in disc cutting—mastering":

> **There are only three possible degrees of separation on the master tape that we now use: those elements that are panned to the left, those to the right, and those in the center. With Rudy's stereo spectrum the way it is, he would be able to enhance the equalization on just the left side—where Trane's signal is—without adversely affecting Elvin, and the same goes for Elvin on the right. And if he wanted**

to enhance McCoy's parts, he would invoke an equalization on both left and right channels that would mostly affect the music panned center—which would, to a lesser extent, also affect Elvin and Coltrane as well.

As was his practice, Van Gelder "would run a master tape and a copy for [Coltrane] to take home." While recording the master tapes, as Van Gelder notes, "I made [lower-quality] 7½ ips mono tapes for all clients, so they could play back the session." Normally, "client" would denote the record company paying for the session; that Coltrane was allowed to keep the mono reels containing a full record of the session, including all false starts and outtakes, was another privilege Thiele granted his banner artist.

Thiele assigned the first track to be recorded with an Impulse catalog number: *A Love Supreme*'s as yet untitled opening section was referenced as "Part I," or master #90243. It contained a theme Tyner and Jones may have recognized from past gigs; Coltrane had been rehearsing the melodic line of the theme in the restroom of Boston's Jazz Workshop only a few weeks before the session when a startled member of the club's staff happened upon him. Saxophonist John Slate, whose career included stints with Woody Herman's big band of the late sixties and teaching positions in Pittsburgh, was then only eighteen, studying at the Berklee School of Music:

Tape box A1 (of original four) containing one of only two surviving 7" reels of full session recordings from December 9 and 10, 1964

I had a job as a busboy at the jazz club just so I could hear the name players come in. When Coltrane came in it was really unique: Jimmy Garrison fell down the steps with his bass and they had to get another bass. And Elvin was there with the two Dobermans, and McCoy was playing piano. Before the gig even started, Trane was in the bathroom, just woodshedding. He was practicing these chromatic patterns and [sings theme to "Acknowledgement"]. And they got up and played what ended up being parts of *A Love Supreme* for almost an hour set.

Coltrane completed his instructions and preparations for the first take of the evening. At the appropriate moment of readiness—with a full evening of recording ahead—Coltrane signaled to Van Gelder behind the control-booth glass.

The reel-to-reels started rolling.

Acknowledgement

From the very first sound that was recorded, *A Love Supreme* raised expectations.

Elvin Jones leans to his left and, striking a Chinese gong, opens the album with an ethereal, exotic splash. "It's the signal of something different," remarks Ravi Coltrane. "You don't hear that instrument anywhere else on any other John Coltrane recording. He never had one on a gig before." In one stroke, the hammered metal's distinctive shimmer clears the air of standard jazz practice. "Those guys were influenced by classical music, and brought in elements that sounded of grandeur—orchestral instruments like the gong and tympani."

As the metallic ring of the gong begins to decay, Coltrane is ready at the microphone Van Gelder had placed before him, tenor saxophone raised to his lips. It would be the only instrument (save for his voice) he would play on the session—a departure from his habitual inclusion of at least one soprano feature per album. Given his propensity for experimentation, why only tenor?

Jones answers decisively, noting that "he didn't play soprano saxophone just because he had it. He played it because it was appropriate." The suite was doubtlessly conceived with a tonal and textural unity; to Coltrane, the warmer, earthier tone of the tenor—plus its vocal-like range—made it the appropriate choice. "I don't know if it's because the tone of the instrument is very close to the human voice—his solos on *A Love Supreme*, they're like small sermons to me," Tommy Flanagan observed. "But the tenor can express a lot, it has a lot of range. It touches deep."

Coltrane enters with a brief fanfare. Whether blown from minarets or at military barracks, as a call to prayer or to arms, it's a time-honored device with a timeless function. Fanfares demand attention, heralding the importance of the message to follow. On a classic jazz recording like Louis Armstrong's "West End Blues" from 1928, the opening statement sounded a virtuosic wake-up call; in 1945, on Dizzy Gillespie's "Salt Peanuts," it was a giddy nudge in the ribs.

Elvin at the drums, with
the gong behind him

In the context of *A Love Supreme*, Coltrane's warmly stated opening figure—in E major, which, though briefly played, was an unusual key for Coltrane—serves as a benediction, a spiritual welcome. He repeats it with a fading effect, as Tyner, Garrison, and Jones join in and softly add to the earnest tone of the opening. "If you say *A Love Supreme*, that's what I hear first, every time," says Alice Coltrane:

> **It's like a beautiful city, but we don't enter, because we have to go through the portals, the corridor, and then we reach the entranceway. When that chord hits, that E major, the doors start to open. That's what it's like for me—the very first invitation to this beautiful place that's here, that's in our heart and spirit.**

The invocation lasts no more than half a minute but leaves a longer, levitating impression. Before the feeling of suspension dissipates, Garrison enters, anchoring "Acknowledgement" with a four-note motif that literally sounds out the cadences of the album's title.

This famous "a love supreme" riff is a phrase that is, essentially, a blues building block. A more common element of jazz—of African-American expression in general—does not exist. Because such phrases are an integral part of the music's grammar, it is not surprising to find at least one antecedent to the "love supreme" figure in the jazz annals.

"Mau Mau," a 1953 recording by trumpeter Art Farmer (co-written by Quincy Jones), falls into a Latin jazz category, and features a section with the same melodic and rhythmic stamp as "Acknowledgement." Given the eleven-year gap, it's a safe bet that Coltrane, Farmer, and Jones were simply drawing inspiration from the same deep, blues-filled well many others have visited. Branford Marsalis:

> **You know Led Zeppelin's "Whole Lotta Love"? [Sings, shifting rhythm so it sounds like "a love supreme" riff] Or Willie Dixon's song "The Seventh Sun"? [Sings, does same] That's the bass line in the first section of *A Love Supreme*—it's just a blues lick.**

It's the paradox at the heart of Coltrane's mid-sixties flight: the apparent simplicity yielding the deep and timeless. "The blues is the common denominator in jazz, however much harmonic finery may be employed to dress it up," writes Gary Giddins, distinguishing the conventional twelve-bar form from the impromptu tour de force "Chasin' the Trane" in 1961. But three years later, the view that "the more Coltrane limits himself . . . the more he seeks" still applies. "He pushes himself and the blues to the limits of endurance, drawing light from dark, pleasure from pain, liberation from constraint."

Assigning the role of invoking both melodic line and rhythmic pulse to the bassist was nothing new for Coltrane. On his recording of "Olé" in 1961, he had Art Davis supply the minor-key opening. Two years before, he was present when Paul Chambers performed the famed introduction to Miles Davis's "So What." On Coltrane's first date as a leader in 1957, Chambers had utilized a similarly seductive opening pattern on "While My Lady Sleeps," echoed by pianist Mal Waldron's left hand.

It's a credit to Garrison's timekeeping ability that he hit the right mix of tempo and sentiment on the first take. But then, he was often marked as one of the most economically fervent bassists of his generation. Critics praised "Garrison's swing [as] a contrast to the often violent charge of [bassists Charlie] Haden and [Scott] LaFaro," and came to laud him for "never slicing the rump roast off the bottom of the beat." Garrison himself was aware of his reputation:

> **There are some musicians who are characterized as guys who can really swing and there are some that are thought of as technicians . . . I'm not saying that a technically equipped player can't swing, but I've been thought of as one who swings and that's where the emotional tag comes from.**

Garrison continues stating the theme as Jones neatly layers in accents on snare rim and sock cymbal. The two allow the sway and swagger of the piece to establish itself. Tyner enters with a series of sharply hit, offbeat chords, goosing the rhythm forward.

Then, with added bluster, Coltrane returns, blowing in time to the rhythmic component of Garrison's bass line, but introducing a new, three-note melody—ba-*dwee*-dah—that asserts itself as the tune's primary line. The quartet swings into a groove, unveiling the open-ended, vamplike structure of "Acknowledgement."

From the opening moments of his first solo on *A Love Supreme*, Coltrane cuts a wide emotional swath. Like an orator warming to his task, his saxophone starts gentle, grows insistent, building from a simple lyrical riff to levels of joy and grace, solemnity and sorrow. Coltrane finds his distinctive rasp, adding a tone of urgency. As he raises his "voice," leaning on the end of a passage, so Jones and Tyner increase the intensity to match his emphasis.

Garrison and Tyner—particularly in the latter's left hand—seem intent on suggesting a 4/4 rhythm. Meanwhile, Jones is playing double-time, even triple-time patterns on the cymbals; fills on the snare rim and tom-toms simultaneously define a 6/8 meter with a slight Latin lilt. Years later, a focused listening of "Acknowledgement" elicited comment from Jones on his Afro-Caribbean influences:

> I used to listen to Xavier Cugat's band a lot because they were on the radio and in the movies. And of course, Cole Porter wrote a lot of compositions that implied Latin rhythms. So I always wondered what it would feel like to do that myself, as part of what I was supposed to do. Some parts of Latin music are very rigid, as are some aspects of African rhythms. The flexibility comes from the number of people that are playing the rhythm. It is not always synchronized, so that gives it a certain movement that makes it more fluid. When I applied it, I opted for the fluidity rather than the static portion of the rhythms.

Jones offered a key to grasping the foundation of his approach:

> I always try to sustain some kind of continuity with the cymbal. That's where the consistency really is, because we no longer use a strong 4/4 bass beat, or that rigid, up-and-down, 2 and 4 on the hi-hat. So the emphasis is on the consistency of the tempo and, of course, on the continuity of that cymbal. That provides what would be the clave [the central pulse] in a Latin orchestra.

The end result was a loose rhythmic base Coltrane found inspiring in its elasticity. "I especially like his ability to mix and juggle rhythms," he said of Jones, his partner in pliancy. "I guess you could say he has the ability to be in three places at the same time." "Acknowledgement" offers a fine display of the Coltrane-Jones dialogue, a teaser for the album's later dynamic interplay.

Toward the tail end of his "Acknowledgement" improvisation, Coltrane achieves a plateau of intensity, as Tyner frames the moment with a rich tonal palette. "That section is always my favorite part of the solo there, when he plays these natural thirteenth notes [an interval of a sixth above the tonic]," remarks Ravi Coltrane, noting how his father would reserve the use of certain harmonic gestures to enhance their value. "It's the first time he really outlines that in the solo, and it has a cool kind of sound—like the music is opening."

Coltrane now begins to downshift: ruminative pauses steal into his playing. He starts to hang on to phrases, playing long tones, nudging the music into a more meditative pocket. He falls in line with Garrison, adopting the now mantralike "a love supreme" phrase.

Then, in another of the album's most celebrated—and startling—moments, Coltrane blows the four-note pattern thirty-seven times in methodic succession. With exhaustive precision and apparent randomness, he transposes the phrase from one key to another. What was an "opening" effect to Ravi is now raised to an extreme: it sounds as if the tune is being unraveled, and reinvented moment by moment.

A word about modulating, or changing keys, is in order. In the context of contemporary pop songs, modulation is an oft-used trick that effects a final push to a melody, adding one more level of intensity before the song ends or fades out, as in the Beach Boys' "Good Vibrations," even Celine Dion's "My Heart Will Go On." But modulating—almost always one full step up—is not key-hopping. To rapidly change the harmonic base of a melody, not once but repeatedly, is to invite an unsettling effect, if not confusion. Yet in the context of *A Love Supreme,* Coltrane's transposition of the signature theme fulfills a number of functions.

To some, Coltrane's exercise in key-hopping is just that: a mere expression of his self-directed academic drive. To Lewis Porter, however, it resonates with deeper, spiritual significance: "he's telling us God is everywhere—in every register, in every key." To minimalist composer Steve Reich, it's an extreme example of the saxophonist's equal-opportunity approach to harmony:

> **In a nutshell, what knocks me out about Coltrane is that he's the most harmonically static player and the most harmonically adventurous at the same time. I listened to it [sings modulating "a love supreme" theme] and that one point just made me wonder, "What is he doing?" So I went back and wrote some of it out, about fifteen different times that he played it. I couldn't figure out any particular pattern. But what really strikes me is the tension between a very tonally fixed anchor and finding out that that anchor makes it possible to go literally anywhere in the twelve keys and return. That's a worthwhile lesson.**

Ravi agrees: "It's deliberately random—he was not following any harmonic pattern." To Dave Liebman, the key-hopping section portends the final, experimental extreme of Coltrane's career:

> **It's really looking towards what he's about to go into, which is very, very free and non-key-centered improvisation. The way he takes that "a love supreme" motif, and transposes it through all the keys over the ostinato pattern that Jimmy is playing, is a real study. And McCoy is sort of in between, chasing Coltrane, and staying on the one key.**

Coltrane returns to repeating the mantra in one key. A moment of stasis settles in—he removes the tenor from his mouth and leans toward the microphone. With extra emphasis Tyner plays a long, resonating chord, as if to signal the start a new musical event. With a focused ear, it is possible to discern Coltrane's own voice entering in just after Tyner's bold stroke with the word "supreme." It's an unrehearsed move that has never been corrected or erased. Coltrane had begun his chant off-microphone; the words "a love" were lost, but "supreme" remains. Van Gelder quickly adjusted Coltrane's microphone level to catch the next full utterance:

> **"a *love* supreme . . ."**

There's an air of inevitability in Coltrane's vocalizing the riff he's just performed on tenor, as if it's the only logical choice. In Porter's view, Coltrane's reed-to-tongue maneuver "brilliantly executed a reverse development," drawing the listener further into the album's musical journey:

> **You can't just hit someone over the head by chanting right at the outset—the listener has to experience the process . . . we realize that there is a method behind the unusual structure and sound of the piece—Coltrane's music is not abstract, but is dictated in part by the messages he wishes to convey.**

Coltrane's incantation certainly raises a high-flying banner even higher, and leaves no question as to the origin of the four-note motif. But would it not have been more evocative to refrain from making it all explicit, to leave the words implicit in the melodic line, like the "in the mood" bridge section of Glenn Miller's swing-era anthem? Or Miles's famous "soooooo what" horn riff?

Alice Coltrane sees her husband's choice as a purposeful stepping off the pedestal of instrumental prowess, a spiritual self-leveling. "It's as if he's saying, 'It doesn't matter what we think we play that's man-made. God, you gave all of us an instrument. We can also offer you praise with the use of the voice that you created in us.'"

Wayne Shorter, an avowed Buddhist given to the power of chanting, agrees:

> **I know that his grandfather was a preacher, and he came from that experience. When he started singing the words "a love supreme" he didn't solicit the vocal expertise of some well-known record-selling singer. I think he was saying you must rely on yourself for communication. I think he was going back to square one where the voice is the first announcement of your humanity—your humanity is your instrument.**

Matching the lugubrious phrasing of the saxophone, Coltrane's deep voice repeatedly intones the four syllables. But just how many voices are there? Certainly more than one. Shorter notes that it sounds like Coltrane chants "along with Elvin Jones and someone else maybe." Van Gelder confirms that "he did the voice live [though] I don't believe his voice was overdubbed."

But closer examination would explain otherwise. As the chant begins, an audible dimension of reverb opens up, typical of the effect of overdubbing, or multitracking. It seems the additional voices were taped later. The voices sound layered, more alike than disparate. One further clue supports the argument that after a full day to think about it, Coltrane decided to add another voice: his own. A briefly jotted line on the audition tape box from December 10 reads: "900243—Part I—voice overdub."

After the fifteenth repetition of "a love supreme" Coltrane's voice drops a whole step from F minor to E-flat minor, a carefully planned modulation that the band follows, and which sets up the link to the next section of the suite. He chants the phrase four more times and stops. The reverb effect from the overdub disappears, Tyner slowly drops out, and eventually Jones as well. Garrison carries on alone, first with the four-note mantra, then with a bass line that maintains the rhythmic pulse yet works toward a new melodic area.

Garrison's ending to "Acknowledgement" is not so much a solo as a seam. Or better yet, half of one. Like other jazz recordings meant to flow from one track to another sans interruption (*Miles Ahead* comes to mind), at least one part of *A Love Supreme* was constructed so that the tail end of the opening section matched the head of the next: same solo instrument, same key, same tempo. Van Gelder would later suture the two parts together. A brief silent pause marks the splice (and a barely noticeable bit of sonic crackling signifying tape deterioration on the master tape).

Resolution

As "Acknowledgement" had been performed by the quartet prior to the session, so the second section of *A Love Supreme* had been road-tested by the time the musicians hit the studio on December 9. But unlike any other part of the suite, a recording of an earlier, live performance of "Resolution" does exist. It was captured on September 18, 1964, a Friday evening at a small neighborhood drinking hole not far from Coltrane's old home in Philadelphia. For the saxophonist, what the Half Note was to New York City—a low-key haven from the more formal environment of higher-priced nightclubs and concert halls—so Pep's was to Philadelphia.

Sitting on one of the benches in the upstairs gallery, a local saxophonist and Coltrane enthusiast was in attendance with a small reel-to-reel recorder perched on his lap. Frank Tiberi, later to hold the lead tenor seat in the Woody Herman Orchestra, had been following and taping his hero since 1960. "When I first saw Coltrane, he was with the Miles Davis Group at these Showboat dates. It just amazed me of what he was doing. I just knew this was going to be the future."

With stealth and slight discomfort, Tiberi began recording in venues like Pep's:

> **I'd be sitting on this sort of church bench with people right next to each other. On my lap I'd have my bag with the tape recorder inside— a TR-100, made by Howard W. Sands & Company in Indianapolis, Indiana—and the wire to the microphone coming out. It was just a relaxed situation there, you know—a funky bar, dollar beers. I think his playing in the club was a lot more accepted by musicians that had been hearing all of his recordings. All his friends and everybody were at the bar and he just played as much as he wanted to and as much as he felt.**

On that mid-September evening, Coltrane performed a new tune he had recently written. He counted off the work-in-progress. Over half an hour later, Tiberi had evidence of the magic that a comfortable, late-night environment could engender. Beyond the tape's value as an antecedent to *A Love Supreme*—one can hear the distinctive "Resolution" melody line already in place—there are stunning examples of the ways and means of Coltrane's exploratory style of late 1964.

"My man is definitely trying to find something," quips saxophonist and reissue producer Bob Belden, pointing out the bottom-to-top, harp-influenced scales Coltrane plays in his first solo on the tape. (Coltrane had in fact recently installed the classical instrument in his home and encouraged Alice "to study the harp.") On his second improvisation—taking the bandleader's prerogative to return to the bandstand and deliver the final, high-energy solo—Coltrane leans on his signature midphrase register leaps, jumping from the saxophone's low to high end and back again: a mesmerizing one-man call-and-response that elicits audible gasps and cheers from the crowd.

Belden also notes Coltrane's extensive use of his self-dubbed "landmarks"—moments when long, exhilarating periods of tension seem to resolve with a breath of harmonic relief. "Hear how he puts extra emphasis on the E-flat tonality when he wants to bring it home? Then the band joins him—he hits the root, and plays off it."

Ten weeks later in the more sedate setting of the studio, the tempo is slightly sped up. The lengthy 32:30 workout in the key of B-flat minor from Pep's has been distilled to a punchier, seven-minute-plus performance in E-flat minor. And as the cover of the 7½ ips tape box of the session shows, the final take of "Resolution" was the end result of seven tries. Given that audition tape, "Resolution" is the only performance from the session that allows a glimpse into its development; no outtakes of "Pursuance/Psalm" are known to exist.

Bob Thiele: 90244, part 2 . . . take 1.

Thiele's noticeable Brooklynese announces ("slates," in studio parlance) a first take that only includes a few halting notes on bass, an initial effort by Jimmy Garrison to lay down the song's introduction. Thiele responded by writing "bd" ("breakdown") on the tape box, indicating that the performance was called off well before a full performance was completed. Take 2 lasts just as long, and take 3—with Garrison now introducing a more jaunty feel to his bass line—reaches the tune's horn line, only to be fumbled by Coltrane.

BT: Take 4.

In less than two minutes, over four brief tries, Garrison has developed his introduction from a mere single-line run to a more deliberate and satisfyingly complex improvisation. Rhythmically, it now has a more interesting, push-pull motion; echoing his lengthy solo from the nightclub, he now injects a number of what are known as double stops (two notes played at the same time).

"You want to know what started me on that?" Garrison revealed. "I heard Charlie Haden play something on a piece of music that Ornette [Coleman] had written . . . he was using double stops. I had heard bass players use double stops a thousand times but not quite that way, so I experimented with that. I discovered a way I could finger three notes at one time and get a chord . . . what I did then was devise a way to play scales like that."

Much like Coltrane, the bassist was looking to extend the chordal possibilities of his instrument by stretching standard fingering practice: implying a full chord by simultaneously plucking two, even three notes. The net effect was an engaging way of allowing the harmonic structure of the composition to ring out.

Take 4 is the first full performance of "Resolution," clocking in at 7:15. Compared to the final version used on the album, it is less compelling: at a slower tempo, with reduced steam and focus. The theme is competently performed, and the structure and feel of the tune are more than adequately delivered. Though Tyner stands out during his own solo, the pianist and Coltrane seem to joust more than join together when the latter takes the lead. From bandstand experience, Coltrane knew his quartet had a better take of "Resolution" within them.

Thiele often spoke of the saxophonist's propensity for recording take after take:

> **Coltrane would make 30 takes on a tune when I first recorded him. They got worse. Then, he wanted to go home. You gotta capture it when it happens. That's jazz.**

Thiele was given to exaggeration, a factor that added to Coltrane's perfectionist reputation. If a producer slates every breakdown or false start as a full take, as Thiele did, it would appear that a musician was rather take-happy. In fact, "Resolution"—including all breakdowns and full performances—easily fit onto twenty minutes' worth of tape. Furthermore, by 1964, Coltrane was a studio professional, well acquainted with the concept of diminishing returns. Van Gelder himself marked the saxophonist's unusual ability to *not* over-record:

> **The thing about him that really is outstanding to me—and this is really in the latter part of [the sixties]—he had a command of his own music, knew what he wanted, to where he could say, "That was a good take." I admired musicians who can do that. Sometimes they want to keep going after it, just making take after take, to see if they can do better. But he had a way of knowing when it was right.**

After the tape stops, Coltrane confidently informs Thiele they will try again.

> *BT: Are you ready? OK—we'll call it 5. Anytime you're ready . . .*

Take 5 swings with a little more energy. Coltrane's statement of the "Resolution" melody is again embellished and changed; the saxophonist was forever testing, interpreting. Toward the end of his statement, he slips into the wrong key, stops, and utters a quick apology.

> *John Coltrane: Excuse me . . .*
> *BT: Six when you go.*

Faintly, Coltrane can be heard telling Garrison the degree of consistency he is looking for in the bass accompaniment after the introduction.

> *JC: Keep that going exclusively when the melody comes . . . you can elaborate on it some, but most of the time . . .*
> *BT: Six.*

Thiele's voice precedes another jettisoned effort, and unfortunately so, for—in its 2:58 duration—Coltrane smokes through the "Resolution" theme; mid-statement, he determinedly repeats an improvised phrase that lends the take an air of exigency. But the energy drops measurably as Tyner starts his solo. A minute into his improvisation, the take is called off. With apparent displeasure, Jones sharply hits the snare.

> *JC: Excuse me . . .*
> *BT: Seven.*

Coltrane and the quartet refocus, and deliver the complete, final version of "Resolution."

As a guitarist might strum the chords to an impending number, promising more orchestration and volume, so Garrison's introduction sets up expectation. Deceptively hushed, his preamble is a slow-burning, blues-tinged fuse to the detonation that follows.

Coltrane explodes into the tune's theme. The carefully planned pacing of the tune trumps the more subdued fanfare that opened "Acknowledgement." When the drama of the music called for it, Coltrane was more than willing to manipulate—to lull and then jolt—his listener. "For me, when I go from a calm moment to a moment of extreme tension, the only factors that push me are emotional factors, to the exclusion of all musical considerations," he explained, speaking of *A Love Supreme.*

Following the less-than-traditional structure of the opening section, Coltrane's eruption on "Resolution" returned most jazz listeners to familiar ground: a blustery tenor leading his quartet through a swinging, 4/4 jazz tune, with a hummable theme, a finger-snapping pulse, an identifiable structure. "The first part doesn't call for a fixed number of measures," Coltrane admitted, adding that "the central section ['Resolution'] is composed of three groups of eight measures."

To musicians as well, the second part of the suite offers a more standard structure, "a great set of chord changes," according to saxophonist Pat LaBarbera, who would later perform the tune as a long-running member of Elvin Jones's group. "You've just got these few chords, and when you think about it, 'Resolution' is just 'Bernie's Tune' [a late-forties bebop standard] in another key. But Coltrane's melody is just so different. If you weren't a musician you'd never pick up on that, because he made it such a great melody."

Tyner's ensuing solo—his first of two on *A Love Supreme*—takes lyrical advantage of "Resolution," first playing off the melody with a marked ebullience, then dipping moodily. Inventive, supple lines flow from his right hand as his left drops in spontaneous chords that echo the boosting effect of Jones's sporadic cymbal crashes. In contrast to Coltrane's slurred note-stretching, Tyner's phrases ring clear and true. Telegraphing a change, he sets in motion a rhythmic barrage of block chords, his left hand ascending then descending. Ravi raves over Tyner's influential effect:

> **There's just so much personality and originality in all of McCoy's left-hand stuff, that it's a model, so many pianists now do that—but to hear where it comes from—it lifts everything up! When you're a horn player and you hear a pianist do that, you think, "Man, I wanna do the same thing on the saxophone!" I love it.**

And so did his father:

> McCoy is a beauty, isn't he . . . there's so many things he does and I
> don't [have] to tell him to do. I couldn't tell him because when I hear
> it I say, man, that's just like I would want it, I would have done it
> myself if I'd have thought of it. And it happens so often . . . he's just
> that sensitive.

One of Tyner's intuited tricks was to raise the passion of the performance as
his improvisation approached its close, so that the transition to Coltrane's
solo could take place just as anticipation and energy crested and con-
verged. It was a well-practiced maneuver, requiring an equal degree of fer-
vor both before and after the high-intensity handoff.

Coltrane's improvisation meets the challenge. He takes over, blowing on
the fifth full step above the E-flat-minor root of "Resolution," intent, as
always, on avoiding cliché. In the late fifties, his trademark way of kicking
off a solo had been jarring and controversial. By 1965, it was less so, but
critic Joe Goldberg was still uncertain of the melodic surprise that had
become the saxophonist's calling card:

> Excitement is there, certainly, of an incomparable nature, and sur-
> prise. Most often, at the beginning of a solo, Coltrane enters from an
> unexpected place, creating a shock effect in the first phrase that
> leaves the listener limp for two or three choruses.

For many musicians, such as Miles Davis, there was nothing disaffecting in
Coltrane's manner. The trumpeter, in fact, assumed partial credit for some
of his unorthodoxy: "I'd tell him to begin in the middle, because that's the
way his head worked anyway."

As Coltrane's solo surges and falls, Tyner lays down an accompaniment
matching his bandleader's dynamic sweep, using chords chosen for their
harmonic ambivalence, affording the saxophonist a less restrictive choice
of direction in his soloing. Tyner explains:

> You're allowing yourself to do a lot of things with sound when you
> leave your voicings open. You see, a long time ago, a lot of the piano
> players used to lock, close everything up, you know. Play all the notes
> in a chord. They left no space. But I'm finding space, and the spaces
> between the intervals are just as important—more important some-
> times—than filling the chords up.

Coltrane's solo speeds through a sequence of blues-flavored licks, pushing the entire quartet toward a series of powerful climaxes spiked by rough-toned screams on the tenor, urged on by drum rolls and cymbal splashes from Jones. A master instrumentalist *and* an accomplished dramatist, Coltrane had developed an arsenal of passionate phrases and riffs, and he knew how to maintain their value by holding them in check. On "Resolution," Bob Belden notes how the saxophonist waits for just the right moment before unleashing an intense two-note call that achieves a high B-flat ("it's a very vocal note to play on the tenor saxophone—it just leaps out"), marking the peaks near the end of his solo:

> **For a sax player, you really have to know your instrument. That B-flat is way up there in the altissimo register—to get there requires overblowing a certain fingering. It's one of the hardest notes to nail and it's loaded with overtones. But it's not part of the standard way you're taught to play the instrument.**

With another B-flat blast, Coltrane reaches one more summit and—unleashing the built-up tension—replays the "Resolution" melody. As the saxophonist allows more space to breathe into the performance, Garrison hops jauntily alongside him; it's a moment that provides an opportunity to discern the bassist's irregular yet fluid beat, as Ravi describes:

> **I always liked that—it's not just like the walking thing. It was this drive where he sounds to me like he's walking and pedaling at the same time, so things don't sound like "ching-ching-a-ching." He was just the perfect bass player for this band. I don't think it sounds the same with Reggie [Workman], and Reggie's great, of course, but this is really Jimmy's thing.**

Garrison's style distinguished itself further by the juggling of short, sharply played staccato notes with those that were longer and more resonant. As the bassist explained, the technique derived from a search for a more resonant sound, and from the influence of a fellow Philadelphian:

> **One day I was listening to Percy Heath, and his notes were so long, man . . . I had a picture in my mind that the strings were like rubber bands [and] had that kind of resilience and warmth. From that time on, that's how I wanted to sound . . . warm, long, one note flowing into another one . . . more legato.**

Listening to a playback: Tyner and Coltrane at Van Gelder's in the early sixties

Coltrane lingers over the final phrase of the "Resolution" theme, resolves it by closing on E-flat minor, and steps back as Tyner sweeps up and down the keyboard. The final punctuation is left to Jones. A roll on the snare drum and a crash on the ride cymbal bring the take to a halt.

Satisfied with take 7, Coltrane proceeds to the final recording of the evening.

Pursuance

Though composed as two separate sections, "90245—Part 3/Part 4" is still listed as just that: one master, one recording. No stranger to extended studio efforts, Coltrane made the decision to tackle the remaining part of his suite—nearly eighteen minutes' worth—without interruption. Excluding any false starts, "Pursuance/Psalm" was almost assuredly another one-take wonder, as its length would have almost filled one of Coltrane's 7" audition reels (presumably reel A2).

When *A Love Supreme* was released, Coltrane's audience might have marked the symmetric construction of the suite's four parts: the first and last are more mood-oriented and structurally unorthodox, while the middle two are more in the established jazz vein. To those familiar with classical music, the album's overall shape suggests aspects of a concerto form, contrasting segments of varying meter and mood, with moments set aside for soloists.

Whether Coltrane consciously built *A Love Supreme* on such a model, "Pursuance" certainly follows that paradigm, kicking off with a tempo-shifting solo turn by Elvin Jones.

"The trend I see taking place in this music," said Jones in 1963, "[is that] it doesn't have to be in one tempo":

> **It's reverting in a sense . . . that is, there are movements in classical compositions, and it's natural to change the tempo when you get to a new movement . . . there has not been much of this [in jazz] but enough to lead one to wonder why a performance must be in only one tempo and why a tempo shouldn't change if this enhances the artistic merit of the music.**

The opening of "Pursuance" is Jones's moment on *A Love Supreme*—a relatively brief, ninety-second solo that sparkles with a melding of patterns typical of the master percussionist's patented polyrhythmic approach. In

1981, Jones traced his interest in multiple rhythms—particularly in folk music from foreign lands—to one particular listening session:

> In my first trip to Europe in 1957, I was living in a friend's house in Belgium and he brought out some tapes that he made in Haiti of an artist there. At that point the guy had just got out of jail, and he was sitting on a street corner drinking rum and playing the conga drum. I thought he was five people, listening to him. This really intrigued me, so from that point in time I began to pursue African traditional music. The quest led me to [music of African] pygmies and [of the sub-Saharan] Dogon. There's a lot of music in the Belgian Congo, and these were tremendous sources of inspiration.

Jones was already known for a "busy" style before any cross-cultural sounds exerted their influence, and his distinctive translation of African and Caribbean polyrhythms onto the traditional jazz trap kit involved a democratic use of all its elements. "The conventional thing is to use the hi-hat for the after-beat and use the bass drum for the underlying 4/4 or 3/4 rhythm to keep the steady pulsation," Jones commented, "[but] I just think you have to use all of the drum set all of the time."

For "Pursuance," Jones recalls that though Coltrane "didn't give me any instruction," the drummer understood "the way the melody was geared to start. I thought I had to play something that was simple and clear. So I played half of an Afro-Cuban beat, and it worked out." His grasp of the tune's melody paralleled the saxophonist's rhythmic sense. In the context of Coltrane's group, argued the drummer, a heightened demand was placed on both:

> The drummer and horn become full partners . . . not just one supporting the other. The horn player therefore has to be as secure in his knowledge of the rhythm as the drummer has to be secure in his understanding of the melodic and the harmonic. This is the balance that is struck.

Jones's sparkling intro—which wastes no time in setting up a rhythm alternatively skipping then strutting—builds to a succession of rolls immediately before Coltrane's entrance. Jones's solo never really ends; it sharply turns with a quick snare roll to a steady 4/4 rhythm on the cymbal, setting off the hottest tempo of *A Love Supreme.* As on "Resolution," Coltrane awaits the proper dramatic opening to enter and sound the theme to "Pursuance." Like similar melodies from his past recordings—notably "Mr. P.C." from 1959—"Pursuance" is stark, simple, and yet another blues set in a minor key. ("Perhaps my main fault at the moment is that I have a natural feeling for the minor," Coltrane apologized in 1965. "I'd like to do more things in the major . . . and there are many other modes I've got to learn.") As lyrical as the theme may be, the saxophonist's treatment of it seems almost perfunctory; Coltrane barely blows the "Pursuance" line twice before Tyner kicks off his second solo on the album.

Tyner lays down a line that responds to the phrasing of the "Pursuance" theme, repeats it, then waves it away with a succession of freely played motifs startling in their impromptu originality. "First, there is his melodic inventiveness," Coltrane once stated. "And along with that, the clarity of his ideas." On "Pursuance" Tyner does indeed weave together, clearly and crisply, a fleet solo that outlines and extends the tune's form. Coltrane explained it further:

> **Invariably, in our group, [Tyner] will take a tune and build his own structure for it . . . he doesn't fall into conventional grooves . . . because of the clusters he uses and the way he voices them, that sound is brighter than what would normally be expected from most of the chord patterns he plays.**

The key was the pianist's favoring of fourths—notes and chords that jumped three full steps above the root of the melody at any given moment. "He's got the voicings!" Coltrane once enthused. To Lewis Porter, it was a cornerstone of the Coltrane group:

> **Tyner developed a particular type of voicing in fourths that characterized the sound of the quartet . . . whereas triads [or thirds] have a certain earthy familiarity, fourth chords are abstract . . . perhaps because they avoid the familiar ring of popular songs.**

Tyner admits that "the reason why I may have used fourths [and] began to use them more and more" was that it was one way he could continually elevate the music and avoid quick resolutions to his statements. His solo on "Pursuance" is remarkably light and buoyant; halfway through this improvisation—as on "Resolution"—he grows restless, leaning on a series of left-hand chords warning of another shift in focus.

Impending, of course, is Coltrane, but Tyner's declaration occurs a little

early, pulling Van Gelder to the control board in anticipation. One can hear the engineer fading up the saxophone microphone in anticipation: an increased level of room sound—Jones's cymbals most discernibly—is evident. It's a moment that reveals Van Gelder's hands-on studio style: as the performance unfolded in the studio before him, so the engineer closely manipulated the controls. Ravi, who has studied a substantial number of his father's master recordings, recognizes the Van Gelder touch:

> **The more I listen, the more I'm aware of Rudy's presence during the tracking. Back then, most engineers set the levels before time, and gave themselves enough headroom so that even if a guy hit the loudest note on the horn or the drums it still would not distort. But I noticed on almost all the John Coltrane Impulse recordings that Rudy was in there almost everywhere. When somebody finishes a solo, you can hear the faders come down. You've got all these open mics in the**

room, and as soon as he pulls the faders down on a certain set of mics, the whole atmosphere changes, because maybe some drums were echoing and jumping into the horn mic. . . . Nowadays with CDs, they reproduce the masters pretty accurately, so things that maybe no one ever noticed before, you're more aware of them. When you put on the headphones, you really notice it.

It was perhaps the most delicate aspect to Van Gelder's craft, and it followed one basic, timeless rule of recording: the more information preserved, the more accurate the reproduction. By 1964, Coltrane's favorite engineer had perfected his technique in order to capture as wide a sonic spectrum as possible; in the acoustic setting of a jazz quartet, that meant all the tones and overtones, the timbre and depth that defined each musician's sonic signature.

As before, Coltrane reenters at just the right instant, boosted by a crescendo of chords from Tyner. But this time it's different; in the tight geography of *A Love Supreme,* which climbs from meditative valleys to rousing, tumultuous peaks, this is to be the crowning moment of the album. The studio clock is running, and Coltrane faces the task of distilling the dizzying assurance and unbridled feel of a twenty- to thirty-minute nightclub improvisation into a mere two and a half minutes.

Coltrane's dexterous "Pursuance" solo is his onstage spiral of melodic runs and harmonic leaps delivered in miniature. Twisting through a number of in-the-moment motifs, he unhesitatingly carries his frenetic lines toward a number of heated summits, leaning on his rough-throated rasp to push the spikes even higher. At one point he develops an idea that, to at least one saxophonist, rings of past experimental ideas. "That's basically the 'Giant Steps' cycle," Ravi points out, referring to the chordal pattern of one of his father's better-known compositions:

The "Giant Steps" cycle is more a reference to the harmony than the actual theme [sings familiar "Giant Steps" melody]. I think it's something he really checked out and tried to utilize and manipulate in different ways. You hear it a lot in his music in this period, this minor, major, minor, major, descending-in-whole-tones pattern. You never hear it in an obvious way—I just think after he wrote "Giant Steps," that was always an element of his playing.

As Coltrane's solo reaches its apex, Jones is a sympathetic blur of activity on the drums, firing off a fusillade of rattles, rolls, and crashes matching the saxophonist's tumultuous arc. At certain moments it seems he almost over-reaches in order to retain a footing next to Coltrane's creative stampede; yet as the drummer admitted, it was in the bandleader's very prowess that Jones found a strange freedom:

> **When I worked with John Coltrane . . . he had such forceful time himself that it allowed the drums to do a bit of deviation. You can play around with it more, with a person who has so much forcefulness.**

Upon listening to "Pursuance," Jones offers that despite his reputation as an inspired soloist, "I was just as content to listen to John play":

> **I was more listening to him than trying to accompany as a drummer. I was just fascinated by this guy and the way he played. He had so many ideas. It seemed like he was sitting on a mountain of ideas, and they would flake off every three or four seconds.**

If—as many contend—Coltrane reached his career pinnacles in the company of his Classic Quartet, the nucleus of that structure was undoubtedly the saxophone-drums partnership. According to Dan Morgenstern, the Coltrane-Jones pairing stood among the most rhythmically charged unions in jazz:

> **There were certain people who worked together—Louis Armstrong and Big Sid Catlett. I mean, that was a marvelous interrelationship. Dizzy [Gillespie] had a thing with drummers. I think the one who probably did it best was Kenny Clarke. Max [Roach] and [trumpeter] Clifford Brown, Max and Sonny Rollins when he was in that band. And later, [Thelonious] Monk and Art Blakey were very different from Elvin and Coltrane because the music was different—but they had a kind of connection that was remarkable.**

Morgenstern explains it further:

> **There was a kind of telepathy between them—they worked together so well. Elvin's a remarkable rhythm player—his dexterity, the independence of limbs, unique in the way that he can set up so many different things at the same time. But Elvin makes so many sounds, it's not just rhythm, it's sonic. With Coltrane, whose music is very intense and in a way can be unpredictable, Elvin not only follows him but it's**

like you can't say who the leader is and who's the follower. Look—I'm doing this with my hands [rolls one fist repeatedly over the other]; they're so entwined. That level of complexity from both of them, the melody instrument and the rhythm, certainly happens on "Chasin' the Trane." That's probably the closest we come on record to what it could be like live. *Crescent* is a terrific record, I think, for that. And of course, "Pursuance" on *A Love Supreme*.

Like a spent runner, Coltrane returns to, and breathlessly skips through, two readings of the "Pursuance" theme. The entire performance feels ready to wind down, as Jones hits what sounds like a final drum roll, but refuses to let the momentum melt away. One might label it a false ending, but it's more like an alternative one. In a manner that he had developed over years of intense nightclub work, Jones clips on his own explosive denouement: explosions of cymbals and rapid-fire strikes to the snare.

Jones eventually drops away, revealing Garrison already in mid-improvisation. A three-minute solo ensues, in which the bassist at first feeds off the driving pace of "Pursuance," strumming double stops while sliding the pattern up the neck of his bass. As if to tie together how far the suite has come with where it began, Garrison hits a four-note sequence suggesting the rhythmic "a love supreme" pattern. To another bassist like Ron Carter, it's an intriguing solo that might have been improved with "additional harmonic support, or rhythmic support, or any extra impetus to try something different":

My broad concern is when the bass player plays, everybody stops, man. You've got to hear these things to play against them. You've got to hear two kinds of rhythms for them to have an impact on you. When Jimmy would slow or speed up the tempo during his solo, or play different changes, he needs the same kind of emotional support, and the physical presence of having [the band's] attention, to take some ideas from comping [accompaniment]. That way no one feels that he's so self-contained.

In 1967, Garrison himself commented on performing while the band laid out:

I like the idea when I soloed of not having any accompaniment. The bass has been stifled for so long; I don't think people have been really aware of the possibilities of the instrument, and I think we are now

finally becoming aware that the bass can be just as melodic as any other instrument.

Garrison proves his point, laying down a lyrical pattern of single-note runs and chord strums: a veritable one-person call-and-response. A still-bristling Jones can be heard, nervously snapping his sticks together, then brushing a cymbal. The bass solo slows and develops into a meditative, almost melancholy walk from the upper register of the instrument to the lowest strings. He strikes a low note, then pauses. In the silence one can actually hear his left hand loosen and the bass strings snap back; testament again to Van Gelder's penchant for close-miking.

With a minor chord from Tyner, Jones leans to his right with mallets in hand, ready to strike the kettledrum near his drum kit.

Psalm

After listening to *A Love Supreme* and sitting briefly in silence, Jones resurrected an on-the-road memory from 1964 that presaged his unusual instrumental role on the suite's closing section:

> **I remember one time when we were in a station wagon coming back to New York from San Francisco. I was driving, and we got lost in the Mojave Desert. It was a new highway that was still under construction, and it suddenly ran out. So I had to drive back about 15 miles to a gas station. When we got there, I said, "We're trying to find Route 66. Apparently I missed the turn somewhere." And the guy said, "Just cut through here, and when you get to Searchlight, Nevada, turn right" [laughs]. Searchlight, Nevada, was a trailer with a gas pump. That was the *whole city*!**
>
> **Anyway, we were driving along and John asked me if I could play tympani, and I said, "Yeah, I can play tympani." He started talking about some of the things he wanted to do when we went in the studio again.**

In fact, Jones had played tympani on one of the best-selling jazz albums to date, the Miles Davis–Gil Evans collaboration *Sketches of Spain*. Coltrane may have been unaware of that historical detail, but no matter; Jones's competence on all percussion, in all styles, developed from an education that began in a classical setting. "I wasn't so interested in jazz in the beginning, but I did want to know everything there was about the drums—to be as professional as possible—play the tympani in a symphony orchestra." But not just any orchestra:

> **I was always taught that I would be the percussionist in the New York Philharmonic or something like that. I started studying with that in mind and *then* I got interested in jazz . . . and [began] thinking in terms of putting that kind of [classical] knowledge and training into ahhh [laughs], the blues.**

Jones recalls that the idea of adding more orchestral instruments to his work with Coltrane had come to him before. "I thought some of the compositions that we played would sound much better if I used tympani [rather] than a drum set. I had brought tympani out to the studio to another Coltrane session but didn't use it, but I always use mallets, if I can think of it ahead of time!"

With mallets in hand, Jones sets to the large, resonant skin of the drum, producing a low rumble like the sound of distant thunder. Almost immediately, Coltrane enters, whispering loose, melodic fragments off a C-minor scale, his ethereal tone betraying his early reverence for Lester Young's wistful take on the blues. And again, like the rest of the suite, it's blues in flavor.

But in form and function, "Psalm" is separate and distinct. It is the subdued, poignant conclusion to *A Love Supreme*. After the fire and fury of "Pursuance" and the assured swing of "Resolution," it stands out all the more distinctly, offering no hummable melody or complete lyrical line. "Psalm," in fact, reveals little structure at all: no metric consistency, no time signature to speak of—completely, purely rubato.

And purely emotional. Coltrane had already explored similar mood pieces in the past. In early 1963, he recorded "After the Rain" with Roy Haynes's cymbal strokes painting an effective ambience, a loosely shaped precedent to "Psalm." "You can pick anything in classical music—*Adagio for Strings* by [Samuel] Barber—that Trane could have probably listened to when the melody carries the song," offers Branford Marsalis, mentioning another possible model with which Coltrane was surely familiar:

> **Ornette Coleman's "Lonely Woman" [from 1959] is a perfect example of that [rhythmically free effect]—in a lot of ways it's even more incredible because the drums and bass kept the rhythm going at the same time. But the song wasn't in their rhythm; the song—the chord**

changes—shifted and moved based on what the soloist played at the time, separate from their rhythm.

"Psalm" has a strangely isolating effect. Even in the presence of the quartet, Coltrane seems all the more alone, carrying the weight of the performance by himself. Garrison's strumming and Jones's cymbal splashes lend atmosphere more than beat, while Tyner's sporadic accents fall gently, like random raindrops before a downpour, saying more in the silence between his notes than in what he actually plays. "You have your exclamation marks, your question marks, your periods. All those things make up a good sentence," the pianist once explained. "That's the same thing with music, you have to punctuate . . . it's like a conversation."

The vocal metaphor fits. "Psalm" does indeed seem an intensely private, one-to-one conversation. Coltrane's hushed delivery sounds deliberately speechlike: he hangs on to the ends of phrases, repeats them as if for emphasis. He is in fact "reading" through his horn. "The fourth and last part is a musical narration of the theme 'A Love Supreme' which is written in the context," Coltrane explained in his liner notes. "It is entitled 'Psalm.' " His plan was to sound the words through his saxophone; in the case of *A Love Supreme,* he noted that "that's the longest [poem] I've ever written."

Wayne Shorter points out that in choosing to employ spoken language as the basis for the closing section, Coltrane unveils a further, subtle symmetry to the construction of *A Love Supreme.* As music gave way to words in the chanting of "Acknowledgement," so "Psalm" calls for a similar transferral, only in reverse: from words back to music:

> **I think he was . . . adding on to what he already had—even to the meaning of the instruments, whether they were made out of metal or wood, or vocal. He was doing something to show that, actually, there's no difference.**

"Words, sounds, speech, men, memory, thoughts, fears and emotions—time—all related . . . all made from one," Coltrane himself wrote in the album's liner notes.

Had Coltrane been clearer in his liner notes, the poem's subtle structural role would undoubtedly have been more widely understood and appreciated. As it turned out, this aspect of the composition became part of the album's mystique; a secret to be discovered and shared by a few. Those who had had personal exposure to Coltrane's methods, like Reggie Workman, did not take long to catch on. " 'Psalm' *is* a psalm—you can hear that in the music, if you listen closely. Of course I heard it the first time because that's the way he played, that's the way he thought." It eventually became accepted jazz lore, passed from musician to musician. "Somebody hipped me to that," says Branford Marsalis. "When I moved to New York [City in 1980] cats were talking about that and that's one of the things that was said."

Lewis Porter was the first to share the lyrical aspect of "Psalm" with a larger musical community, first in his treatise "Jazz Improvisation As Composition," delivered to a 1980 meeting of the American Musicological Society, and then in his full-length Coltrane biography in 1997. His line-by-line analysis noted that the sax solo begins with the words "A Love Supreme," and even caught a few ad-libs that departed from the script:

> **You will find that he plays right to the final "Amen" and then finishes. There are no extra notes up to that point. You will have to make a few adjustments in the poem, however: Near the beginning where it reads, "Help us resolve our fears and weaknesses," he skips the next line, goes on to "In you all things are possible," then plays "Thank you God" . . . towards the end he leaves out "I have seen God."**

Coltrane did not make his use of a prewritten text obvious, even to those in the studio. "Elvin Jones indicated to me that he was unaware that Coltrane was reciting the poem on his saxophone," Porter recalled. Given the number of lines in the poem (fifty-seven) and the duration of "Psalm" (5:55), it is likely that he would have glanced at the words as he performed.

Like a libretto, the words to "Psalm" (eventually titled "A Love Supreme" and printed on the inside of the album cover) define the lyrical flow of the music; one can follow syllable by syllable. Each line crests and resolves, implying punctuation. Some lines—like "God is / He always was / He always will be"—convey an almost operatic sense of drama. The words "thank you God," which appear a dozen times in the text, achieve a greater weight each successive time the three-note incantation sounds through the bell of Coltrane's horn. Three minutes into his recitation, as he delivers the line "the universe has many wonders . . . ," Coltrane sounds hoarse, even tired.

"It's the wear and tear of the session," Bob Belden opines. "It's an effective use of a straining effect, but it wouldn't have sounded that way if he had recorded 'Psalm' first."

"Psalm" ends dramatically with a rich sonic swell—cymbal crashes,

A rare glimpse of Coltrane and
Thiele in the control room,
early sixties

measured vibrations on the tympani, a rolling piano figure, and a melancholy cadenza from Coltrane—then a slow, receding wave. Garrison's bow bouncing on the bass strings and a whispering cymbal are the final sounds heard as *A Love Supreme* fades to a close.

Psalm Overdub

The musicians settled back to listen to what they had recorded. Though his syllable-by-syllable "reading" on "Psalm" was near perfect, down to the last "amen," Coltrane was not satisfied. A more dramatic denouement seemed called for. What to do? Another try at the full eighteen-minute "Pursuance" and "Psalm"? Another take only of "Psalm" to be edited in later?

"The saxophone at the end of 'Psalm' *was* overdubbed," asserts Van Gelder:

> **He came into the control room with Bob Thiele and asked me if he could add something to the end of the piece, which we did. The idea was his. He just wanted to fix the end. There were a couple of ways to do it, and I had to decide which way to go. I could have asked for an insert, then edited it together, or I could have asked him to overdub the extra part at the end of the piece. At that time I was already familiar with the overdubbing process. I had been overdubbing back in Hackensack—one album [I used overdubbing on] was by Bobby Sherwood, a bandleader in the fifties. He played fifteen parts.**

Ultimately, Coltrane asked that the session tape be rewound, and stepped back in the studio to accent the swell and fade of the final seconds of "Psalm." Thus, on opposing tracks, it is possible to hear Garrison's bowing blend with his strumming, Jones's cymbal crash accompany the thunder of his mallets, and Coltrane's wide, upper-register vibrato mix with his own low-end phrasing: a virtual—if momentary—septet. Van Gelder adds: "The original saxophone you hear is on the left-hand side [of the stereo separation], and the overdub saxophone is on the right-hand side."

The session's participants departed Englewood Cliffs. Though the music for a complete album was in the can, plans had already been made to return the following evening at the same time. Coltrane spent no more than a few hours—four at the most—rehearsing and recording in Van Gelder's studio that evening; the session was over before midnight. ABC-Paramount records reveal that each musician was paid union scale plus a half-hour overtime for four hours on the clock: a gross total of $142.33. As leader,

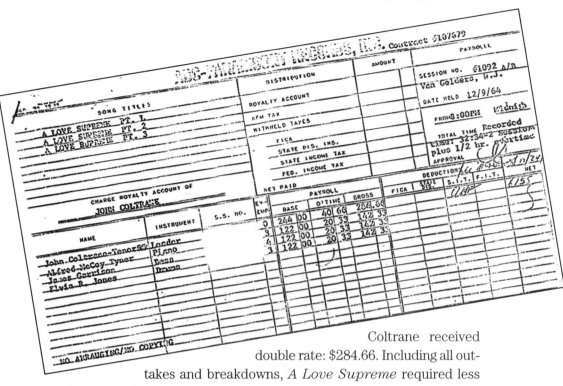

Coltrane received double rate: $284.66. Including all outtakes and breakdowns, *A Love Supreme* required less than one hour's worth of recording tape.

"In one sense, it seemed that we played for an hour, and in another sense it seemed as if it were two or three minutes," Jones would later comment. "Even when I listen to it now, I lose the sense of passage of time. I'm completely submerged in the music."

Archie Shepp and Coltrane: Back at
Van Gelder's, December 10, 1964

December 10, 1964: A Second Try, a Year of Triumph

Nothing fascinates like protracted unknowing. For years an air of mystery has swirled around and elevated Coltrane's second studio recording of *A Love Supreme*. Aficionados and general music fans alike have long known of the session, and that it featured two basses, two saxophones, and allegedly an extra percussionist, but little else about it. One book refers to it as the "lost version," another the "original version"; recent articles perpetuate its reputation as "long-lost" or "long-rumored." The master tapes of the December 10 recordings disappeared, presumably sometime in the late seventies, only adding to the session's mythic reputation and raising more questions than answers.

What motivated Coltrane to expand upon what already seemed artfully crafted and complete? Which session reflected his original vision? Did Elvin Jones receive help on percussion, and if so, who was the mystery musician? Why did Coltrane ultimately reject the results of the second evening?

"There's all kinds of stories why Archie [Shepp] and I weren't included on that," bassist Art Davis states. Coltrane himself was partly to blame for planting the seed of speculation when he dropped a reference into his *Love Supreme* liner notes:

Also, to Archie Shepp (tenor saxist) and to Art Davis (bassist) who both recorded on a track that regrettably will not be released at this time—my deepest appreciation for your work in the past and present. In the near future, I hope that we will be able to further the work that was started here.

In the upside-down logic of memory, none of Coltrane's usual studio colleagues remember December 10 with the clarity of his special guests that evening: bassist Davis and saxophonist Shepp. Tyner admits that "I kind of remember that, but . . . my consciousness was more like on what I was doing," then suggests, "talk to Elvin and see if he can fill in the gaps." Jones seems equally hard-pressed to recall details: "You know, it's a funny thing about it, I know Archie Shepp was there, but I don't remember anything that he did [laughs]. It just didn't register with me." Van Gelder notes succinctly, "No recollection of that session."

In contrast, Shepp remembers getting the call to join Coltrane in the studio "out of the blue—John was very spontaneous at that time. He would usually do that, 'Hey, Shepp, how you doing? You want to do something?' That's how he called me for *Ascension* [in July 1965] and how I got the Chicago Armory date [a concert performance in August 1965]." The last time Shepp had seen Coltrane at Van Gelder's was on August 10 when recording his debut LP for

An animated Coltrane: comfortable and conversant

Impulse, *Four for Trane*. On a phone call from Thiele, Coltrane had driven out from Long Island to peek in and pose with Shepp for the cover photograph.

Four for Trane found Shepp re-arranging four of Coltrane's best-known tunes from 1959–60, all familiar to an entire jazz generation. But on December 10, he faced the challenge of interpreting original Coltrane material he had never heard before; in fact, he was provided little information beyond the time to arrive:

> **You have what the French call the "bouffe"—it's not necessary to know who's there, it's even better if you don't . . . otherwise that's really a jive party. The moment of surprise was all part of the ultimate experience. I was totally unfamiliar with *A Love Supreme* until that day.**

Art Davis had likewise received a call from Coltrane, and recalls arriving at the studio to meet the evening's attendees: "Archie was there, McCoy, Elvin, and Jimmy, then of course, Rudy. I think [photographer] Chuck Stewart was there too."

Stewart, whose six rolls of black-and-white film are the sole visual record of that evening, recalls the session as not being part of any album. "Yes, I was there on December 10 but I did not shoot *A Love Supreme*." He assumes that, as per the norm, he got the call from Thiele to bring his camera down to the studio.

"In those days, photographers worked for producers," recalls Stewart. "If a producer liked what you did, he would call you for the session. And Bob liked my work. I think that's what helped my session photography so much, because I worked for producers as opposed to art directors, who had preconceived ideas of what things should look like."

Stewart had become familiar with the conditions at Van Gelder's studio, having been hired to shoot many Impulse artists in medias res:

> **Each studio has its own photographic sound, so to speak. [Rudy] had designed his for acoustics, and it turned out to be ideal for photographics, the way I did it. I used to use a strobe unit, with the light bouncing off the ceiling. That's why most of my pictures at recording sessions look like they were taken with natural light. I think it might have been a little more difficult if I had used natural light. I don't think the photographs would have the lasting quality they have.**

Note tympani in foreground

Stewart's portfolio from December 10 candidly conveys the relaxed atmosphere at the studio that evening—Jones at his drum kit, paging through a magazine; Thiele kicking back with a cigarette on the steps leading from the studio to Van Gelder's home; Art Davis and Tyner in conversation; Coltrane gesticulating . . . puffing on a pipe . . . reclining on a piano bench.

Many frames also capture the edge of readiness, just before the tapes rolled—Coltrane writing on a music stand as Davis and Garrison look on; the two bassists, side by side, Garrison dwarfed by the more substantial Davis; Coltrane standing next to protégé Archie Shepp, horns in hand; Tyner at the piano, framed by the two saxophonists.

Perhaps the most compelling aspect of the photographic record from that evening is when Coltrane is seen with others: all attention centers on him. For one reputed to be so tight-lipped, he appears quite conversational. The session tapes may have recorded little of his leadership role, but Stewart's images show him in charge and comfortably so.

Coltrane was equally at ease playing the musical alchemist, mixing elements that might catalyze and yield something new and exciting . . . or not. By December 1964, his predilection was for chance-taking, as Alice Coltrane recalled:

> Someone might say, "Well, it's only a quartet," [but] see, his thoughts were more lofty, his vision more broad, he was seeing higher dimensions in sound. Who knows, maybe the man was hearing fifty instruments at a time, or a hundred, like many of the great classical composers. They have to be able to hear it to be able to conduct it. He was slowly going toward that—two basses, two tenors, he was thinking about it in bigger terms.

It was more than simple expansion. "He was always looking and listening for that special sound, special blend. How would it sound with one bass on this side, one bass on the another? What is the interplay?"

His widow's contention is confirmed by Coltrane's decision to mix and match his quartet with Art Davis, a classically trained professional well versed in a broad range of popular jazz and experimental improvisation, and Archie Shepp, a relative neophyte specializing in avant-garde expression. Yet other than Coltrane, few in the group embraced the idea of adding to what was already a winning—and complete—combination.

Tyner reports that he "didn't know what was going to happen to that [*A Love Supreme*] material. When we were doing it [on December 10], it was like, 'Oh, John's experimenting with that' . . . but we felt that the quartet was self-contained, we were very partial to that." Jones concurs: "It was a complete musical entity, and I didn't see any way that he could enhance that."

Shepp himself confesses, "I felt daunted—I was in the presence of the man who, for me, in the context of my musical system, had exhausted all the frontiers. He was the Stravinsky, and I was a novice." Shepp sees his inclusion that evening as evidence of Coltrane's growing infatuation with the raw, emotionally charged sounds—influenced heavily by his own unfettered style—emanating from a new breed of saxophonists:

> At that time, he was listening to some of the younger players [and] found different things in different young people. Albert Ayler, for example, was a very mature player and was doing something with sound and the range of the horn that he found some affinity with. Wayne Shorter was also a more evolved player [than myself] at the time, in the sense that he was solidly in the tradition.

"He'd write down the symbols to a set of very basic chords" (Tyner): Davis and Garrison watch Coltrane at the music stand

Shepp feels two reasons spurred Coltrane to call him for the session:

As I look back, I think John liked me. I wasn't sure as a young cat, because there were so many young cats around him, but I think it was both a musical and perhaps a genuine friendship. I think that's why he gave me a chance and that's why I played the way I played.

Both Shepp and Davis recall having received spoken instruction before the recording began, and Stewart's camera caught many instances of such discussion. Shepp maintains that though Coltrane "had a small scrap of paper himself with some chords on it, he gave it to McCoy, but as for myself, John didn't give me any music." Davis likewise remembers that, despite his seeing some music on paper, the direction was mostly verbal. "Jimmy was to play the bass notes, the basic notes, and then I was to go higher from there. There'd be bowing, as well. Then when the time came to roll things we just started to play."

Coltrane's 7½ ips audition tape seems to be the only existing recording from the second *Love Supreme* session. Inside the box marked A-4 is a tape whose quality has sadly deteriorated, and has actually proven to be tape A3, containing takes 1 and 2 of "Acknowledgement." On the outside of the box, Thiele's handwriting lists takes 3 through 6 and two takes of a "voice overdub." Between faded memories and a lack of any other records, there seems little choice except to take Coltrane at his word as he wrote in the album's liner notes that Shepp and Davis "both recorded on *a* track" (emphasis added), and that December 10 found them working on "Acknowledgement" only.

More than the music from the day before, the two surviving takes provide an accurate snapshot of Coltrane at the Great Divide of '64/'65: one foot on a more melodic platform, the other pointed toward atonal territory. On the carefully constructed foundation of "Acknowledgement," he grafted ideas both new and tested. The recordings prove both prescient (Coltrane solidified the twin tenor idea in 1965, recruiting Pharoah Sanders into the band) and familiar (casting the same tune in both quartet and larger-group molds, as he had with "Greensleeves" in 1961).

Jones's gong strike opens the first take of "Acknowledgement." A moment later, Coltrane and Shepp sound off, and the change is immediately apparent. The previous day's meditative call to prayer has now become a bubbling conversation: Coltrane's smooth lyrical strokes are answered by Shepp's roughly hewn asides. Jones's rapid cymbal taps urge the intro forward; the horns fall silent as he works into a marked Latin beat using the cymbal bell, tom-tom, and bass drum. (If there is any point in the take that the presence of a second percussionist might be inferred, it is here; but Jones's adept polyrhythmic talent—and the lack of any photographic evidence of, or payment to, another musician—argue against it.)

Garrison and Davis enter together, doubling on the album's defining four-note mantra, and Coltrane blows a soaring line portending the melody to come.

Shepp, meanwhile, searches for an entry point. "I had to sort of try to rise to the occasion. I think in the first take, I did something that's interesting to me even now." Like a one-man R&B horn section, he locks into the powerful bass line, slurring and honking the "a love supreme" riff with a punchy rhythm. With growing confidence, he alternates the emphasis in his phrasing.

In a spontaneous complementary stroke, Coltrane produces a new idea to match Shepp's staccato contribution: a raspy, three-note call-and-response that jumps registers—high, low, then high again. It's a particularly revelatory moment that points to both Coltrane's acute gear-shifting ability, and his willingness to forgo even his own carefully constructed melody for a greater cause: the chance to hear and respond to a different interpretation. From Coltrane's perspective, Shepp's playing did not alter "Acknowledgement" from its intended approach but provided a valid alternate idea. According to Alice, her husband was determined to find value in any musical statement:

> He always showed an appreciation for what was not always just about himself, his story, but he liked hearing other people's expression, and how *you* would interpret this idea, how do you respond to these chords. I thought it made him even greater, because truthfully, he has never criticized any musician, no matter what his field was.

Shepp himself offers a sharper, self-critical view:

> Well, I wish I had listened more. When John does the intro, I think I'm completely off, I play something that doesn't sound at all related. If I

Coltrane's tape box containing reel A3. Judging by Thiele's notes, four full takes of "Acknowledgement" were attempted on December 10. Two survive on reel A3, the other reel presumably lost forever.

had used my common sense, I would have played more—I didn't approach it as honestly as I should have because ["Acknowledgement"] is very beautiful, very plain, very minor. I did something which was to really replace melody with sound, so in fact, I created a texture of minor sound.

Out of deference to his fellow saxman, Coltrane cedes the first solo to Shepp, who—true to his words—plays more reactively than reflectively, bristling with emotion and a throaty tone faintly reminiscent of a classic tenor sound, not unlike Ben Webster's in the forties. Coltrane follows on Shepp's heels and, while returning to his usual lyrical flow, deliberately starts off under the influence of Shepp's energetic, vocal-like cry. It's an effect others have noted. Ravi Coltrane, studiously familiar with the music of the December 10 session, admits that "at first, I thought of this as the 'Quartet Plus' with the 'Plus' getting in the way of the 'Quartet.' But after hearing those solos again and again, I realize that it's much more an energy thing—it's about building each other up." Shepp concurs: "I think I was a sort of catalyst for [Coltrane], because he had done so many things by himself."

The "two-bass concept" Ravi points out another peculiarity to this version of "Acknowledge-

ment": "Trane's key-hopping is much more organized—it starts off the same as the day before, but then sticks to a cyclical pattern that returns him harmonically to where he began. It's a great example of him just trying out new things."

As Coltrane's solo ends, the chanting is noticeably absent, replaced by an extended section given over to the two bassists—Garrison maintaining the tune's low-end riff as Davis develops an arco (bowed) improvisation, which takes the reworking of "Acknowledgement" to the extent of its nine-minute length. Davis saw his participation as yet another step in the evolution of Coltrane's bass-on-bass idea.

"I call it the two-bass concept," says Davis, recalling how Coltrane had directed him in 1961 on "Olé": "he wanted me to play sort of in a solo capacity, and that would drive him, and then another bassist would play the regular 'bass parts,' having a drone sound, just like in Indian music." In 1964 on A Love Supreme, "it was more of an experimentation of new ideas and novel ways of approaching improvisation. It was more advanced, more explorative, more experimental—a sense of keeping the reins more open, rather than a set pattern."

As with the quartet version, Garrison ends the take alone with a bass line to be spliced to the lead-in to "Resolution."

A second full, more refined take of "Acknowledgement" immediately follows, lasting another nine minutes. The introduction follows the same general pattern as before, with one notable exception: a slightly more comfortable Shepp opts for a sparse, lower-register path, while Coltrane plays a long-winded, high-end tone; as the rhythm section lock in together, Coltrane returns repeatedly to the three-note idea of take 1, developing it into a more fluid trill.

Shepp again shares a self-effacing opinion of his performance:

> **Some of the things that I did on the first take really impressed me more than the second take. I found much more variety in the texture of sounds I was using. I seem to be more locked into the bottom on the second take—I'm not into the swing as much. But what I played was more relevant when Coltrane played the introduction. I didn't like my solo as much on the second take.**

To his defense, Shepp's second improvisation is actually more generous in both time and trademark style, ripe with his rootsy snarls and growls of that era, a compelling example of his role as a "lyrical banshee, full of everything the blues has always meant" (as writer Amiri Baraka described it that year). Coltrane's solo is also more than that on the first take, filled with inflections and cries, as he toys with—at times displaces—the rhythmic flow of the tune. Even the two-bass portion reaches a relative peak of intensity, with Davis's arco workout reaching the vocal-like timbre of the saxophones.

It's a tantalizing, too-brief sample of what Davis could do with a bow in his hand when asked to meet the emotional requirements of a Coltrane recording—of what he *would* do in two short months when the quartet-plus-one recorded "Nature Boy." Davis

credits Coltrane for providing the necessary environment—and consistency—of support.

> Elvin and I discussed this at the time—that you could wake up John in the middle of the night and he was still John Coltrane, a real person, very sincere all the time. Because of that there was warmth there, there was encouragement there, there was creativity. The atmosphere that he provided was an infusion of energy—I never got tired, I don't think Elvin got tired, of working.

Take 2 of "Acknowledgement" ends, and so apparently does the attempt to record any further sextet versions of *A Love Supreme*; it was a much shorter evening than the night before. The ABC-Paramount requisition for session #1093 shows the expanded lineup—with no second percussionist listed—receiving payment for a two-hour session with overtime. Shepp, Garrison, Tyner, and Jones each received $101.66. Davis, whom Coltrane held in special regard, collected the same as the bandleader: $203.32. Davis explains further:

> For both this date and later for *Ascension*, John called and said he wanted me; both times he told me to name my price and not to be bashful. He was aware of some of the problems I had had when working on other Impulse albums— [arranger] Manny Albam, and Freddie Hubbard. I hadn't been paid right away; they fooled around with the money. So I made certain demands and, as a result, Thiele "whitelisted" me.

One vocal overdub to go . . .

I was too uppity. I didn't have to tell John about it even—he was very aware of these things. So I kind of put the ball back in his court and said, "OK, I'll do it . . ." Paying double scale was his idea. I would have played for free just to be on John's dates.

The last tracks listed on the surviving tape box from December 10 are two takes of Coltrane's vocal overdub for the quartet version of "Acknowledgement." Once the chant was recorded, the session ended, Van Gelder held on to the master tapes for later editing, and Coltrane, with his own 7½ ips copies under his arm, returned home to audition the results of the past two evenings.

It was mid-December 1964, and the year was ending for Coltrane much as previous years had: busy in New York City. Immediately following the *Love Supreme* sessions, the quartet played a week-long engagement at the Half Note in Manhattan. On December 27, the Sunday after Christmas, the group appeared at a matinee benefit for the civil rights publication *Freedomways* that also featured Max Roach, Abbey Lincoln, and Dick Gregory. As the new year approached, Impulse's premier jazz artist was busy putting the final touches to an album that would help launch his most successful year ever.

■ Editing the album came down to choosing the best takes and splicing them together in the correct sequence; Coltrane had already made the decision to use the quartet version of "Acknowledgement." "Well, the first part, Archie Shepp played on it, and . . . I had another bass on there, but I

Rudy Van Gelder and his Scully mastering lathe

didn't use this part," he told a New York deejay in early '65. "We talked about that," recalls Alice Coltrane, and though he "liked [the sextet version] very much . . . he said 'this is the final, it will be the quartet.'"

Once the album was sequenced, Van Gelder set to creating an acetate album master. Cutting the master was the first step in the process of transferring sound from recording tape to a flat vinyl platter. Laden with potential problems—carving grooves too deep or too shallow, resulting in the loss of high fidelity; failing to maintain a consistent volume level from track to track—mastering was a delicate

Poetry and Prayer

Coltrane did not normally invest much confidence in language: he avoided interviews and preferred his music to speak for itself. "I think it was an instinctual as well as conscious conviction of what he felt, that words don't do it," says Nat Hentoff, whose words grace the covers of myriad jazz albums, including *Giant Steps, Live at the Village Vanguard, Crescent,* and *Meditations.* He recalls the effort necessary for each of the Coltrane titles:

> I'd call him up and say, "John, I'm going to do the liner notes," and he'd always say the same thing, "Man, I wish you wouldn't, because if the music doesn't speak for itself, what's the use?" And I said, "John, it's a gig." And he said, "OK, what do you want to know?" He was a very generous fellow.

Hentoff explains further:

> It's awfully hard to get words to say what the musician had in mind, and when the musician is articulate, you're one step ahead. It's a word that's used very loosely these days, but Coltrane was an intellectual in his way, sort of a theosophist, I guess. I mean, he thought all the time. That's why the notes I've done that made any sense are the ones that are simply interviews.

For *A Love Supreme,* the normally skittish Coltrane opted for another, well-established liner-note option: he wrote them himself. He divided his thoughts into two sections: a prose letter to his listener, and a poem serving double duty—as prayer to the Divine and a libretto for the final musical section of *A Love Supreme.* The former was well thought-out, arranged with a logical flow much like the progression of the music inside: from greeting and opening benediction; to statements of purpose, dedication, structure, and gratitude; to closing prayer, salutation, and signature. Not known for his writing, and given to halting statements when asked to

He was baring his soul on the back of *A Love Supreme,* in that letter and that prayer. He put a lot of thought into those notes before he decided to put it down. It's the last part—the fifth part—of the suite.

—Elvin Jones

speak, Coltrane revealed a surprising eloquence with pen in hand. His notes showed he could be florid ("May we never forget that in the sunshine of our lives, through the storm and after the rain . . ."), dramatic ("As time and events moved on, a period of irresolution did prevail"), poetic, and syntactically adventurous ("for in the bank of life is not good that investment which surely pays the highest and most cherished dividends").

Coltrane's text told the classic story of personal redemption with a musical twist: man fallen, man saved, man dedicates self to God through horn. He gave a general date—"during the year 1957"—of his rebirth, when he "experienced, by the grace of God, a spiritual awakening which was to lead me to a richer, fuller, more productive life." The evidence was certainly there to back him up. The cold-turkey end to his drug addiction, his intense musical studies, alone and with Thelonious Monk, and his debut on record as a leader all occurred in that same fateful year.

Had the "merciful hand of God" been extended only then, Coltrane would have been content. But "in gratitude," and with a messianic urge, he tells his listener that he "humbly asked to be given the means and privilege to make others happy through music." That he had received the ability, "granted through His grace," was the sole, simple reason for *A Love Supreme.* The album was his "humble offering to Him. An attempt to say 'THANK YOU GOD' through our work."

On *Kind of Blue,* an album Coltrane helped create, the structure of each track was explained in detail by Bill Evans. Coltrane did not provide as much in his notes, simply naming the four parts of the *Love Supreme* suite, and attempting to clarify the role of the poem to follow. "The fourth and last part is a musical narration of the theme, "A LOVE SUPREME" which is written in the context." Despite Coltrane's obtuse explication—confusing for those with little musical background—the relation of written word to sound in "Psalm" is today more widely understood.

The title of the musical section "Psalm" (as opposed to the title of the poem itself: "A Love Supreme") points to a poetic form with which

Coltrane, and most of his audience, was familiar. Psalms is the nineteenth book of the Bible, and contains 150 songs praising God ("Song of David," "Song for the Sabbath"), each proffering devotion in a lyrical, rather than narrative, flow. They are bold, melodic declarations of faith coupled with admonitions to follow God.

And so is Coltrane's poem. "A Love Supreme" delivers a litany of devotional oaths (to God) and spiritual counsel (to the reader) in a manner that suggests a tuneful rhythm, intoning the Lord's name forty-two times over the course of fifty-seven lines, like a refrain. The words reveal Coltrane drawing guidance from, and a familiar ease with, various schools of belief: American preacher-speak ("Keep your eye on God"), Eastern principles ("all related . . . all made from one . . . all made in one"), sixties mysticism ("One thought can produce millions of vibrations . . ."), and biblical terminology: "He is gracious and merciful"—divine attributes repeated often in the Old Testament. Coltrane even quotes Scripture directly: "May I be acceptable in Thy sight" (Psalm 19:14); "I have seen God" (Genesis 32:30).

(Of the liberties Coltrane assumed with his church-based upbringing, the idea of meeting God face-to-face most distressed his mother. Pianist Bobby Timmons, another jazz great from Philadelphia, recalled, "I remember her telling me about *A Love Supreme* and how she was wishing he'd never written it . . . she was worried to death because she said, 'When someone is seeing God, that means he's going to die.'")

"Acknowledgement," to "Resolution," to "Pursuance," to "Psalm." As interrelated as are all the written and musical elements of *A Love Supreme,* so the four successive stages of redemption mapped by the suite are plotted—albeit in free, random order—into the poem. "The fact that we do exist is acknowledgement of Thee O Lord," to "I will do all I can to be worthy of Thee O Lord," to "Seek Him everyday. In all ways seek God everyday," are lines implying the same spiritual progression leading to emotional release and repose. "ELATION–ELEGANCE– EXALTATION" are Coltrane's climactic words at the close of "A Love Supreme," written with a poet's flair

A Love Supreme

I will do all I can to be worthy of Thee O Lord
It all has to do with it.
Thank you God.
Peace.
There is none other.
God is. It is so beautiful.
Thank you God. God is all.
Help us to resolve our fears and weaknesses.
Thank you God.
In You all things are possible.
We know. God made us so.
Keep your eye on God.
God is. He always was. He always will be.
No matter what . . . it is God.
He is gracious and merciful.
It is most important that I know Thee.
Words, sounds, speech, men, memory, thoughts,
    fears and emotions—time—all related . . .
    all made from one . . . all made in one.
Blessed be His name.
Thought waves—heat waves—all vibrations—
    all paths lead to God. Thank you God.
His way . . . it is so lovely . . . it is gracious.

It is merciful—Thank you God.
One thought can produce millions of vibrations
    and they all go back to God . . . everything does.
Thank you God.
Have no fear . . . believe . . . Thank you God.
The universe has many wonders. God is all.
His way . . . it is so wonderful.
Thoughts—deeds—vibrations, etc.
They all go back to God and He cleanses all.
He is gracious and merciful . . . Thank you God.
Glory to God . . . God is so alive.
God is.
God loves.
May I be acceptable in Thy sight.
We are all one in His grace.
The fact that we do exist is acknowledgement
    of Thee O Lord.
Thank you God.
God will wash away all our tears . . .
    He always will.
He always will.
Seek Him everyday. In all ways seek God everyday.
Let us sing all songs to God

To whom all praise is due . . . praise God.
No road is an easy one, but they all
    go back to God.
With all we share God.
It is all with God.
It is all with Thee.
Obey the Lord.
Blessed is He.
We are all from one thing . . . the will of God . . .
    Thank you God.
I have seen God—I have seen ungodly—
    none can be greater—none can compare to God.
Thank you God.
He will remake us . . . He always has and He
    always will.
It is true—blessed be His name—Thank you God.
God breathes through us so completely . . .
    so gently we hardly feel it . . . yet,
    it is our everything.
Thank you God.
ELATION–ELEGANCE–EXALTATION–
All from God.
Thank you God. Amen.

JOHN COLTRANE—December, 1964

for capital letters and alliteration.

In 1891, a sermon delivered by a Scottish theologian was published as a thirty-two-page tract by a small evangelical press in the United States. Within a few years, the Fleming H. Revell Company had a bestseller on its hands: Dr. Henry Drummond's *Love: The Supreme Gift.* In it, Drummond, a highly regarded lecturer in both Europe and America, preached the argument that among the Christian qualities deemed most divine, love—of God and of fellow man—is "the greatest thing in the world." His proof was the Bible: 1 Corinthians 13, in which Paul holds that without love, hope, charity, and even faith are meaningless. "If I have all faith, so that I can remove mountains, and have not love, I am nothing."

It was a simple idea that boldly countered centuries of church doctrine: "We have been accustomed to be told that the greatest thing in the religious world is faith . . . well; we are wrong." Yet it struck a popular chord in an era striving to reconcile old and new—like biblical dogma and Darwinism—in the Age of Industry and Science. It was also a concept with universal appeal: the role of love—as the defining divine characteristic and the highest gift from God—is a basic belief shared by most religions. By the mid-twentieth century, Drummond's pamphlet had been translated, read, and discussed by millions; over a century since its publication, it has never been out of print.

Whether Coltrane was inspired by the title of, or ideas in, Drummond's book—whether he even picked up a copy through his own reading habits or in his grandfather's well-stocked library—is today impossible to verify. The titular and thematic parallels of *Love: The Supreme Gift* and *A Love Supreme* could be the result of direct influence as easily as spiritual commonality. Perhaps it was one of those "things in the air at certain times," as Coltrane once described common jazz styles: "a number of people reach the same end by making a similar discovery." Establishing a direct link seems less important than simply marking that, with Coltrane's proclivity for borrowing from the lessons and language of religious writing, a deeper meaning and precedent to the superlative phrase "A Love Supreme" probably exists.

One thing is for sure: Coltrane, favoring music far over language as his chosen means of expression, never again put as much effort into public writing. The letter and poetic libretto he penned constitute the highest yield of his investment in the power of the written word; to this day they remain as inherent a part of *A Love Supreme* as the phrasing of his saxophone. Says Joshua Redman:

> [*They*] *did affect how I listened. I remember the experience of listening to the music, holding the record cover in my hands and reading the depth of his convictions in the liner notes. That's still attached to my experience of the music.*

art that required patience, concentration, and a good ear. Van Gelder, with hundreds of masters to his credit by 1964, could boast of all three. (He still owns the original Scully lathe on which he created many masters, including *A Love Supreme.*)

Mastering was more than just another service offered by Van Gelder's one-man operation; it was a procedure he insisted on providing:

> **It's purely a question of maintaining the quality of what I do for my client. If someone came to me to do an album, how could I say to them that I'm going to do for them what they want me to do if they have to go somewhere else to do the mastering? It's impossible.**

It was a process that endured for almost four decades, the fragile link between hundreds of thousands of music performances and the final vinyl. Once plated and in the hands of ABC, the two masters of *A Love Supreme*—sides A and B—were used to manufacture the stamps bearing the negative impression of the album, which, when pressed into heated vinyl, created LP copies of the four-part suite. Coltrane mentioned his favorite engineer in the liner notes; Van Gelder's role in the mastering process was similarly memorialized on the original master acetate and pressed on to most American copies of the LP. On the vinyl near the label it still reads in small capital letters: "VAN GELDER."

Coltrane's latest was prepared for market with speed common to many Impulse releases; *Crescent,* for instance, had been recorded in April and June 1964, and was shipped to retail shelves in midsummer. *A Love Supreme* would likewise see a two-month turnaround from studio to store, spurred on in part by Coltrane's concern about his own stylistic pace, of moving too fast for his listeners between albums. "What about giving audiences a chance to catch up?" asked Mike Hennessey, a British jazz journalist in July 1965. Coltrane responded:

> **This always frightens me. Whenever I make a change I'm a little worried that it may puzzle people. And sometimes I deliberately delay things for this reason. But after awhile I find there is nothing to else I can do but go ahead.**

Thiele confirmed Coltrane's active role in scheduling the release of his own recordings. "People like Coltrane, or Duke Ellington, record so much, they almost forget about what was recorded and it literally piles up." The producer added:

I tried . . . whenever possible to give him the time to listen to the things that we had done . . . [sometimes] he would say "let's hold up on what we've done. I've got something new."

Coltrane wanted *A Love Supreme* out, and never mind the holidays. Most of the necessary post-production work—mastering, marketing, album cover design—was complete by the end of December. To Thiele's delight, Coltrane decided to use as the cover image an old black-and-white photograph of himself that the producer had taken during the 1962 session with Duke Ellington:

Actual print used for the original album cover. Note Thiele's handwriting on reverse, and wrinkles left by various hands over the years

this shot for cover

> I always get a kick out of the fact that he used my picture on the cover.
> I had taken his picture . . . for my pleasure and I had some 8×10s
> made, blowups, and I had them on my desk and he was looking at
> them. He wasn't smiling and he said, "Who took this picture?" I fig-
> ured, "My God, he's going to kill me that these are so terrible." But
> before I could say I took the picture, he said, "This is the best picture
> of me, ever."

Thiele's unschooled lenswork produced one of the best-known portraits of
Coltrane. It caught the saxophonist, in the parking area outside Van
Gelder's, looking off toward the studio door, lips tight, pensive, with Garri-
son's distinctive patterned sweater in the foreground. When it came time to
choose an image for the album cover, Coltrane had brought a couple of
Thiele's shots home to show Alice:

> Interestingly, there were two. You know how you can take one snap,
> and then you take the next snap right after—the same man within sec-
> onds? So he showed them to me and said, "Which one do you like?"
> And I said, "I like this one . . . which one do *you* like?" And he said,
> "That one." I said, "Well, that's the one it will be." The one he didn't
> use there was a lightness. But the one they did use is a great, great
> photo. I see everything in it. Ev-er-y-thing. The seeker. The devotee.
> The musician, father, son. The man.

Thiele hired Viceroy, a firm that had helped define the Impulse look by creating the majority of the label's covers; George Gray, one of their designers,
was assigned to the job. Working with a limited color palette, Gray chose
not to add, but to maintain a monochromatic look, reaching for a simple
elegance that would, for the first time, break from Impulse's tradition of
using a standard orange spine. On the front cover, a smartly tilted line of
bold sanserif script, parallel to the railing in the background of the photograph, announced title and artist: "A Love Supreme/John Coltrane."

Wishing the inside of the gatefold to be as evocative as the album's
outer cover, Thiele hired jazz enthusiast Victor Kalin to create an appropriate portrait. Kalin, a noted illustrator famed for album and book covers as
well as magazine work, had played trumpet and saxophone in his younger
years, and was a Coltrane devotee. Working from a photograph he had
taken of the saxophonist in live performance, he produced a stark, black-
and-white portrait that seemed to artfully exaggerate the bottom bulk of
the saxophone and extend Coltrane's tapered fingers.

Joe Lebow, another experienced designer, integrated Kalin's rendering into the vertically aligned layout for *A Love Supreme*'s inner gatefold. The text of Coltrane's letter to the listener was run alongside the portrait, justified to match its curving contour. The main stem of his saxophone defined the design's center line, pointing down to the hymnal-like lettering of the album's title and Coltrane's poem/prayer, which was neatly centered and divided into three columns below. Quite a few music fans were inspired to unfold the album and hang it on their walls; its posterlike dimensions (24″ × 12″) more than suggested it.

Defying common practice, the proper titles of the sections of *A Love Supreme* were never clearly and separately listed on the sleeve. "Acknowledgement," "Resolution," "Pursuance," and "Psalm" were only mentioned by name in the text of Coltrane's letter and on the label of the record itself.

■ In early 1965 the Beatles, the Supremes, Barbra Streisand, and Petula Clark were all jostling for the top of the pop charts. Among the Top 30 popular albums sat titles by bossa nova jazzmen Stan Getz and João Gilberto, and New Orleans trumpeters Al Hirt and Louis Armstrong. *Billboard*'s R&B LP chart revealed the concurrent tastes of black record buyers, listing Lee Morgan's *Sidewinder* at number 10. The R&B singles chart showed ABC-Paramount enjoying soulful hits by Ray Charles ("Makin' Whoopee") and the Impressions ("Amen").

ABC was hot, and proudly bought a two-page spread in *Billboard* designed around a bowling metaphor ("a smashing group of albums that are right up everybody's alley!") to advertise the label's year-opening push. The top hopefuls among the featured LPs were *Ray Charles Live,* the Impressions' *People Get Ready,* Frank Fontaine's *I'm Counting On You,* music from the ABC TV show *Shindig,* and—with the first public showing of the album cover—*A Love Supreme.*

In 1965, as all Impulse titles received marketing and promotional push from the same department that handled ABC's more pop product, Coltrane's latest was boosted by the success of his better-known labelmates. But as Thiele described it, when it was his turn at the monthly new product meetings to introduce his releases to ABC's sales staff, he felt like the odd duck:

> **You know, ABC at the time was a major record company, and Impulse was a jazz label, and I guess outside of myself, there was no one in the company that understood jazz music. They didn't know John Coltrane from Benny Goodman.**

Victor Kalin's 1961 photograph
of Coltrane at the Newport Jazz
Festival, on which he based his
portrait for the inner gatefold of
A Love Supreme

In any case, as Thiele added, Coltrane's ability to move albums was at least established and respected:

> **His records were selling. So they figured that anything that he did, as long as it had John Coltrane's name, that they'd sell some records. And that's how a major record company would look at it—sales, dollars—that's all.**

Despite Thiele's contention, an ever-present concern with the bottom line was not in fact limiting ABC-Paramount's ecumenical efforts at the start of 1965. If anything, rapid expansion and chance-taking were in the air, an attitude from which *A Love Supreme* benefited. Partly in reaction to the explosion of the Beatles and the subsequent "British Invasion," recently appointed label chief Larry Newton reactivated Apt Records, a teen-music subsidiary, in the first week of January. Before the month was out, ABC introduced a new budget classical label called Baroque with no fewer than forty titles. At "The Big Drive in '65," a three-day national convention organized and funded by ABC in January, the company unveiled new incentive programs for its distributors ("one free album for every six bought," "100 free singles for each 500 bought," reported *Billboard*) and "announced the first release of ABC-Paramount, Impulse and Westminster four-track stereo tapes."

Buried in the *Billboard* story was mention that "Allan Parker, ABC-Paramount-Impulse album sales director, detailed 17 ABC-Paramount and 12 Impulse

packages, playing selected bands from each." It's hard to resist a smile guessing what track from *A Love Supreme* he must have chosen to play to a roomful of suntanned salesmen at the Eden Roc Hotel in Miami Beach. But Parker's effort must have paid off, for the company happily reported that the convention climaxed with "the largest sales volume of any distributor conclave in the label's history."

If "The Big Drive in '65" ultimately was worth the investment of ABC flying its distributors to Florida, the label had little choice but to sponsor such events: unlike other major record companies with their own branch distribution systems—Columbia, Capitol, and RCA—ABC-Paramount was totally reliant on independent distributors. If the company's music was to make it onto retail shelves, those annual expense-paid junkets were simply a part of doing business: it was fete or fail.

Former ABC A&R director Sid Feller adds that in getting its music played on radio, the company was also dependent on the services of outside specialists. "It was up to each label to decide on who they used to plug their music. We [ABC-Paramount] had our choices, and Bob [Thiele] had his. Of course, if there were over a hundred deejays in the country at that time, only ten would have been playing jazz."

This process, called independent promotion, is a music industry tradition that was and remains prevalent, despite recurrent attempts by major record companies to break free of a reliance on freelance "hit men." In 1965, Thiele worked with a few promotion veterans, boisterous souls who loved the music, never represented fewer than several labels at a time, and made it their business to know every deejay and radio station in their territory.

Veteran jazz producer Joel Dorn was a deejay in Philadelphia in 1965, spinning jazz "on one of the pioneering FM jazz stations: 'WHAT-FM, jazz at 96.5.' " With candor, he provides a behind-the-scenes look at the local world of jazz promotion:

> **The record promotion guy's job was to get the record on the radio, and there were two ways to do it: by paying cats off or by force of personality. The jazz stations were not places where you could get great payola, so we worked other deals, we got free records, we sold them, we did what we had to do. The guy who was the promotion guy for Impulse was Matt "Humdinger" Singer—if he was five foot two, five feet of it was mouth. He was a beloved character, and when he came in, he respected what it was you liked. I'll give you an example— Matty would bring you a record, like Chico Hamilton's *Man from Two Worlds* on Impulse [1962]. But for some reason, I didn't listen to it. He called me up, and he always called everybody "Mr.," though I was like twelve years old, and he was fifty. "Mr. Dorn, how come you're not playing the Chico Hamilton record? 'Forest Flower: Sunrise/Sunset'!" "I listened to it, Matty, I don't know . . ." "Play it! PLAY IT!" So I played it. We broke "Forest Flower" in Philly and then it broke all over the country.**

When Impulse delivered the white-label deejay copies of *A Love Supreme* in January, "[Singer] didn't have to do anything," Dorn reports. "He just brought it and said, 'Here's the new Coltrane.'" But not every market proved as easy to conquer; record spinners at Southern California's KLON did not embrace Coltrane's new album as immediately as those at WHAT. Radio promotion notwithstanding, deejay Chuck Niles explains the resistance:

> Coltrane and *A Love Supreme*, the Albert Aylers and the Pharoah Sanders . . . didn't knock me out too much—there wasn't as much excitement in it for me. I was still in the early sixties—still with Lee Morgan and Hank Mobley—just trying to preserve what I thought was true, good, straight-ahead stuff, with no gimmicks and no wild modal experiences. Maybe that's a selfish outlook. I didn't completely ignore [*A Love Supreme*], but I dug tunes with changes, you know?

Release of the music to radio was coordinated with various mentions of *A Love Supreme* in magazines, drumming up pre-sales anticipation. *Billboard* flagged the album for its music industry readers, deeming it worthy of a "Jazz Spotlight" on February 27, noting how it defied certain preconceptions of jazz musicians:

> To the world outside (and inside, we expect) the jazz artist is not one who closely identifies with God. Coltrane is one who now does, and has dedicated this most interesting jazz treatise to Him. A special emotional projection (John calls it "A Love Supreme") prevails throughout. Good jazz is creative, innovative and emotional. Coltrane, with God, plays excellent jazz.

Jazz readers were first alerted by a full-page ad in the February issue of *Jazz* for Shepp's *Four for Trane* album that also teased, "as for Coltrane himself, the 1964 Down Beat Poll's 1st Place Tenor Man has again produced a performance of unequalled distinction." The following issue, Impulse's full-page ad trumpeted *A Love Supreme* in name and image, employing Kalin's portrait and the album cover to herald, "Coltrane's new album is his personal monument to the forces that gifted him with self-expression and the power to please others."

Wayne Shorter recalls needing little more than the jazz community grapevine to be aware of the album's imminent arrival:

> I was sort of in the circle of people where we would be notified what would be coming out soon, and I was hearing about *A Love Supreme*—musicians might say, "Hey, did you hear about the next record by Trane," and all that. My antenna was always up, but it got to me without a radio broadcast—just word of mouth.

Copies of *A Love Supreme* began to appear in stores by the end of February, and were immediately snatched up by eager Coltrane fans. One of them was David S. Ware, a fifteen-year-old African American living in Newark, New Jersey, who already had his sights on becoming a saxophonist:

> I used to work a lot for my grandfather, man. He had a wood yard in Newark, and he used to sell wood and coal, and we used to go around and pick up scrap in his truck, and cash it in down at the scrap yard. I got money like that. I remember the day that my grandfather went to take me to get the album—I was so excited. I had waited for it to come. I don't remember if I had pre-ordered it or not, but I remember him taking me over on the highway, and buying that record at—it's not there anymore—it was called Harmony House, in Springfield, New Jersey, on Route 22. It was probably three dollars, four dollars and something.

Not far away in one of Philadelphia's more affluent suburbs, another fledgling saxophonist, Michael Brecker, had fallen under Coltrane's spell and was primed for his next album:

> I was in high school at the time, and in my little circle of musicians, we were all listening just to Coltrane. I was getting my hands onto any record I could, and trying to learn from it. I remember going out and buying *A Love Supreme* and listening to it in my bedroom. That record was powerful from every aspect, including the photograph on the front. It was a very intense kind of picture—more than intense: serious, focused, and clear.

Like Brecker, many of Coltrane's contemporaries recall that their first impression of *A Love Supreme* was focused on specific aspects of the album. Tommy Flanagan noted the chanting ("I didn't know his voice was so deep . . . Coltrane's voice is really a standout there"). Frank Foster was drawn to the text ("I fell even more in love reading the liner notes"), as was Yusef Lateef ("I think that was a pristine attitude, thanking the people who had helped him achieve what he did—and his love for God—it was wonderful, it impressed me very much").

For those closely charting Coltrane's progress, for whom each successive album competed with his previous release, *A Love Supreme* was neither explosive nor surprising—impressive, certainly, but not as immediately jolting as the titles that preceded it. "In those days in New York, it was like, *A Love Supreme* was just one album . . . OK, what's next," says saxophonist Dave Liebman. "I don't think it had the effect on the musicians as it might have had on the public a little bit later. I don't remember a gigantic buzz about it as much as would come with *Ascension.* I mean, *Ascension* blew everybody out of the water."

On university campuses, future rock recording artists found Coltrane's new album strengthening an already entrenched enthusiasm. "By the time *A Love Supreme* came out I was in community college [in New Jersey]," says Patti Smith. "Most people were into the [Rolling] Stones, Bob Dylan, and the Beatles. I shared those interests but I listened to it alone—my love of Coltrane developed at that time into a deeply personal experience." Steely Dan's Donald Fagen had just arrived at Bard College and recalls meeting and asking another piano player if he had heard *A Love Supreme.* "He said, 'Heard it? That's the Bible, man.' "

In San Francisco, Frank Lowe—Vietnam-bound after completing school—was already bowled over by the album that preceded *A Love Supreme.* "*Crescent* is like a perfect musical portrait, I mean, *that* recording was almost perfect to me." Then came *A Love Supreme*:

> **I got drafted into the army in '65 so before I leave [I'm thinking], "OK, this is where we're at now. This is the state of the music now." Instead of just the spiritual stuff, he had urbanized the spirituals, you know what I'm saying? Instead of compositions being "Steal Away" and "Old Rugged Cross," they became *A Love Supreme.***

Another musician who divined the spiritual message inherent in Coltrane's new album (and with whom Lowe would soon perform) was Sun Ra. But it did not make the avant-garde composer and bandleader happy. "Since I was the first person to do certain things, they think that, if I do something, it's the direction to take. Nine or ten years ago, I was the first to play music at a spiritual level. Recently, Coltrane has done a piece, *A Love Supreme,* with spiritual intentions." Having openly shared his musical theories with the saxophonist, Sun Ra felt some credit was due. "[After my group] moved to New York [in 1961] and . . . stayed in a hotel, Coltrane would come by, and I'd talk to him again about things . . . he never gave me a cup of coffee."

Predictably, for those who were studying jazz at the time, *A Love Supreme* had momentous effect. Saxophonist Pat LaBarbera—then a student at Berklee School of Music—remembers an evening gathering that became an ad hoc classroom:

> When that album came out, I remember we were all sitting around the dorm there, about six or seven or us. I remember there was a drummer—George Nebesnick—he had bought the LP, and a sax player named Tom Pastor, he's now president of the musicians' union in Vegas. And David Mott, a saxophone player who lives in Toronto, and Joe Calo, another saxophone player who played baritone with Buddy Rich were there, and maybe some other guys. Somebody put this record on, and all of a sudden, we're going, "What is *this*?" And then we played it back—"let's see if we can pick up on it." Because back then, if a tune was in F minor, you stayed in F minor, you didn't go to F-sharp minor or A-flat minor, but all of a sudden there's the harmony shifting, Coltrane's going all over the place and McCoy's doing all the movements. It was stuff Coltrane had done before, but it hit me that it was a really unique way of playing. I remember going to Ray Santisi, the piano teacher at Berklee, and I said, "Ray! What's going on here?" And he started showing me these fourth voicings that McCoy was using. I had been really into *Giant Steps* so the modal thing was really a stretch for me. But then we caught on, and everybody bought that album, sat there and tried to play it.

Other musicians, still working through the musical complexities of Coltrane's earlier work, were similarly puzzled by *A Love Supreme.* "My first reaction to *A Love Supreme*—I have to tell you—I thought it was simplistic musically," remarks arranger Sy Johnson:

> I had no connection at that point with the spiritual aspect of it. It's incomplete without the rest of the picture—the underlying intent of the music. I wasn't ready for that when it first came out.

As controversial as Coltrane had always been, various reviews in music journals reveal extreme responses—positive or negative—to the album and its message. Some critical reaction mirrored Johnson's initial inability to embrace the album as an integrated whole:

> **While the religious celebration which he wishes us to share in the recording cannot be questioned on any grounds of sincerity and integrity, it is still possible and necessary to ask whether a musician as gifted and capable as Coltrane is serving his talent well in this manner when *Crescent* offers so much more. The insistent incantation of *A Love Supreme* is moving in its devoutness, but wearing in the absence of any real development.**

Other academically inclined jazz pundits hailed the music in spite of its heart-on-sleeve spirituality. "John Coltrane has made it very difficult to discuss this disc with any objectivity," wrote Joe Goldberg in *HiFi/Stereo Review,* calling the album's spiritual dedication "almost embarrassingly open and fervent." Musically, he found *A Love Supreme* "a good record . . . and I think the listener might enjoy the music without need of the philosophy that accompanies it."

Not surprisingly, *Jazz* magazine—still close to Thiele and relying on Impulse's monthly ads—printed a review overflowing with superlatives. Written in free-form style by Detroit-based music writer and political activist John Sinclair, the piece lauded *A Love Supreme* as everything from "an enormous musical, emotional, *personal* statement by a genius of modern music" to "the most ambitious [music] Trane has yet undertaken." To his credit, Sinclair did mark Coltrane's departure from "traditional songform," but even in his ovation, he found it necessary to play the apologist. "Don't let the religious connection Coltrane makes bother you at all—you should rejoice in it."

With ears wide open, *Down Beat* delivered the most perceptive contemporaneous appraisal of the LP. Editor Don DeMicheal alloted it five out of five stars and deemed it "thoroughly a work of art," and his balanced analysis offered context (Coltrane's career path), detail (the suite's structure, the quartet's role), and—in dealing with the album's disarming spirituality—honesty:

> **I don't know how Coltrane's rediscovery has changed him as a man, but there is a change in his music—not a radical change, but one that has produced a peace not often heard in his playing previously, and Coltrane's peace induces reflection in the listener.**

How was *A Love Supreme* first received by jazz fans, by music consumers in general? *Billboard,* then lacking a chart to specifically track the sales of jazz albums, did highlight Coltrane's album as showing surprising retail strength by including it in their "Breakout Albums" category for March 13. Under the heading "New Action LPs" ("these new albums, not yet on *Billboard*'s Top LPs Chart, have been reported getting strong sales action by dealers in major markets"), *A Love Supreme* joined company with Johnny Cash's *Orange Blossom Special,* Lawrence Welk's *My First of 1965, The Animals on Tour,* and others.

As a jazz deejay with his own in-house system of taking measurements, Joel Dorn perceived a different character in the response to Coltrane's new album from the first spin:

> **There were three ways we, the disc jockeys, knew that an album would sell. Contact with the record company; record shops calling the station saying, "we're getting a lot of response to so and so," and the one I trusted the most: the phone in the studio. Listeners could call in and talk to any of the disc jockeys while we were on the air. So you knew what people were thinking pretty quickly, because we'd say, "we have a new album by Ray Charles, by Cannonball," whatever it was, and [snap fingers] in a half-hour you knew whether or not that album was going to make it.**

A Love Supreme—in Philadelphia at least—was reverently received:

> **There was a different sound in people's voices—an extra-musical response—that album evoked. "You going to play *A Love Supreme*? You going to play the whole album?" There was a spiritual response to that. It wasn't just the record—*Giant Steps* and *My Favorite Things* were big jazz records, and established Trane as a legitimate giant—but he became this spiritual slash political slash iconic something.**

From Dorn's perspective, Coltrane defined and seemed powered by the spirit of the day; *A Love Supreme* not only reflected a growing spiritual and political awakening, but reached across long-standing cultural boundaries:

> **In 1965, I'd say that the [radio] audience was half white and half black. There was a tremendous response to John Coltrane among the**

> young hipper white kids, but among the young black kids, he was *Trane,* he had another meaning. There was a response to *A Love Supreme* like you would have to Malcolm [X], like you would have to the march on Washington, like you have with the emergence of a black consciousness.

According to Archie Shepp, the timing of the album's release matched a palpable step-up in the assertive nature of black protest. "When *A Love Supreme* was released, people weren't singing 'Mercy, Mercy' anymore. Then, people were marching in Selma. Then, Malcolm X was preaching in the temple."

To black America, the album's appeal to the Divine, riding on a strident, emotional wave of sound, fit the season only too well. Malcolm X had been assassinated on February 21; on March 28, following a series of mass arrests and violence, Martin Luther King Jr. led 25,000 on a fifty-mile "March on Alabama" from Selma to the state capital. "I think that's what you hear in that music," says writer Amiri Baraka of Coltrane. "You hear the struggle against opposite forces, but you hear a kind of transcendental embrace of what is, and what is going to be, in his music":

> So much is made of Trane's link with Malcolm in the sixties, because those periods are when art of that kind does emerge. You have social upsurges, and for every social upsurge, there's an artistic upsurge that corresponds with that.

For those on both sides of the racial divide, *A Love Supreme* yoked the spirit- *and* fist-raising energy of the day. For bassist Rick James—then leading a rock 'n' roll band in Toronto that also included his roommate Neil Young—the album was a link between the city's black and white music scenes:

> Most of the white boys I was hanging out with in Toronto in 1965 were down with Coltrane. I mean, David Clayton-Thomas—he became lead singer of Blood, Sweat & Tears—Joni Mitchell, Gordon Lightfoot, Neil Young. That's one of the good things about the musical experience there. They were folkies, and folk and jazz went hand in hand. Everyone had *Sketches of Spain,* everybody had *A Love Supreme.*

Joel Dorn adds, "You gotta understand, at that time, it was the first time there was a black consciousness that the white audience knew about."

While some—including Coltrane himself—tried to explain his stridency, the perceived fury actually increased his cross-racial reach.

"I'm attracted to music that frightens me," confessed Donald Fagen, "like Coltrane's tone on the saxophone." To Roger McGuinn, founder of the group the Byrds (then enjoying their debut number 1 hit "Mr. Tambourine Man"), Coltrane's music "was assertive, it was strong, and it did have an anger to it, and so did rock 'n' roll":

> I'd listen to KBCA in L.A., a jazz station at the time, and they played an awful lot of Coltrane, they played everything he ever did. My initial reaction was one of physical pain. After I got past that, I said, "Yeah!" It was rebellious, it sounded like he was going, "I'm not going to take this anymore. I'm just going to do what I want to do, and that's it."

To his ears, *A Love Supreme* sounded tame compared to what came before:

> I did buy *A Love Supreme* and listened to it, but I really liked the '61 [Village] Vanguard sessions the best—*A Love Supreme* seemed more mellow by comparison. Obviously he had gone through a spiritual change and he was praising God . . . and I was going through a similar kind of thing at the time, so I could relate to it.

McGuinn points to the album's less-edgy sound and unifying message as the key to its success with "the flower-power hippie movement [which] was obviously based on love as opposed to any other emotion or spiritual feeling":

> I think [*A Love Supreme*] attracted them because it wasn't specific, it was not trying to shove a particular religion down your throat. And it gave people an opportunity to experience spirituality on a general level.

Saxophonist David Murray—later to record with the Grateful Dead—agrees that Coltrane "had pierced into the whole 'flower-child,' hippie base. They might not even know about any other jazz album, but they knew about *A Love Supreme.*" Like McGuinn, Murray credits the palatability of Coltrane's message. "They connected to spirituality in music, and I don't necessarily mean religion—he was taking the whole religious thing into pure spirituality, and that's where he plugged in, big time."

Grateful Dead bassist Phil Lesh, who first made his bandmates aware of Coltrane's music, recalls the sounds threading through San Francisco's quiet, multiracial Haight-Ashbury district in 1965, a year before it exploded onto the national radar as a locus of youth culture:

> **That's one of the records I would hear walking through the Haight on a spring night, all over town. You'd be walking, and somebody'd be playing [Bob Dylan's] _Bringing It All Back Home_, and somebody'd be playing [Miles Davis's] _Sketches of Spain_, and another time it was _A Love Supreme_. It was all just coming out of people's windows.**

As hallucinogenic backdrop—and as musical primer—_A Love Supreme_ was channeled by a crop of new rock groups. "I took LSD and listened to John Coltrane a lot; a lot of people did," admits Sam Andrew, founding member and guitarist with Big Brother and the Holding Company, who recalls hearing _A Love Supreme_ as walk-in/walk-out music at the city's most legendary venue. "It was definitely on the soundtrack at the Fillmore [Auditorium]."

Guitarists in particular, the premier soloists of the San Francisco music scene, were drawn to the album, and Coltrane's extended improvisations. Carlos Santana, then cutting his teeth on the electric blues of B. B. King and Jimmy Reed, was introduced to Coltrane through _A Love Supreme_:

> **What is really amazing [is] it was a pimp that turned me on to John Coltrane, I think he's still alive, but I haven't seen him in a long, long time. He had a lot of great music in there—Howlin' Wolf and Muddy Waters and Olatunji—but for some reason, he just put on _A Love Supreme_ and went into another room to make phone calls, keep up with his chicks or whatever. And here I am, smoking a joint, still in high school, and checking out _A Love Supreme_. It was one of the first times that I realized a paradox of music—being so violent and peaceful at the same time. I looked at the album cover, and saw his face being so intense. It was like . . . his thoughts were screaming.**

In Cincinnati, meanwhile, William "Bootsy" Collins, who would rise to fame as bassist in James Brown's legendary backup band, the JBs, in 1970, recalls, "I had to be around fifteen when I heard that album." Collins was already performing in various black clubs and bars around the city playing a mixed bag of R&B, blues, and jazz for whomever would pay—and soaking in the most unusual music he and his bandmates could find. "We looked at Trane as one of the 'outside musicians'—like Jimi [Hendrix] was later. We were really into that. But at that time we couldn't afford albums. We would listen at people's houses, on the radio, at the clubs." Collins remembers hearing *A Love Supreme* for the first time:

> It was at this little jive jazz club, the Blue Note, downtown in the West End—kind of a rat hole. We didn't actually know how to put it into the music or how to express what he was doing but we felt—I guess it was both musical and spiritual mode. We could see with the people who were listening to it there was some kind of connection there. But we were looking more at the musical side of it 'cause it just *freaked us out*. At that time we were into getting freaked out.

Up in Chicago, drummer Maurice White, future leader of the R&B group Earth, Wind & Fire, was similarly struck but for different reasons:

> I remember when *A Love Supreme* was released—I heard it at a friend's house. I went over to Rose Records, under the El, and at that time they allowed you to take records in a booth and you could listen to 'em. That was a record I didn't even have to take in the booth. Coltrane always had a lot of emotion in his playing, but that particular one—man, it was incredible. That record sounded different from the rest. I was trying to gather my spirituality together, trying to get an understanding of life, because I was a little bored with the misinterpretation of the Bible and the whole thing that was being taught in America. I felt Coltrane was the first musician who made a transition from one side to the other.

Even beyond R&B, rock, folk, and jazz circles, Coltrane's new album had pull. Composer Terry Riley, then laying the groundwork for the minimalist movement with music based on repetitive cycling of basic patterns, was more than ready for the saxophonist's latest:

> I heard him several times in San Francisco, when he would come with the quartet. When I moved to New York in '65, I had just written *In C*—which is probably the work I'm best known for—and I saw Coltrane getting deeper and deeper into the spiritual realm of music. On *A Love Supreme,* you get this kind of insistent rhythm that is just

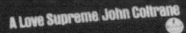

Posing with a Yamaha electric saxophone for a promotional photograph in late 1965, Coltrane stands in front of his signature album

very riveting—he uses it like a mantra. I was very much influenced by that and by Coltrane's approach to the permutation and combination of intervals, and to modality.

■ Just before Coltrane composed *A Love Supreme,* he had met with jazz writer Leonard Feather between sets at Shelly's Manne Hole in Hollywood. Feather noted that his "most devoted followers are young listeners, many of whom are musically illiterate." The writer wondered how—and if—these non-jazz types could fully appreciate music that "demands technical knowledge and intense attention." Caught off guard by the question, Coltrane replied:

> **I never even thought about whether or not they understand what I'm doing . . . it isn't necessary that it be understood. After all, I used to love music myself long before I could even identify a G minor seventh chord.**

In the months following the release of *A Love Supreme,* Coltrane was in and out of town—Boston, Chicago, Washington—and back in New Jersey recording the music for an album that would be titled *The John Coltrane Quartet Plays . . .* Early summer arrived, and plans were made for festival dates in the United States and a brief European tour returning the quartet to France, and then Belgium. To Coltrane, *A Love Supreme* was a fast-receding concern, and he was not one to look back for any measure of success. "He did call every once in a while to find out if there was an acceptance to a new album," Thiele recalled a few years later. Then he qualified his comment: "I guess I am oversimplifying his lack of interest in the public, but I don't think he was *that* concerned."

Coltrane had faith—in himself, his art, and his audience—that he would achieve the level of communication and uplift he intended with his music.

"Eventually," he told Feather, "the listeners move right along with the musicians."

Suite by the Sea

The practice of promoting one's own recordings—of shaping one's live repertoire to match the selections on a recent album—is an ambivalent enterprise for many jazz musicians, as artistic sensibility squares off against commercial demand. For those lucky enough to have landed a minor hit—like Adderley, like Coltrane—it only exacerbated the issue.

Coltrane's set lists had always sought a balance. He treated most clubs as greenhouses with a cover charge—supplying the opportunity to nurture new material while satisfying regulars with requests.

Yet among many live dates in the months immediately following the release of *A Love Supreme,* no evidence exists of the suite being performed, either in part or in its entirety. Coltrane, neither obtuse nor stubborn, seemed determined to ignore rather than revisit the album. So why slight his own success? If anything, Coltrane was more sensitive to the demands of his material than most; his music began to veer more to suitelike efforts, testing his audience again.

"The Trane who was into the major long extended composition . . . was difficult for people who were not accustomed to hearing that kind of music," remarked journalist A. B. Spellman. To Ravi Coltrane, 1964 marked the turning point:

> *I think that* A Love Supreme *affected the way a lot of live performances were going after '64. Most of the gigs in '65 were like suites . . . maybe a set would be two tunes. He would play a melody, then leave the stage, then McCoy would play, and then there would be a drum solo, and then Trane would come back and play a kind of a shorter solo like "One Up, One Down," and then that would go into a bass solo, and Trane would come back for the head for another tune.*

If I went into a nightclub like the Sutherland Hotel in Chicago and played a John Lewis–type "Fontessa" thing . . . it would actually lose customers for jazz . . . if you drop long things—serious works—on them where there are cash registers ringing and the waitress is hollering "two bourbons," and all that's going on, it just does not work.

—Cannonball Adderley, 1962

New music demanded new venues, and Coltrane himself felt the change acutely. The Half Note was not going to cut it anymore:

> *Now there was a time when it felt all right to play clubs, because with my music, I felt I had to play a lot to work it out . . . the music, changing as it is, there are a lot of times*

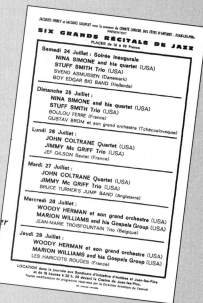

it doesn't make sense, man, to have somebody drop a glass, or somebody ask for some money right in the middle of Jimmy Garrison's solo . . . I think the music is rising into something else, and so we'll have to find this kind of place to be played in.

In late July 1965, as tapes rolled and TV cameras caught the action, Coltrane found the "kind of place" for *A Love Supreme.*

France's Côte d'Azur was a busy, bustling place in 1965. The fishing villages dotting the coast west of Nice—Cannes, Fréjus, St.-Tropez—had long ago seen the higher value in their blue skies and flat, crescent-shaped beaches, and begun actively competing for tourist revenue.

In 1960, businessman and music fan Jacques Hebey convinced local leaders in Antibes to invest in his idea: a weeklong series of concerts struck in the mold of the Newport Jazz Festival, mixing seaside atmosphere and world-renowned musicians on an outdoor stage. To help book major talent, Hebey partnered with Barclay Records executive Jacques Souplet. From June 6 to 14, 1960, the first Festival International de Jazz in Antibes was held, with an eclectic mix—Charles Mingus, Helen Merrill, Bud Powell, Albert Mangelsdorff, Sister Rosetta Tharpe—attracting audiences to a secluded, shaded beachfront called Juan-les-Pins.

The festival exploded in reputation and pull. In its first few years, it presented Ella Fitzgerald and Sarah Vaughan, Ray Charles and Lionel Hampton, Miles Davis and Fats Domino; it produced live recordings that became solid-selling albums; it boasted the primary state media

outlet, ORTF (Organization of French Radio and Television Production), as its co-sponsor. André Francis was there from the beginning as on-air commentator, program producer, and stage emcee:

I was the MC from 1960 to 1990 . . . my voice is on all the records recorded there, like with Miles Davis, where I pronounce Herbie Hancock, "Hancook." In '65, Juan-les-Pins was the king of the jazz festivals. It was a very international audience who came from Germany, England, Belgium, Italy, which is something that doesn't exist today because every country has its

own festivals. It was the only one in the summer.

For their sixth year, the festival promised a varied lineup; among the first-timers to Antibes would be Nina Simone, Woody Herman, gospel singer Marion Williams, and, for two consecutive nights, John Coltrane.

Having just completed an extended run in New York at the Village Gate, the quartet boarded the plane for a three-city sweep through Europe, kicking off with Antibes, then Paris, and a festival in Belgium.

The group arrived on their first performance day, Monday, July 26, to unseasonable weather. "It was a

Antibes Jazz Festival, July 26, 1965

JEAN-PIERRE LELOIR

little chilly at that time—real nippy," recalls Tyner. "None of us were prepared for that kind of weather," adds Jones. "It was miserable and muddy." The quartet would be sharing the evening with organist Jimmy McGriff and French pianist/bandleader Jef Gilson, who found himself face-to-face with the saxophonist after performing that afternoon:

When I finished, backstage, Coltrane came and he said, "Very good, young man, very good." He said that he liked my music. I thanked him, and I spoke of the playing of Elvin [which] for me, in 1965, he was the future for the drums. And Coltrane was very satisfied that I thought so.

Based in Paris, with friends in the music business, Gilson had heard an advance copy of an album that he was inspired to mention. "*A Love Supreme* was my idea because I heard the test pressing before Coltrane came . . . [Michel] Delorme was my *témoin*—my witness." Delorme himself does not recall the encounter, but confirms that Vega—the record label releasing Coltrane's Impulse titles in France—would have received copies of *A Love Supreme* by that summer (though it did not issue it until spring of the following year). Whatever Coltrane's motivation, he was often open to outside suggestion, and a request for an album-length composition would surely have stood out. "People didn't request suites that much," laughs Jones, "even after the record was distributed."

With more than a hint of civic pride, Francis has his own theory why Coltrane chose to honor Antibes with the only public performance of *A Love Supreme*:

I think that it's because Coltrane and the other musicians found themselves in a place that was extremely important at the time. It was a place that was very sacred for the artist, a feeling of atmosphere, of well-being, and of confidence.

Could the quartet accurately recall the structure of music first struck almost eight months before? According to Tyner, unquestionably.

The material really wasn't the challenge. It's funny—I think A Love Supreme was a culmination of everything we did prior. If we were a new band that had just been put together, then I think it would've been a tumultuous challenge, but it wasn't like that. All we had to worry about was, "let's just get in there and play, and see what happens."

Jimmy McGriff finished his set to warm applause while Coltrane and the quartet stood waiting in the wings. Jones still recalls marking a sellout crowd and the white-gloved doyennes in the VIP section up front. "That part of the Riviera, there's a lot of retired folks, and they just live there year round, and they're always going to a concert or ballet or whatever. We were the entertainment that night!"

With the Mediterranean behind them and a packed audience of European jazz fans, local gentry, and television cameras in front, the tuxedoed quartet took the stage, ready to offer their only live per-

La Pinède Gould, Juan-les-Pins, France, July 1965: Marion Williams and her gospel group onstage

breezes to stormlike fury—were swept away; in the words of Michel Delorme, a jazz journalist in attendance, "He played only forty-eight minutes, but those forty-eight minutes were really a thunderstorm."

From the outset, Coltrane assumes a traffic-cop role, cueing transitional passages, nudging the band along. "Acknowledgement" kicks off with an urgent fanfare, as Coltrane delivers the signature four-note mantra, then hops the theme through a succession of keys, with no chanting offered. ("I opened my mouth, and nothing came out," he joked the next day.) The surviving concert footage captures the performance losing focus as Garrison fumbles his cue to take the tune out. Coltrane deliberately crosses to the microphone to reboot the energy with the opening notes of "Resolution," which is played in an easy-swinging tempo, mellower than the studio take.

Tyner's solo is a five-minute

formance of Coltrane's suite. Francis, in his mother tongue, introduced the players one by one, then explained, "John Coltrane will play a theme—rather, a composition in several movements—that he recently recorded in the United States. It is titled *Love Supreme*." Without a word or a glance, Coltrane launched into the opening flourish of "Acknowledgement."

A faithful rendering of the studio recording it was not. A six-month gap and an expanded canvas—thirty-three minutes in the studio, forty-eight on stage—stretched the suite's concentrated cohesion. As the group members reacquainted themselves with the material, sharply defined peaks of intensity spread into high-energy plateaus. The weatherlike shifts of mood on the album—warm, gentle

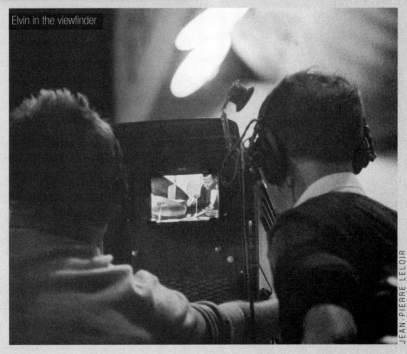
Elvin in the viewfinder

standout, the pianist fluctuating single-note runs from his right hand and chordal bursts from his left. Coltrane's improvisation follows, and a change is immediately, startlingly apparent. The lyrical phrasing of late '64 has grown a more brittle bite, evolving into unresolved flurries of notes favoring the upper register of his horn. Breathlessly emotional, Coltrane's altissimo cries screech forth, seemingly determined to locate some lost note. At one point, he pulls himself off-mike and the swell of his solo lowers noticeably; the saxophonist restates the blues-tinged melody, then retreats from the microphone, allowing "Resolution" to trail off.

Applause overlaps the start of a brief drum solo, the close of which Jones develops into a rolling figure as Coltrane blows the theme to "Pursuance." For many, the saxophonist's ensuing performance is the unpolished jewel of the evening, more liberation than abandon. "You can feel the creative tension that Coltrane is going through during that period," David Liebman comments, "the tempo is faster than they usually play." Branford Marsalis agrees. "That's a very, very fast tempo for that group . . . ["Pursuance"] has a freedom that the studio recording doesn't have." Saxophonist Andrew White, noted for transcribing an extensive array of Coltrane performances, labels it "solo number 527" and says, "That is the hardest solo out of 650 that I've done . . . the complexity and depth of his linguistic contribution is incredible. It's really substantial—a real high-water mark."

In Coltrane's free-sounding exhortation lies an uncanny range of style and texture from a rich, twenty-five-year palette—low-end honks that speak of R&B gigs in the

Tins holding the tapes of the only live performance of the suite

'50s; scalar sweeps that bring to mind his "sheets of sound" phase with Monk; upper-register cries from his more recent, spiritual phase; densely packed lines that presage the free period to come. Two minutes into Coltrane's solo, Tyner, then Garrison, drop out, leaving saxophonist and drummer in a tight, mano-a-mano duet.

Coltrane ends his solo and restates the melody to "Pursuance." Piano and drums share an extended cadenza and take the piece out. The next eight minutes belong to Garrison, during which he coaxes an exhaustive variety of sounds from his instrument. Following a skipping beat, he plucks, chords, strums; he first raises his bow to play in a classical manner, then slides it up and down the strings rapidly, bounces it pizzicato style, and finally uses the back of the bow as a hammer, eliciting a timbre reminiscent of a dulcimer. He returns to a Spanish sonority and signals the end of his solo.

With practiced synchronization, the last low note on the bass leads to the downbeat of "Psalm": Coltrane, Tyner, and Jones join together on the free-rhythm mood piece. As Coltrane works from memory, his somber, eloquent tone implies the word-based phrasing of the album. But frequent embellishments to the former syllable-by-syllable reading betrays either Coltrane's inability to recall the text of his poem or simply

an intentional melodic departure. In either case, Coltrane sermonizes with a compelling rasp, then answers his acclamations with more purely musical runs. An intense inner dialogue reveals itself: at times, both preacher and saxophonist seem to inhabit the same sonic space.

Stepping back from the mike, Coltrane closes with a drawn-out, fluttering figure. A shimmering cymbal and a sustained piano chord maintain the spell of the tune. Clapping and cheering begin to swell, then a round of whistles and boos is heard among the huzzahs demanding more music. But Coltrane has already led the group off stage, tired and spent. "A third of the audience was yelling because they wanted more," explains Delorme. "They thought forty-eight minutes was not enough. Another third was yelling because they didn't like it, and the last third was yelling because they loved it." The chorus of confusion continues until Francis hurries to the microphone. Deep in the Paris-based archives of the National Audiovisual Institute, France's national TV and radio agency, lies the small reel containing the emcee's remarks, which begged understanding from the crowd.

That's it for this concert [jeers] . . . You can hear Coltrane again tomorrow evening [more jeers] . . . Understand, my friends, that this music is not measured by

the timepiece—more than anything John Coltrane's musical talent . . . he wanted to give us of his deepest self, so allow him to avoid repeating himself and to get some rest [applause] . . . Tomorrow night then, again— John Coltrane, Jimmy McGriff, and also the British band of Bruce Turner.

Within a few months, Europe's leading jazz critics helped spread the word of Coltrane's memorable performance of *A Love Supreme.* "You really had to be there," wrote an Italian journalist. "Like a furious hurricane, Trane grabbed the crowd with the force of a cyclone, traversing a long series of choruses that I can only describe as stupefying." "His playing has developed into a much more 'further out' sound, intense, fascinating, at times charging like an angry bull," opined a Norwegian writer. "The audience were a little puzzled and disappointed to hear just one piece," noted a British reporter, while a Spanish colleague explained the crowd's disappointment in terms his home readers could grasp: "The minority that always demands more from their idols—much more if they are famous—were disappointed. That's how bull fighters die."

Arguably the most informed overview appeared in France's *Jazz Hot*, in which Delorme placed the performance within the context of Coltrane's career, and described a post-concert conclave:

The audience who left the Pinède

171

JEAN-PIERRE LELOIR

He studied the image, whispered, "That's my boy . . . ," and, propping it up on the mirror, serenaded it with his horn.

That night Coltrane acquiesced to the festival's request and performed more familiar material: "Naima," "Impressions," and "My Favorite Things." His next two concerts found him in Paris, then Belgium, and then home. He would never return to France or even Europe again. Nor did he ever choose to perform *A Love Supreme* again, not in its entirety.

Decades later, those fortunate enough to have been in attendance still hail the evening's impact and importance. "I saw so many performances at Juan-les-Pins . . . I heard practically everybody in many places," states Francis. "But what's certain is that *A Love Supreme* concert was for me the summit of the career of the man." Delorme remembers, "I was just so shocked after the concert, it took me about five minutes to recover and talk to people."

Even McCoy Tyner, after many years and countless gigs, accedes: "I remember it was a very exciting and firey performance by the band. If you see the footage, you can see the animation that was going on."

On July 27, the day after he performed *A Love Supreme* for the last time in its entirety, Coltrane was typically self-critical. "I did not play as I wanted last night. I know what I was trying to do, but it is not always easy to achieve." Then he added:

I want to get to a point where I can feel the vibrations of a particular place at a particular moment and compose a song right there, on the spot— then throw it away.

Gould on the right-hand side will certainly remember a small gathering of men engaged in a heated discussion. They happened to be some of our foremost critics, some venting their outrage, whilst others asserted that their faith in John Coltrane had in no way been shaken. The former admittedly had their reasons. No one had yet heard the record, and this hardly helped towards the success of the performance given at the festival. Already committed to the next stage of his development, the John Coltrane of Antibes '65 had already covered over half the distance that separates the record A Love Supreme *from the* Ascension *album. Was it not symptomatic that he spent his days listening to recordings of Albert Ayler?*

And that's exactly what Coltrane did. While the rest of the band hit the beach the following afternoon, he remained yards away in his hotel room, practicing as usual, playing along to a tape of an Ayler concert. Among the guests he received was Jean-Pierre Leloir, a noted photographer, who presented him with a concert shot from 1962 showing the saxophonist and Eric Dolphy. Dolphy had passed away only a year before, and Coltrane still felt the loss.

Coltrane steps back, December 26, 1966, Village Theater, New York City: Pharoah Sanders takes center stage as Coltrane expands the band.

Every time I talk about jazz, I think of prizefighters. One year it's your year, like it's mine now, and the next year everybody's forgotten you. You only have a few years, and you have to stay up there as long as you can . . . and be graceful about it when it's somebody else's turn.

—JOHN COLTRANE, EARLY 1960s

Chapter 5

Avant-Garde, a Force for Good

Perhaps it was a four-year itch.

Not that Coltrane planned his career turns with any exactitude, but the timeline of his most creative period does imply a certain regularity: one year bursting with diverse activity and unsettled exploration—1957, 1961—followed by three of relatively focused progress. By that schedule, 1965 promised another creative eruption.

On cue—while the sound of *A Love Supreme* threaded its way into the cultural tapestry—Coltrane again accelerated his experimental drive in contexts large and small, in the process testing the bonds that held his core group together. Before the year was out, the reign of the Classic Quartet would come to a close, and Coltrane would front a new band and a new sound.

The signs of his future direction were already present in the *Love Supreme* sessions. Coltrane's measured key-hopping on "Acknowledgement" presaged a harmonic approach in his playing bordering on—and soon embracing—a passionate atonality. His penchant for chanting would resurface on recordings like "Om"; his love of poetry on the album cover of *Kulu Se Mama.* His explicitly hymnlike titles became an unbroken theme among the many tracks recorded in 1965—"Dear Lord," "Welcome," "The

Father, the Son and the Holy Ghost"—and their meditative sonority a looser reflection of that on *A Love Supreme*.

A Love Supreme also left its trace in the extended, suitelike compositions Coltrane brought into the studio throughout 1965. He even chose the title "Suite" for a five-part work with sectional names again suggesting spiritual focus—"Prayer and Meditation: Day," "Peace and After," "Affirmation." The album *Meditations* (and the later release *First Meditations*, among the final sessions with the Classic Quartet) furthered Coltrane's trend to multisectioned constructions presented in continuous performance. *Meditations* also elicited questions as to whether he was consciously following in his own footsteps. Coltrane's response leaned more to the spiritual than the musical, as he saw his current efforts as points along the same continuum:

> **Once you become aware of this force for unity in life, you can't ever forget it. It becomes part of everything you do. In that respect, [*Meditations*] is an extension of *A Love Supreme*, since my conception of that force keeps changing shape. My goal of meditating on this through music, however, remains the same. And that is to uplift people, as much as I can. To inspire them to realize more and more of their capacities for living meaningful lives.**

As Alice noted, "From *A Love Supreme* onward, we were seeing a progression toward higher spiritual realization, higher spiritual development."

Notwithstanding the unreleased quartet-plus-two experiment of December 10, 1964, Coltrane seemed taken by a need to augment his forces. In February, he revisited the two-bass idea at a session again matching Garrison with Art Davis, which yielded two deeply hypnotic takes of "Nature Boy." The tenor-on-tenor concept inspired Coltrane to consider recruiting another tenorist into his group. By that spring, the bandleader was frequenting various Manhattan clubs, and began following a young tenor player from Little Rock, Arkansas, whose unfettered style was clearly in the Coltrane mold. "This was before I was working in clubs nightly," Farrell "Pharoah" Sanders recollects:

> **I was playing at this place called Slugs on a Saturday, and I think it was seven-ish. It was only for about an hour and a half before the regular bands came out. I didn't even know he was in the room—I looked up and he was at the bar. I was into a more modal kind of thing and he**

heard me play some of those tunes I wrote—"Upper and Lower Egypt"—that was before I recorded it. He came up, and we talked very briefly. He said that he enjoyed the music.

Sanders, like Dolphy, would soon become the second horn in Coltrane's band, his presence having an undermining effect on the tight solidarity of the quartet. But the most striking example of Coltrane's expansive drive took place in early June, in his first big-band effort since *Africa/Brass,* and arguably his most daring effort since "Chasin' the Trane."

Take a roomful of players of varying experience and abilities and, sans rehearsal, allow them to improvise simultaneously over a loose series of themes and modal frames. Turn on the tape machine, and let it roll for forty-odd minutes. Coltrane called on no fewer than seven horn players (trumpeters Freddie Hubbard and Dewey Johnson, alto saxists Marion Brown and John Tchicai, and tenors Shepp, Sanders, and himself), plus Art Davis again, to supplement his quartet. Short of finding a few swing-era stalwarts friendly to the avant-garde cause, Coltrane could not have picked a more disparate group, from those with conservatory training (Davis, Tchicai), to those with a strong bebop background (Tyner, Garrison, Hubbard), to "New Thing" newcomers (Shepp, Sanders, Johnson).

The fact that the session threw together players of unequal experience and different temperaments both excited and daunted Coltrane. "He was just very quiet and concentrated . . . very much occupied in his mind with what he wanted to do," Tchicai remembers. Coltrane seemed to demand from the group the same unspoken dialogue his quartet had achieved, giving "small directions, he didn't say a lot—'OK, we have this little theme here, and then at a certain point you come together in the piece and play this theme, and then you take a solo, and then after you it's . . . Freddie Hubbard.'" Coltrane himself recalled being happier with the results than with the session itself:

> **I was so doggone busy; I was worried to death. I couldn't really enjoy the date. If it hadn't been a date, then I would have really enjoyed it. You know, I was trying to get the time and everything, and I was busy . . . to hear the record I enjoyed it; I enjoyed all the individual contributions.**

It had been an adventurous effort, and would have been even more so had Coltrane realized his wish to have two drummers on the recording. He had originally asked a Philadelphian he met, Rashied Ali, who had managed, through youthful persistence, to sit in for Jones on a few nights at the Half Note. With incredulity, Ali recalls turning down Coltrane's invitation:

> **I had an ego bigger than this building at that point . . . I was young, I was ridiculous, and I said "Yeah, I would like to play. Who else is gonna play?" . . . "Well, I don't think I wanna play with two drummers." He said, "Oh, you don't?" . . . so I blew the date on *Ascension*!**

Coltrane points the way—
the *Ascension* session: (from
left) Coltrane, Archie Shepp,
McCoy Tyner, John Tchicai

Nonetheless, Coltrane continued to pursue the idea of multiple percussionists, along with his other additions. Upon returning from his European tour, he peppered live and studio dates with unlikely combinations of instruments. He invited Archie Shepp to a *Down Beat* Jazz Festival appearance in Chicago. A subsequent West Coast tour found him working with Pharoah

Sanders, flutist Joe Brazil, two bassists, and someone playing a thumb piano in Seattle. Upon reaching Los Angeles, he doubled every instrument save piano—including bass clarinetist/bassist Donald Garrett and percussionist Juno Lewis—and recorded the African-flavored, chant-heavy "Kulu Se Mama."

Upon his return to New York, Coltrane was determined to honor the past and yet face the future—to maintain the quartet, but augment to it at will, as he described the following year:

> I figured I could do two things: I could have a band that played like the way we used to play, and a band that was going in the direction that the one I have now is going in—I could combine these two, with these two concepts going. And it could have been done.

Alas, given personality clashes (Jones and Ali never saw eye-to-eye) and divergent musical paths (Tyner especially was not in accord with Coltrane's more atonal experiments), it was not to be. One night in November, Coltrane walked onto the stage at the Village Gate carrying his soprano, tenor, a bass clarinet, percussion instruments, and even a bagpipe—accompanied by Sanders, Ali, alto saxist Carlos Ward, and the quartet. It was one of the last times he would play with Tyner and Jones. As 1965 drew to a close, the strain on the senior members was proving too much, and in short order, Tyner left, to be replaced by Coltrane's wife, Alice; Jones soon followed, leaving Ali alone in the drum position. Only Garrison remained from the groundbreaking quartet. Years later, the Tyner and Jones explained their respective departures matter-of-factly:

> *Q:* **What prompted you to leave . . . ?**
> *Tyner:* **I felt if I was going to go any further musically, I would have to leave the group, and when John hired a second drummer, it became a physical necessity. I couldn't hear myself.**
>
> *Q:* **Do you think you [and Ali] were compatible as drummers?**
> *Jones:* **I think that I was. I don't think he was . . . I didn't think my leaving would have any debilitating effect on the group.**

■ The winter of 1965–66 delivered the full windfall of *A Love Supreme.* Of the public citations crowning Coltrane's artistic *and* commercial achievements over the years, none matched the awards and attention this album engendered in the few weeks that came exactly a year after its recording and release. A popular poll conducted by *Down Beat,* the country's leading jazz publication at the time, resulted in Coltrane's being inducted into the magazine's Hall of Fame (a first for a living musician) and receiving awards for Tenor Saxophonist of the Year and Album of the Year. The music industry took notice as well, nominating *A Love Supreme* for two Grammys. And though ABC-Paramount never officially secured the gold-record distinction for the album, Impulse's parent company had a gold replica of Coltrane's best-selling disc made, and hung it proudly in their New York corporate offices. "Gold before it went gold," laughs Archie Shepp. "It's a good marketing technique." He explains:

Our thanks and appreciation to everyone who voted for

JOHN COLTRANE

and, especially, our gratitude to this great artist himself.

"A LOVE SUPREME"-RECORD OF THE YEAR
JAZZMAN OF THE YEAR
BEST TENOR SAX
HALL OF FAME

i! impulse!

A Product of ABC-Paramount Records, Inc., A Subsidiary of American Broadcasting Companies, Inc.

Coltrane and
Impulse return the love

Jimmy Garrison told me a really strange story of how on the ninth floor of ABC was the jazz office and they had the glass cage there with gold records, and he used to see *A Love Supreme* beside the all the others. He couldn't believe it, and finally went to Bob Thiele and Bob acknowledged that it was in fact a gold record.

Not since the heady success of "My Favorite Things" in 1961 had Coltrane enjoyed such a wide and warm embrace as he did at the close of 1965; yet not since the harsh critical reaction of 1962 had he faced as dramatic a reversal of support as he did following the changes he effected in his lineup. But unlike the "anti-jazz" storm, this one was neither headline-grabbing nor loud. Tyner and Jones left with little fanfare (their departures eclipsed by Coltrane's far-ranging explorations of later 1965); and a flock of fans and fellow musicians began to slip away.

"That was really cataclysmic to me," submits Dave Liebman. "Seeing Coltrane starting to use two drummers, then Elvin not there anymore, and one tune for an hour and a half with three or four guys playing at the same time. I'm used to 'Impressions' and that certain vibe that Elvin and McCoy had, and here he was breaking that." Coltrane's music became more challenging than ever:

It was disturbing, but fascinating—like a bunch of maniacs just screaming at the top of their lungs. This doubled the ante because the

energy level and intensity of the free stuff live was beyond description. It was hard to believe it was Coltrane.

Liebman recalls one gig in particular. In February, at the Philharmonic Hall (now Avery Fisher Hall) in New York's prestigious Lincoln Center, a night devoted to the tenor saxophone was scheduled. Coltrane joined a lineup featuring Coleman Hawkins, Zoot Sims, Sonny Rollins, and others playing with their own bands. His slot would be the final one of the evening:

> I recall the last part of the first half was Sonny Rollins—he was in one of his not-really-into-it moods, walking around the stage playing in the corner. He only played about fifteen minutes and then he got on the microphone to say "I'll be back later with John Coltrane." Everybody went crazy, you know. Then there was a break and after, Coltrane walks on the stage holding Alice's hand—[with] about ten cats who look like they're off the street, holding shopping bags with bells, shakers, and tambourines. It was [drummer] J. C. Moses and Rashied [Ali], and [trumpeter] Don Ayler and Albert Ayler, [and Sanders, Garrison, and Carlos Ward]. And people are very excited. Coltrane gets on the microphone and he starts chanting "Om Mani Padme Om," which [was]—by that time I knew a little bit about that stuff—a heavy Tibetan chant of the dead. Alice starts rolling into a tremolo, and the group starts shaking the tambourines and everything, and people start to look at each other weird. Then he goes into "My Favorite Things." He plays the melody over this rolling rubato and people applaud. But of course, after the melody there was nothing that was recognizable, and it went on for an hour and a quarter, or so it seemed [25 minutes, in fact]. I'm not exaggerating—at least half the audience got up and left. He had his head down and he was playing near the ground and in those days he was, he got very low and was kneeling, off mic. It was just a barrage of sound. I was there with a very good friend—we used to go together to see Coltrane a lot. We were just speechless. I couldn't talk for a couple of days.

Meanwhile, *Ascension* had been released in the final weeks of '65 and was gathering a momentum of its own. The collective tour de force culled a largely positive critical reaction ("massive and startling," the normally buttoned-down *New York Times* declared), and as Liebman recalls, "was the torch that lit the free-jazz thing. I mean, it really begins with Cecil [Taylor] and Ornette [Coleman] in '59, but *Ascension* was like the patron saint saying, 'It's OK—this is valid.' I think that even had much more of an effect on everybody than *A Love Supreme.*" Yet it also had an effect as divisive and alienating as the Philharmonic Hall concert, according to Frank Foster:

> **The main complaint came after the album *Ascension*. That was the turning point for some musicians who had been Coltrane enthusiasts up to that time; after that they turned off. I thought it was a little extreme, but he was always my man. I agreed with some who said, "Coltrane's experimenting. He's done just about everything that can be done with a tenor saxophone, so now he's trying to reach out for something else." It wasn't even about the tenor sax anymore, it was about exploration. It was more about finding oneself spiritually than trying to turn the tenor saxophone into something.**

Village Theater, New York, December 26, 1966: (from left) Lionel "Sonny" Johnson (bass), Alice Coltrane (piano, hidden), Jimmy Garrison (bass), Pharoah Sanders (tenor), Rashied Ali (drums), Coltrane (soprano), Omar Ali (conga), unidentified (tambourine), Algie DeWitt (tamboura)

In 1966, Coltrane's saxophone "sound was changing dramatically," writes Lewis Porter, pointing to "a richer tone, with fuller vibrato . . . he also extended his altissimo range . . . didn't hesitate to produce squeals . . . [and] increased his control of multiphonics." Dissonance and atonality—freely hopping from one key to another—were the new hallmarks listeners came to expect from his horn.

The startling shift went beyond Coltrane's own sound and pervaded his band. Gone was the drama of Tyner's rich, hammered chords; Alice's facile sweeps along the keyboard provided a more diffuse rhythmic accompaniment. Sanders favored Coltrane at his most forceful and vocal-like: his unabated energy was both trying and exhilarating. Jones had always suggested a steady swing, even at his most polyrhythmic. Ali, whom Coltrane praised as "one of the great drummers . . . laying down multi-directional rhythms [that] allow the soloist maximum freedom," had substituted an intuitive, improvised drive for any sense of regular pattern.

To David S. Ware, who frequently traveled into Manhattan to catch Coltrane in 1966, the loss of that pulse, be it explicit or implied, was the reason for many of the empty seats he saw. "You can get almost as avant-garde as you want to be, as long as you keep that steady pulse, but Coltrane lost a lot of people when he broke that time, and went into that other world and started messing with that multidirectional time."

It certainly was not about jazz—not in the commonly accepted definition of the term in 1966. Coltrane still spoke of his group's music in terms of specific melodic and harmonic structure, but began to refer to more general sonic qualities ("the right colors, the right textures . . . the sound of chords") and more abstract characteristics ("human foundations of music" . . . "integrity" . . . "essences").

Various writers, committed to keeping abreast of Coltrane, strove to find a vocabulary to describe his new, adventurous leap. Some opted for a confessional route. "This music . . . opens up a part of myself that normally is tightly closed, and seldom recognized feelings, emotions, thoughts well up from the opened door and sear my consciousness," wrote Don DeMicheal in a *Down Beat* review. Others, like A. B. Spellman and Nat Hentoff, offered disclaimer and instruction. "A caveat for the casual listener. Be advised that this record cannot be loved or understood in one sitting . . . it's like Wagner—it begins on a plane at which most performances end and builds to a higher plane than the average listener considers comfortable," wrote the former on *Ascension.* "Listening to Coltrane work through his own challenge may well stimulate self-confrontation in the rest of us," Hentoff noted on *Kulu Se Mama,* adding that "each listener, of course, will himself be challenged in a different way."

As Coltrane's 1965 recordings were released (in a fashion mixing quartet and augmented sessions), what most fans and musicians noticed was that his sound *and* stance became those of the avant-garde. No longer the reluctant leader aware of, but not involved with, the new improvisers showing off his influence, he began to actively champion the younger players he came to know. He took advantage of his stature at Impulse, playing an A&R role, urging Thiele to consider signing many of the newer artists. "It was certainly through Coltrane that I became aware of Archie Shepp and many of the younger players," recalled Thiele. "I think that if we signed everyone that John recommended we'd have four hundred musicians on the label."

Most noticeably, whereas Coltrane had in the past sporadically used younger players, his albums and live gigs now started to rely on them. With his new quintet—Sanders, Garrison, Ali, Alice—he performed through 1966, intermittently adding African percussionists and a second bassist to the mix.

With a wave of his hand, Coltrane had legitimized the angry, discordant sounds of the New Thing, forcing serious attention to be paid to a subgenre that might otherwise have been dismissed. Critics scrupulously explained their terms ("free," "avant-garde," "New Thing") and cited precedents (Coleman, Dolphy, Ra), and, certifying their acceptance, began to distinguish various players—Ayler, Shepp, Sanders, Brown—as deserving particular consideration and praise. "Let me make the necessary observation that it is impossible to talk of the new jazz as if it were a homogenous movement," argued Hentoff. "On the contrary, there has never before been a time of new jazz directions during which so many different routes are being taken by so many implacable individualists." "I must say that you can't put them all in the same bag," agreed Cannonball Adderley. "They are playing what they believe in and what they hear, what they feel."

Another sign of arrival, as Shepp recalls, was that even among the brotherhood of the New Thing, a standard of ability had developed: "The term 'free' was often a euphemism for, in my estimation, people who were total novices in some cases. There were certainly levels of this music, and a player like Coltrane was the consummate horn player within that African-American improvising tradition."

In addition, Coltrane's duty as standard-bearer helped affix his own brand of spirituality and well-being on the larger group. Not that the disposition did not preexist with many avant-gardists; "I think you'll find that the spirituality of the music during the '60s wasn't something exotic. It was coming directly out of the church, especially the Holiness church," commented Marion Brown. But Coltrane did stand out as more than a musical role model, as Don Cherry recollects:

> **It changed the whole scene because of him being a vegetarian and meditating and everything. And everyone became aware of health and balance and life . . . he was one of the main persons to really set an example. He didn't speak about [it], he just set an example.**

By December 1966, such was the collective weight of the new jazz rebels that the mainstream magazine *Newsweek* devoted a six-page study to the phenomenon, an article which served as a serious defense of the new guard, interviewing Taylor, Ayler, Ra, Shepp, Coleman, Coltrane, Marion Brown, and writer Nat Hentoff, who emphasized the social consciousness intrinsic to this "jazz revolution." "It believes in soul and law and freedom. There's almost a touching belief in music as a cleansing, purifying, liberating force, as if jazzmen were the unacknowledged legislators of the world. They all want to change the social system through their music." As if to still any fears caused by the word "revolution" (examples of strong black nationalism were in the headlines by the close of 1966; the rise of the Black Panthers was only a few months away), Hentoff added that "the jazz revolution is not a programmatic black-power movement."

And yet the political connection was there, to at least one young African-American. "You couldn't help but pick up on it, being a black kid in America and being in the generation I was in," Frank Lowe points out. "It was already written that I would be interested in cats like Malcolm X, and right after that came the Panthers." Lowe recalls an indelible impression left on him while he was a university student in California that tied together the music, movement, and mood of the time.

> **It was a documentary on this cat named Fred Hampton, who was a big leader of the Chicago Black Panthers, who organized breakfast for the kids [*The Murder of Fred Hampton*, 1969]. He was ambushed one night in his bed—the police shot through the walls, assassinated him right through the walls. As the camera was panning the room that was shot up, under the bed there were some records. Right on top, man, covered with blood, was Dolphy's *Out to Lunch*! That showed me right then that what these cats were saying and what we were listening to were all of the same mind—it was in the body, in the walk, in the air.**

The jazz avant-garde certainly did not speak for black America in general. One had to look no further, Hentoff pointed out in his own article on the New Thing, than the dearth of black clubs booking the new jazz generation. "Their predecessors, at the start of *their* [bebop] revolution, at least were able to work in urban Negro neighborhoods ... but the current avant-garde, also predominately Negro, has stirred minimal interest in the Negro night clubs. Thus the present revolutionaries have even fewer places in which to play than did Monk and Parker."

On at least one occasion, Coltrane himself fell into the gap. Lewis Porter writes of a Newark, New Jersey, club engagement in late 1966—also witnessed by saxophonists Byard Lancaster and Leo Johnson—where "the audience and manager became hostile and insisted that he play some of his old standards . . . the gig was actually cancelled after the first night."

Coltrane, in Hentoff's terms, was both a patriarch and a revolutionary. Notwithstanding the negative reaction in some live situations, his cross-generational appeal to the black community transcended considerations of style—and even the music itself. Like Miles Davis, as Ben Sidran has noted, Coltrane had become an iconic figure:

> **Davis and Coltrane became giants in the black culture specifically because they represented the elder statesmen, black men who had gone through the mill and survived, not empty-handed, but with peculiarly black solutions to peculiarly white problems. Their triumph and their acceptance by the black culture at a time when some of the jazz "avant-garde" were undergoing openly hostile treatment, lay in the fact that they had "paid their dues" in the old school and emerged with their individuality intact.**

In what would be the last year of his life, Coltrane stood as an enduring force in a series of ever-widening circles: from the tight, avant-garde brotherhood to the larger jazz scene to black America in general. In the black community, it's a safe bet that few forty- to fifty-year-olds picked up *Ascension,* just as younger fans may have bypassed Coltrane's earliest Prestige recordings. But the one album that could be found among them all would have been *A Love Supreme.*

"It was like, boom! Knocking the doors down—like a revelation," maintains Frank Lowe. "It was the sixties and *A Love Supreme* seemed to express a lot of blackness. At a time when people were talking black, it seemed like Trane was saying more with the music than the cats were saying with the words." Lowe adds:

> **Sure, it was black music, but it was almost beyond that. It took on a universality that could embrace these other things and still keep its blackness. In other words, it's not like us against the world. It's like all these things are included and we all *are* the world.**

■ In the spring of 1966, if one crossed the Brooklyn Bridge from Manhattan and followed Flatbush Avenue for about ten minutes (fifteen if traffic was heavy), one would have located the center of Crown Heights, a Brooklyn neighborhood rife with New York City jazz players, a stone's throw from Prospect Park, a mere half-hour's drive to most of New York's jazz clubs and even less by subway.

"I lived on Sterling Place, Calvin Massey lived right around the corner on Brooklyn Avenue," says baritone saxophonist Cecil Payne, then one of the senior members of the community and a veteran of Dizzy Gillespie's big band in the forties. "[Pianist] Cedar Walton lived on the same block. Bobby Timmons, Freddie Hubbard—they were on the next corner, and [alto saxophonist] Jimmy Spaulding. They were all there."

Curtis Fuller, a Manhattan resident, recalls the same collective drawing him to Brooklyn. One of his favorite haunts was the home of Cal Massey. "I was at the house all the time with Charlotte, his wife, and the kids. I'd be over there on the porch, sitting around, right across the street from that church."

St. Gregory the Great, a Catholic church, convent, and school centered on the corner of St. John Place and Brooklyn Avenue, functioned as the religious and social heart of the community. Neighboring residents sent their children there, and some, like local television executive Earl Toliver, also volunteered their time and services.

"In 1965–66, I was president of the PTA and an officer in the parish council," recalls Toliver, who had lived in the neighborhood since 1951. "When I moved there, St. John Place and all the blocks around there were maybe ten percent black, ninety percent white. That was true of the whole neighborhood." The sixties, however, brought a radical racial shift:

> **When the change came, it came overnight almost. The flight from that parish was unbelievable. By the mid-sixties, it was eighty percent black. Shirley Chisholm [soon to become the country's first black congresswoman] was our state assembly representative.**

Toliver remembers that the tenor of the time—a more militant black awareness, increased activism—was felt even in the confines of the church:

> **There was a lot of turmoil in the church. I remember [in early '66] there was a sit-in at the rectory, a group of young people who wanted to take over the church, that kind of resistance to traditional kind of organization and structure.**

Despite misgivings from Father Thomas Haggerty, St. Gregory's more traditionally minded pastor, Cal Massey had coordinated a number of Sunday afternoon jazz performances in the school's small auditorium. In April 1966, with the weather turning warmer, Massey was inspired to hold a concert with a very specific purpose, as his son, Zane, then eight years old, remembers:

My father wanted to build a playground—not only for his kids, but all the kids in the neighborhood. There was only one park nearby, but it had been taken over by gangs, so it was kind of dangerous. His idea was to build a playground at St. Gregory's, and since we lived right across the street, he could keep his eye on us. Father Dobson became involved.

Father James Dobson, then a young priest who would later leave the clergy, confirms that the old convent on the church property had recently been torn down, leaving a hole in the ground. He and a fellow priest proceeded to help Massey plan the event, but as Toliver recalls, the church was reluctant at best. Plans nonetheless moved forward for a daylong event on April 24. The auditorium—already in use for a theatrical presentation—was booked. The schoolchildren created musical notes from construction paper to hang on the wall. Flyers and word of mouth filtered out as the day of the event approached. Toliver:

Entrance to St. Gregory's school, Crown Heights, Brooklyn

It was not really publicized. In fact, I think I only knew the week before that Coltrane would be performing there. Massey was really in charge of that: getting Coltrane and the other people.

The flyer promised a concert with a "Religious Theme," featuring the "Top Names of the Jazz World." It was an impressive array for a neighborhood event: saxophonist/flutist Rahsaan Roland Kirk, Cedar Walton, Cecil Payne, McCoy Tyner (leading his own group), Elvin Jones (playing with Kirk), Jimmy Garrison (with Coltrane), saxophonist Charles Tolliver, bassist John Ore, drummer Andrew Cyrille (misspelled "Surelle"), and—positioned first on the flyer—John Coltrane.

Many of Massey's neighbors would be playing in Massey's own band; Coltrane's lineup was expected to include his wife, Alice, along with Sanders, Garrison, and Ali.

April 24 turned out to be a beautiful day. "I remember it was pleasant weather, people interacted in a positive way with each other and with the musicians," says Dobson. An entrance fee of $2.50 was collected at the door, and food and drinks, most supplied by the parishioners themselves, were on sale. By midafternoon the music began, and a crowd soon filled the small auditorium.

"The hall contained room for at least 300 people with standing room," notes Alice Coltrane, who had driven in with her husband and children from Long Island. The well-attended affair brought a mixed crowd, reflecting the generational shifts of the day. Toliver notes that the dress ran from formal to Afrocentric. "It was a hot day, I remember shirts and ties, dashikis, and no polo shirts or anything like that. It was respectable."

To many—performers and audience alike—the most impressive aspect of the day was witnessing the effect of the music on many of the younger attendees, who were more familiar with the then-ubiquitous sounds of James Brown and Stevie Wonder. "I think this was the introduction for many of the young people in the audience to jazz," remarks Toliver. Zane Massey confirms his memory. "It was a whole afternoon of jazz. They did some incredible stuff. I was very young, but I remember Rahsaan [Roland Kirk] played. I had never seen anyone play flute through his nose."

There were no journalists present, save for three French jazz fans—Daniel Berger, Alain Corneau, and Natasha Arnoldi, whom drummer Sunny Murray had brought. "We were the only whites there," Berger notes. "It was mostly families in a non–show business, non–jazz concert atmosphere—quite casual." "They were just regular people from the neighborhood that came—they weren't like jazz fans going out to hear jazz," adds Payne. "And they really enjoyed it, because it was something they would never think of going to see or to hear."

The idea of reaching new listeners, of performing in a location where ticket prices and age limits would not hinder attendance, was a primary concern for Coltrane in his last year. "His goal, shortly before he died, was to get a loft in [Greenwich] Village," explained Bob Thiele:

JAZZ CONCERT
RELIGIOUS THEME
ST. GREGORY'S SCHOOL HALL
991 ST. JOHN'S PLACE, BROOKLYN

"TOP NAMES OF THE JAZZ WORLD"

	Roland Kirk
John Coltrane	Elvin Jones
McCoy Turner	Cedar Walton
Jimmy Garrison	Charles Toliver
John Ohr	Andrew Surelle
Bob Ford	John Stevenson
Cecil Payne	Joey Odom
Romulus	

SUNDAY, APRIL 24th

TWO PERFORMANCES

3 to 5 P.M.   7 to 9 P.M.

Ticket Prices for Each Performance:
Adults — $2.50
(Children under 14) — $1.25

Tickets Available:
St. Gregory's Rectory, 224 Brooklyn Ave.
Reservations: Call PR 2-1244 (after 7 P.M.)
Arranged by: CAL MASSEY
Show for Benefit of St. Gregory's Playground

He wanted to set up a place where people could come in, listen to his music . . . in other words, people could attend rehearsals, no admission, just the price of a Coca-Cola, ten cents if you wanted anything to drink, but this was definitely an ambition of his.

Though Coltrane never found the time to create his dream venue, he did help out a friend, Babatunde Olatunji, performing in spring 1967 at the Nigerian percussionist's Center of African Culture on 125th Street, a performance space based on the same ideals of access and learning. Cal Massey's benefit at St. Gregory's offered a similarly rare opportunity to a jazz star whose schedule was normally overwhelmed by tour commitments, studio dates, and family time. For the event, Coltrane chose a neat, dark suit, and prepared a set list that included a tune appropriate to the setting. "John made his own decision to perform 'Acknowledgement' from *A Love Supreme* . . . and to recite the poem during the program," Alice remembers.

The afternoon had been long. Zane Massey had managed to grab one of the seats near the stage. "I was very close to the front with my brother. Coltrane was the last performance, right after Rahsaan, actually." When Coltrane set up to perform, it was

April 21, 1966: Note paper in pocket, music notes on wall

with a quartet; Sanders was not present. And according to various witnesses, a slightly injured Jones sat in on drums.

"When Trane came on, Elvin had a cast on his foot—I think he had just been in a fire not too long before—and Jimmy Garrison and Alice," Massey maintains. Alice sat behind a "spinet in good condition," as she recollects, obviously provided by the church. Massey:

> I remember they just got up there and played. It was so intense. I was very young, but I was very touched by that music. It was a very long performance—Trane played for over an hour. They played for so long that there were puddles of sweat. Where they were standing—John, Jimmy, Elvin—there was literally water there on the floor.

Whatever the complete selection of tunes Coltrane chose to perform may never be known, but as Massey recalls,

> I remember at one point after he played for maybe a half-hour, he went in his pocket and he read the prayer, the whole *A Love Supreme* prayer. He actually read it—"Thank you God," you know—while the band was playing. Then everybody was chanting [sings], "a love supreme, a love supreme" while he was reading the prayer.

Photographs confirm Coltrane having a piece of paper in his pocket, as Massey, as well as other attendees, claims. "Coltrane was indeed reading a piece of paper," states Berger. Though he played only "Acknowledgement" (Alice: "John did not perform the entire suite"), his performance was enough to touch a communal nerve. The chant from the well-known album—a year old by that point—had certainly become part of the lingua franca of the jazz circle, disseminating as well into the larger black community. Massey adds:

> The band was playing, and he was reading the prayer. And I remember in the back of the room it was all musicians and they were chanting his name, "John, John, John." Rahsaan was actually crying, and I couldn't understand. I was in shock, because I hadn't ever seen anything like that before.

To those who knew Coltrane's repertoire, his performance elicited surprise, Corneau recalling "a soft accompaniment by Alice, Jimmy, and Elvin," and Arnoldi noting:

> After having heard *Ascension* and seen him at the Village Gate when he was exploring his new voice, the concert in Brooklyn was far more subdued . . . it seemed to me like a step backwards to a certain extent.

Even those who, like Toliver, were unfamiliar with Coltrane's music report that the performance was not what they expected:

> It was sort of melodic, just a little different. It wasn't hard jazz—the Gillespie kind of jazz. I was thinking that maybe it was tempered because of the church. His stuff was very . . . it was almost symphonic. I understand now, having listened to some of his music, that that was his jazz.

A warm reception followed the concert. "John spoke highly of all the musicians' performances," Alice comments, while Dobson, who got a chance to thank Coltrane for his participation, remarks, "I had to meet him and thank him for coming. He said he was just happy to be there." Berger states, "I remember after the performance, the mood was quite emotional. Sunny Murray went to shake hands around, but we three had a rather reserved attitude in the middle of such a meditative and religious atmosphere."

Zane Massey recalls the festivities then moved across the street:

> After the concert, everybody came to our house. My mother cooked, and they all came over and ate dinner. I remember being in my father's room and Elvin, Jimmy, and Trane were all sitting on the bed. They were eating, and Trane's saxophone was out—I actually tried to blow in it. My father stopped me—"No! Get away from the horn!" And they were all laughing, "Let him blow, let him blow!" I got a little sound.

In many respects, Cal Massey's event was a success. "The pastor [Thomas Haggerty] was overjoyed, man," recollects Payne. "They were amazed to see that something that good came to them." Zane Massey says proudly, "The playground was built in part because of that concert. Children still use that very same yard behind the school."

■ "I want to be a force for real good," Coltrane stated in 1966. In another interview he expanded on his socially conscious aim:

> I want to discover a method so that if I want it to rain, it will start immediately to rain. If one of my friends is ill, I'd like to play a cer-

tain song and he'll be cured. **When he'd be broke, I'd bring out a different song, and immediately he'd get all the money he needed. But what these pieces are, and what is the road to attain the knowledge of them, that I don't know. The true powers of music are still unknown. To be able to control them must be, I believe, the goal of every musician.**

When asked why Coltrane did not perform his suite more often, Alice shrugs. "To speculate on why *A Love Supreme* was rarely performed opens up many variables." Why that evening in a Brooklyn church? "I believe the sacredness of the event may be a reason."

The next time Coltrane's poem would be read aloud, it would again be inside a church, but for a much more solemn occasion.

July 21, 1967: Albert and Donald
Ayler inside St. Peter's Church

Chapter 6

The Unbroken Arc of
A Love Supreme

"I'll never forget that day."

July 17, 1967, is emblazoned in Zane Massey's memory. "That was the day that John Coltrane died. I was upstairs that morning, there was a phone call, and I remember hearing my father crying."

Coltrane, whose health had been steadily deteriorating through spring of that year, had checked himself into a hospital, where he rapidly succumbed to liver cancer. Cal Massey's shock and grief were shared by a large, diverse community—family, friends, fans. The news was particularly devastating to those who had known Coltrane the longest.

> It was very loud so I came downstairs, and I never saw my father so emotional before. He just kept saying over and over again, "My brother, my brother, John." I didn't really understand. My mother made us go back upstairs and explained to us what had happened. I remember that day, my father just played *A Love Supreme* all day, and records like *Ascension*. It was just John all day long.

The memorial service was held four days later. Over a thousand mourners crammed into St. Peter's Lutheran Church in midtown Manhattan, reported the *New York Times*. "[Albert] Ayler and his quartet were playing 'Truth Is Marching' in the balcony of the Neo-Gothic Church," read the article the next day. Coltrane's casket was covered in yellow and white flowers. As attendees filed past, a nearby easel held Victor Kalin's portrait of the saxophonist, while the simple funeral program carried Bob Thiele's photograph of Coltrane: both images were well known from the artwork of *A Love Supreme*.

Nine Coltrane LPs had appeared on various labels since January 1965; more than twenty-five had been released before that. But none was mentioned at his funeral save for *A Love Supreme*, as the *New York Times* noted:

> **Instead of a eulogy, Mr. Coltrane's friend, Calvin Massey, read a long religious poem "A Love Supreme" written by the dead musician in 1965 [*sic*]. It was used in a Coltrane album of the same name which was chosen the record of the year in 1965 by *Down Beat* magazine.**

Reverend John G. Gensel, the presiding pastor, closed the service with a benediction quoting from the same poem: "May we never forget that in the sunshine of our lives, through the storm and after

The scene outside St. Peter's

the rain—it is all with God . . . All praise to God. With Love to all I thank you . . . John Coltrane."

While the import of Coltrane's words rang with their deepest resonance in a last-rites context, the music of *A Love Supreme* helped many to make sense of his death at the youthful age of forty. Wayne Shorter points to a distinct fatalism in "the tone of the tenor on *A Love Supreme.* I think he knew he was sick—it's as if he were seeing the light—that grand light." Frank Foster also recognizes a sense of foreboding on the album—"that he just had to get himself right with God."

Whether or not Coltrane knew the end was near (he never completed a will), he was certainly aware of his declining condition. Those close to him remember seeing him clutching his side, and even secluding himself during particularly painful episodes. He canceled a series of West Coast appearances. Pharoah Sanders reports that "at that time, he was trying to lose weight. That was what he was trying to focus on, and we would talk about health."

During one of Coltrane's last public gigs, on April 23, 1967, at Olatunji's cultural center in Harlem, Rashied Ali recalls that

[with] all the energy of 125th Street going on right outside the window . . . with incense burning

and the place packed, he did something I had never seen him do before—he sat down on the bandstand. I still didn't think he was sick, because when he put his horn to his mouth, there was no faltering; the fire was up full blast.

To some, the fury of his playing in his final years was sparked by an increasing, innate sense of mortality, which added an urgency to his musical velocity. Says Sonny Rollins, "I have a feeling that he might have had an idea that his tenure on this planet was not going to be extended and so he was really stretching out as far as he could." Coltrane never let up; he was in the fast lane, mid-search, till the end. "There is never any end," he informed Nat Hentoff in late 1966:

> **There are always new sounds to imagine, new feelings to get at. And always there is the need to keep purifying these feelings and sounds so that we can really see what we've discovered in its pure state. So that we can see more and more clearly what we are . . . we have to keep on cleaning the mirror.**

Many have sought the same purification, and through whatever creative process, have achieved it. Yet few have searched as deeply, provoked as consistently, succeeded as profoundly as Coltrane. Fewer have ended as they began: still challenging themselves and their audience. In the jazz tradition—even in the more universal musical sphere—he has almost no parallel. When death claimed Coltrane two years after he released *A Love Supreme,* he was creating music that the world is still trying to grasp and fully appreciate. "People could not follow that music, they still don't know what's going on," Dave Liebman states. "That last stage of Coltrane was an enigma to everybody, including musicians."

Charles Lloyd tells of a brief exchange that neatly summarizes Coltrane's effect:

> **Once I was standing against the wall at Birdland with [pianist] Andrew Hill, [bassist] Richard Davis and [trumpeter] Roy Eldridge. Trane had been playing a solo for about 30 minutes or so. The music was so intensely beautiful, lifting me up to the highest—words can't go there. Roy leans over to Richard and says, "I know Trane is playing, but I just can't get with him." Richard says, "Well, you know, Roy, Trane ain't waitin'."**

The last days: Coltrane performs at the Olatunji Cultural Center, 125th Street, New York, April 1967. (From left) Jimmy Garrison (bass), unidentified (bass), Rashied Ali (drums), Coltrane

■ "One thought can produce millions of vibrations," wrote Coltrane on *A Love Supreme.* So can a song, a sound, and even a catchy record title. References to and echoes of the album abound forty years after its release. Its elements have been borrowed with enough regularity and variety to warrant its current status as a cultural touchstone. By all current indications, Coltrane's count was not far off.

One measure of the album's lasting (and recently increasing) resonance is the number of times the phones at JOWCOL continue to ring with requests from filmmakers and TV and music producers seeking permission to use Coltrane's music. While the most requested single tune is still "My Favorite Things," the number one revenue-earner—from song licensing, publishing, and record sales—remains *A Love Supreme,* according to Alice Coltrane.

Recently, Alice has come to share the role of musical arbiter with her son Ravi, who now knows the relative value of all the recordings in his father's catalog and often joins his mother in passing judgment on who can and can't approach the altar of *A Love Supreme*:

> **A Love Supreme is a very profound and special thing, and it's always been a sensitive zone for a lot of people. Anything like, "I'm going to do a hip-hop version of the A Love Supreme suite," and people would be rioting in the streets [laughs]. Fans from around the world would be marching, trying to hunt me down. That's an extreme, obviously,**

but at some point you have to look back and ask at what point does it become unacceptable?

Often, that's a question no one—Coltrane-related or not—can adjudicate. Ravi Coltrane points to the cross-genre evidence of the album's four-note bass line as its most identifiable, free-use element. "No matter what instrument—you hear that all the time [sings 'Acknowledgement' theme]":

> **It could be completely an unconscious thing—"Wow, why did I play that? Man, it just happened . . ."** **Outside the jazz world especially, you'll discover that bass line. Since it's not a tune, you can't copyright it, just like Beethoven couldn't copyright [sings opening of Beethoven's Fifth]. So musicians are free to use it in rock or rap or whatever.**

A cursory survey of the past twenty-five years finds that simple four-note mantra linking an unlikely collection of jazz recordings and R&B ballads, dance tracks, and rock jams. Guitarist Grant Green, midway through the track "Old Man Moses" from his 1967 album *Iron City,* repeatedly plucked the by-then well-known motif. In 1969, Pharoah Sanders recorded and released his album *Karma* with a lineup featuring vocalist Leon Thomas, bassist Reggie Workman, and various percussionists. In cosmic message, vamplike structure, and bass line, the album's lead tune, "The Creator Has a Master Plan," reworked the more accessible elements of *A Love Supreme,* garnering Sanders and his label a surprise jazz hit. In 1972, Gil Scott-Heron spoke and sang of his indebtedness to not just Coltrane but to the album specifically on his paean ". . . And Then He Wrote Meditations." More recently, soul singer Will Downing's single "A Love Supreme" added lyrics and Stanley Turrentine on saxophone, and launched Downing's career in 1988.

In 1994, in Britain, trance deejay Patterson's "Freedom Now" was a minor dance-club hit: a spooky, bass-heavy reading of the riff, layered with ethereal voices and the twang of a Brazilian berimbau. In the United States the same year, DJ Jake's trip-hop remix of Sanders's "The Creator Has a Master Plan" relied on the same rhythmic signature. Nineteen ninety-five saw guitarist Henry Kaiser highlight the Coltrane–Grateful Dead connection on his *Eternity Blue* album with a jamlike treatment of "Dark Star" and "Acknowledgement." Underground trio Da Nuthouse looped part of a Tyner solo in 1997, rapped lively of their respective street reps, and called the result "A Luv Supream."

LOVE SUPREME

A Love Supreme / John Coltrane

il impulse!
STEREO A-77

A Love Supre

Fanzine of the Year

VAUX SAMSON

Chanté Moore
A Love Supreme

A LOVE SUPREME
Real-Life Stories of Black Love

TaRessa & Calvin Sto
FOREWORD BY RUBY D

LOVE
PREME

PLETE JAZZ
with

CLUDING
TA BAKER
LENNON
SFIELD
TLEY
WINWOOD
TRADING
STEWART
AWFORD
LE FIRE
MANYMORE

A LOVE SUPREME

Black Classics

Pauline Hopkins

The
X Press

Even the simple three-word phrase Coltrane chose for his best-known album now abides in the public domain. Do a Web search. Divorced of any Coltrane connective, one can find the phrase employed as the title of a sampler of eighties love songs; worldbeat, soul, rap, R&B, and psychobilly albums; twelve-inch techno and house singles from Europe; a 1974 hymnal from Tennessee; a retitling of the Pauline Hopkins novel *Contending Forces*; a British soccer fanzine; and a high-quality photographic collection of African-American couples, with permission granted by Alice Coltrane.

There are occasions when access has been denied by Alice. Ever catch the Spike Lee joint *A Love Supreme*? Those who have know it as *Mo' Better Blues*. Ravi recalls:

> **I was on the other side of the coin. I had met Spike Lee—he was young and hot, and I was enthused about the idea. I was trying to convince my mom, "Why don't we think about doing this?" In hindsight, I'm real happy it wasn't called *A Love Supreme*, because it was definitely not in line with some of the ideas we believe in.**

Mrs. Coltrane holds all requests that come before her to strict moral scrutiny—no drugs, wanton prurience, or violence. In her view, Lee's story of a wayward jazz trumpeter would devalue the spiritual integrity of the phrase "A Love Supreme"; he could use the music, hang the album in Denzel Washington's apartment, but he could not share its title. No matter the financial offer, do not expect to hear "Pursuance" spurring an NC-17 soundtrack or "Acknowledgement" pushing a good-time beer ad. Not during Alice Coltrane's watch, nor, perhaps, after the reins are passed on to her children.

■ When it comes to "covers"—reinterpretations—of the tunes on *A Love Supreme*, as long as the songs are properly credited "John Coltrane/JOWCOL Music," the decision to re-record the tunes lies solely with the musicians. But the jazz world can be a very insulated, self-policed community. Undue liberties and infractions of taste—smooth jazz star Kenny G digitally inserting his soprano sax into Louis Armstrong's "What a Wonderful World," for example—hold themselves up for serious rebuke and ridicule. It would seem that anyone approaching *A Love Supreme* does so with an entire fellowship looking over one's shoulder.

To some who were tight with Coltrane, or remain close to his sound, awe and reverence bring further pause. Says Frank Foster, "I was very intimidated trying to play anything of John's, but especially *A Love Supreme*. It was also out of respect for John and the belief that nobody could add anything to the music that John didn't do himself." David S. Ware, one of today's leading "energy" players following in Coltrane's stylistic fooprints, admits other considerations as well:

> **If I were going to do something of Coltrane's, it wouldn't be anything off *A Love Supreme*. According to who I am in the gallery of tenor saxophonists, it's already hard enough. I kind of need to create distance from that. That's like a movie star who has got a son or daughter, and them wanting to have their own identity, so they change their name or something, you know?**

Others, however, regard the compositions on *A Love Supreme* as just that: compositional material free to be reworked, like any standard in the jazz canon. "It's an issue not of music, but of perception and interpretation," insists Branford Marsalis. "If you take off the name, if you take away the fact that it's a tribute to God, then it becomes this great body of work, a great piece of music." "It's like any other music out there," maintains David Murray. "I came from the Church of God in Christ, I know what spirituality is, but I never jibed with that spiritual base with Coltrane that other people might have."

That's today. When Coltrane was alive, no one recorded *A Love Supreme* but he. (One exception: in 1967, Charles Lloyd—already well steeped in the mode of Coltrane—performed a tune called "Tribal Dance" on his first visit behind the Iron Curtain. It was recorded, released on the LP *Charles Lloyd in the Soviet Union,* and proved a melodic twin to "Resolution.") Few approached any of his Impulse material at all (save for Wes Montgomery's live, uptempo version of "Impressions" from the Half Note in 1965). Archie Shepp's *Four for Trane*—the sole tribute album Coltrane ever witnessed—featured only his older, Atlantic-era compositions.

Even after his demise, an apparent reluctance persisted. Perhaps the tunes on *A Love Supreme* were simply too unstructured for most chord-oriented players to approach. Or the material might have been too tightly connected to Coltrane himself, the implicit technical challenge a turnoff to most. Or perhaps it was just too soon.

It was left to Alice Coltrane to first break the ice. In 1971, she recorded her own take of "Acknowledgement" (as "A Love Supreme"), playing organ and harp, along with Frank Lowe's tenor, Leroy Jenkins's violin, Reggie Workman's bass, and Ben Riley's drums. If her recording were a film it might be called a period piece, projecting the cosmic flavor of the day. The performance was the final cut on the album *World Galaxy,* which included a cover designed by sixties artist Peter Max, and was sandwiched between tracks of the voice of Alice's guru, Swami Satchidananda, speaking heavily echoed homilies over a string section.

Two years later, in 1973, guitarists Carlos Santana and John McLaughlin—equally swami-inspired and spiritually focused—pushed Coltrane's music out of the jazz arena, injecting a compelling rock-fusion flavor into Coltrane's classic. While remaining faithful to various elements of the original recording—key-shifting, a chanting section, organist Larry Young referencing Coltrane's primary "ba-*dwee*-dah" melody—"A Love Supreme" (again, actually "Acknowledgement") opened with a twin-guitar explosion, then settled into a balanced, Latinesque groove propelled by drummer Michael Shrieve and conguero Armando Peraza. The two guitarists conversed back and forth, speaking through lightning trills, energetic climaxes, and a constant lyrical invention that brought to mind the forte of the Classic Quartet.

"It was, for all intents and purposes, a simple expression of our individual and collective affection and admiration for Coltrane," notes McLaughlin. "The idea of playing our version of *A Love Supreme* came quite naturally. It seemed to me—it's the same today—that one of the wonderful aspects of Coltrane's music is its liberating aspect." But McLaughlin remains modest. "I look back on it like I look back on all of my recordings: they're all like paintings, full of faults, but the best we could do at that time."

Santana agrees, and submits how he would prefer to do it today:

> **If I did do it, I would do it differently than the way John McLaughlin and myself did it when we just went for it. Now I dream big, man, I don't dream small. I would do it with a symphony, with real African drummers, Brazilian musicians, with Alice Coltrane, [Indian sarod master] Ali Akbar Khan, Wayne Shorter, Pharoah Sanders, Herbie [Hancock], McCoy and everyone in tuxedos. In that way, when people hear it, they'll be dancing in the aisles, laughing and crying at the same time like they have the Holy Spirit in them. Before I leave this planet, that's how I would like to turn on the masses to *A Love Supreme.***

Santana and McLaughlin may already have accomplished that. In its day, as the lead track on the extremely popular *Love Devotion Surrender* album, their version of *A Love Supreme* arguably introduced more listeners to Coltrane than any other single non-jazz track. It certainly helped propel the notion that Coltrane's music—particularly that of his Impulse years—was neither sacrosanct nor exclusively jazz property. (Intriguingly, *A Love Supreme* inspired one other momentous electric-guitar summit; on bassist Marc Johnson's 1985 album *Bass Desires,* John Scofield matched Bill Frisell in an inspired, expansive treatment of "Resolution.")

In 1978, Elvin Jones was touring with his sextet, featuring saxophonists Frank Foster and Pat LaBarbera; the latter recalls the afternoon when the drummer decided to resurrect the material he had helped create:

> **I remember in San Francisco, we were at somebody's house having lunch. We were just talking in the kitchen—Elvin and I. I was asking him about *A Love Supreme,* he said he remembered talking to Coltrane about the work. Then all of a sudden he said, "We should do it." I said, "You know, there's kind of a stigma, because a lot of people relate that to a personal experience. You know how dogmatic musicians can get—'How dare you tread on that!?'" Elvin said, "But it's great music, the songs are great, the whole concept of the album is great. Let's just start playing the thing." So I transcribed it and got all the stuff together to give to the guys. I guess we were the first ones to start playing it live—nobody had ever really touched it before that I know of.**

LaBarbera arranged "Acknowledgement" and "Resolution": "We only played those two movements, because we felt they tied in nicely." Though misgivings still tweak Foster ("I wish I had stuck to my guns and said, 'No, Elvin, I can't do this,'"), LaBarbera reports proudly, "We played it quite a bit in clubs. I've got so many recordings of us doing it live at the [Village] Vanguard and other places. Elvin always got a great response from it. Then we went to Japan, and of course over there they just loved it." A few recordings of their performances—in the United States and Japan—have been released, capturing the two-horn excitement of that period. (Jones's linking of the two tunes inspired another drummer, Andrew Cyrille, to take the same tack in 1994, with saxophonists Oliver Lake and David Murray adding a sharp, avant-garde edge.)

Jumping to the present, it appears that—though Coltrane's record has not yielded a font of new versions—the jazz community has warmed to the idea of interpreting the compositions on the album. "Acknowledgement" and "Resolution" are the clear favorites, while "Pursuance" has rarely been covered, apparently with only three studio versions since Coltrane's—by Tyner, alto saxist Kenny Garrett, and vocalist Suzanne Pittson. "Psalm," despite a structure based on an available text, seems never to have been re-recorded as a stand-alone composition.

"Resolution," with its more traditional structure, has generally attracted a more straight-ahead style of jazz player. From 1993 through 1997, a range of post-bop instrumentalists have covered the tune, including pianist Harold Danko, trumpeter Marlon Jordan, drummer Keith Copeland, flutist Pedro Eustache, and vibraphonist Cecilia Smith. Of particular (and divergent) note is the ear-catching version by trumpeter Malachi Thompson, which fuses elements of bebop and free jazz, and that by the raga-inspired, modal-focused Boston quartet Natraj.

Of the more than half-dozen versions of "Acknowledgement," those deserving special mention are an atmospheric, multicultural reworking by trumpeter Wadada Leo Smith, who sings and plays muted trumpet and thumb piano; trombonist Conrad Herwig's Latin big-band treatment, which unleashes the inherent possibilities in the tune's Caribbean lilt; and David Murray's artfully arranged octet version.

■ And what of the entire suite? "When you go to a gig, and somebody wants to play 'Resolution,' it might be fun," admits Ravi Coltrane,

> **but to me, it's sacred as a whole.** *A Love Supreme* **is not just a tune or a record, it's an offering to God, and not just an idle offering. It's really music for a different purpose, not to be hip or cool, or even nostalgic.**

Whatever the continuing reservations, very few musicians have attempted to perform *A Love Supreme* in its entirety; even fewer have dared record it. Interestingly, two who continue to rise to the challenge are brothers: Wynton and Branford Marsalis.

When performed by Wynton—recorded in a Tokyo nightclub in 1992, and at New York's Lincoln Center for radio broadcast in 1994—*A Love Supreme* took on a formal air. Replacing tenor with trumpet, and featuring Marcus Roberts on piano, Reginald Veal on bass, and

Elvin Jones on drums, Marsalis spoke before the concert of the appropriate balance he sought in tackling the complete suite:

> **You don't try to play what Trane played—I'm not trying to be up there wasting musical time idol-worshipping. But it's an honor, and I'm going to try to play with integrity . . . the most difficult thing is the spiritual intensity and the emotional range of that music.**

To Jones, the chance to perform the suite at Lincoln Center furthered a personal cause. "I always live in the hope that someday, all of John Coltrane's compositions will be played as a matter of course. It shouldn't be anything exceptional for musicians to play this music."

Jones's wish has become more a reality as the current trend of jazz repertory grows. The concept of institutionalizing jazz along the lines of classical music—with orchestras and a canon of great works—has become the controversy du jour. "Jazz is an art form. It must be celebrated and preserved," argues one side. "Not in an environment that prevents an improvised, living tradition from continuing to grow," counters the other.

Coltrane's music, and especially *A Love Supreme*, has become the stuff that tributes are made of. Consider the past few years in New York City alone: 1998 saw Alice and Ravi perform "Acknowledgement" together at Town Hall on 44th Street. The next

February 14, 2002: Wynton Marsalis (trumpet section, far right) leads the Lincoln Center Jazz Orchestra in a performance of *A Love Supreme*

year pianist Misako Kano and Dave Liebman resurrected the entire suite for the Bell Atlantic Jazz Festival. "A Love Supreme: Remembering John Coltrane" was staged at Carnegie Hall in 2001, featuring individual brassy caffeinated treatments of "Acknowledgement" and "Resolution."

Call it homage, celebration, or repertory: by all accounts, festival and nightclub bookers expect sellout crowds with those three words. "I still play *A Love Supreme* when I do these Coltrane tributes that come up all the time," comments Pat LaBarbera.

The same year his brother was performing *A Love Supreme* to a more dress-up crowd, saxophonist Branford Marsalis was downtown at a New York jazz club when he was asked to participate on *Stolen Moments: Red, Hot & Cool.* "We were sitting at the [Village] Vanguard," recalls Branford, whose quartet then included pianist Kenny Kirkland, bassist Robert Hurst, and drummer Jeff "Tain" Watts. "We were talking about this *Red, Hot & Cool* thing and they were going to have contemporary hip-hop artists on it. I said, 'Great, we're going to do *A Love Supreme.*' "

> **We were going to take forty-five minutes, but we did a truncated version—just eighteen minutes because we wanted to get it on the record. We sent them the tape and they said, "This isn't really what we had in mind." What they had in mind was more the Buckshot LeFonque thing [Marsalis's funk/jazz outfit] that I had been doing. It was funny, they wanted to edit it—we told them to take it off the record. They relented and eventually put it on a separate CD [making the release a two-disc set].**

Wynton's and Branford's respective recordings of *A Love Supreme* provide an interesting comparison, speaking as much of their respective styles as their circumstances: live versus studio, expansive and well paced versus confined and slightly rushed. Wynton's playing delivers an emotional focus, while Branford's reveals his more exploratory nature. When the two reach the rubato, knee-dropping entreaty of "Psalm," they both dig deep for a wholly personal take, respectfully avoiding the Coltrane original.

"I just try to evoke the mood but I don't try to play those particular notes," Branford stresses. "To me, that's Coltrane's personal statement, his personal improvisation. I don't even try to duplicate that." "That's *Coltrane's* prayer," echoed Wynton.

Ironically, Wynton eventually did reproduce Coltrane's prayer. In February 2002, the trumpeter led the Lincoln Center's fifteen-piece jazz orchestra in an arranged reading of *A Love Supreme.* The concert climaxed with an orchestrated version of "Psalm" that replicated the exact form of the original: tossing it phrase-by-phrase, from soprano to baritone saxophone, brass to rhythm section.

In a more interpretive manner, Branford also was compelled to return, regretting not having been up to the demands of the suite the first time around. "I didn't have any spiritual trepidation about playing it, but I wasn't ready as a musician to play the music." Accordingly, he released *Footsteps of Our Fathers* as the debut release on his own Marsalis Music label in 2002, reapproaching the suite with a quartet that included pianist Joey Calderazzo, bassist Eric Revis, and drummer Jeff "Tain" Watts. "We're ready now," Branford proudly states.

■ In Coltrane's tide of influence swirl the eddies easily traceable to *A Love Supreme*: the re-recordings, the tributes, the titular borrowings. Then there's that which subtly flows from the album, filters into the general wash of the contemporary music scene, and rests among the music-makers themselves. Today, leave it to the horn section to start the count on the many subjectively distinct ways in which one album continues to leave its mark:

"The young players coming in today are still dealing with that, trying to get at that," notes Charles Tolliver. "I myself always keep that on cassette and throw it on whenever I'm on a long road trip."

"*A Love Supreme* is one of my favorite albums, I always bring it on the road," says Kenny Garrett.

"I probably know all those solos by heart, *everybody's* solos. It's just etched in my psyche," maintains Michael Brecker.

In *A Love Supreme,* Dave Liebman hears musical dedication. "That quartet—they were so professional, they were so good at what they did: *A Love Supreme* is a package with a bow and a ribbon, all that intensity tied up into thirty-five minutes. That showed an incredible artisticness and professionalism." Liebman expands the thought:

What stays with me about the Coltrane quartet is an image of them getting up on the bandstand, not talking to each other, completely burning for two hours without a word to anybody, getting off the stage and sitting down like any other person. Not having an entourage around them or anything. Then doing it again, with unpretentiousness, absolute honesty and matter-of-factness. That was their eight-hour shift—that was not entertainment, not fun and games. I still try to live up to that image: to do your work, do it intensely, with conviction, and be honest with the music.

To Joe Lovano, *A Love Supreme* "was one of the first composed records that, tune by tune, made an impact on me as far as the possible flow of a performance":

Coltrane's music on record always had that aspect of performance to it, but *A Love Supreme* had the complete conception. The music grows from the very first note to the end of the album, orchestration-wise: who solos when, the segues between themes. That really influenced me as far as how I present sets for live gigs and for albums. That's the way I tried to orchestrate my recent recording, *Flights of Fancy*. The music unfolds as you go along, with different sounds and different personalities, making it feel like a full set of music.

Archie Shepp concurs that the extended canvas of *A Love Supreme* proved one of its most inspiring aspects. "He was the first, really, to consistently extend African-American improvisation past five-minute interludes":

Listen to *What's Going On*—Marvin Gaye is clearly taking his lead from Coltrane. It was the first time that a piece of popular African-American music goes on uninterrupted for roughly twenty minutes, for a full side on vinyl.

In the popularity and continuing influence of *A Love Supreme* and other Coltrane recordings, Shepp finds a certain vindication for the avant-garde brotherhood of the sixties. "At the time, guys like Miles dismissed us as bullshitters—motherfuckers who couldn't play. Now I hear young guys—Kenny Garrett, Courtney Pine—and they're doing the kinds of things that we showed them how to do. We're redeemed. Even before Miles died, he had to hire guys who, like us, were the descendents of Coltrane."

Garrett, who acknowledged his musical debt to Coltrane with the tribute album *Pursuance,* notes: "There's one song [on *Pursuance*] called 'After the Rain.' What I try to capture on it is the spirit that Trane has on a lot of his records, but especially on *A Love Supreme.* I listen to that record all the time when I'm trying to keep my music in a more spiritual realm."

Among veterans and newcomers alike, so widespread is Coltrane's influence that it is possible to place his musical progeny along a scale: from those whose vocabulary merely leans to certain screams, shrieks, and arpeggiated runs, to those whose entire approach—including choice of sidemen and material—conjures Coltrane. Some prefer to focus on one specific career step as the jumping-off point—the fiery, modal sonorities of '59–'60 (Frank Foster), the softer-edged Classic Quartet sound of '63–'64 (Charles Lloyd), or the freer, high-energy blasts of '65–'66 (David S. Ware).

As the subjective line of taste and sensibility separates appropriate tribute from misuse of *A Love Supreme,* so is there an indistinct—yet palpable to many—border between stylistic inheritance and infatuation. Yusef Lateef espouses a somewhat hard-line outlook:

> **If one chooses to emulate others, that's their choice, but that's not the history of the music. For an example, once Lester Young was interviewed and the interviewer asked him how he liked tenor player A and tenor player B. Lester replied, "They sound good, but they sound like me." John didn't do that, Lester Young didn't do that, Charlie Parker didn't emulate others. That's the way I see it.**

Whether or not one agrees with Lateef ("When I hear a musician say that he's completely original, then he ain't playing jazz," counters Branford Marsalis), the idea of developing one's own distinctive "voice" is certainly one of the defining threads in the jazz continuum. And when one tenor player—and particularly one of his albums—presents an almost unworldly pull, some admit to a conscious effort to actively avoid its effect.

"I actually had to stop listening to *A Love Supreme*—I think it was very dangerous for me as a musician," confesses Joshua Redman. "There was no way I was ever going to be able to play like that, so I had to say, 'Look, this is so overwhelming as a musical statement, that if I keep listening to it, I won't be able to find any meaning in what I'm trying to do as a musician.' " David Murray expresses a similar concern. "I waited a long time to get to Trane, in terms of getting inside of his music. You know, Trane's music has a way of devastating people. I was watching all of the casualties and was staying away."

Frank Lowe reveals his own reasons for temperance:

> **I had to stop listening to some Coltrane records, you dig, because Coltrane had that bigger grip on me. I had to get away from *A Love Supreme* because I saw people taking to it like a shrine, and sometimes I can't take it. People were like, "Oh, it's so spiritual." It was like the album was losing some of its other essences, like it's just music for you to enjoy, too.**

Given the tone of Redman's further admonition, a spiritual warning sticker might even be in order:

> **I don't want it to sound so utilitarian—"Oh, I had to stop listening to *A Love Supreme*, because I wouldn't be able to get my shit together." It's more than that—it's the sense that it doesn't feel like just an overwhelming musical vision, it feels like *the* vision. That's just a little bit scary, not only to me as a musician, but as a person. I know I'm getting a little mystical here, and I wasn't raised religiously. I haven't had that many what I'd call "religious experiences." Most people cannot spend every waking hour in church. There's a place for that in your life, and you need room for other things.**

For the same reason Redman opts for distance, countless others—including a substantial group of genre-blurring musicians—flock to the spiritual call of *A Love Supreme*.

"I can't say why it is so popular, but perhaps it fulfills people's need for prayer," Patti Smith wrote. "*A Love Supreme* has a feeling of moral authority in the most humble and spiritual way."

"How to praise God and be honest?" Bono was inspired to ask upon hearing the album for the first time. "How to sift through the muddle of choices that is your life and turn it into a prayer? I didn't know how but I was listening to someone who did."

Like a trompe l'oeil image shifting from vase to silhouette and back, *A Love Supreme* seems fated to forever resonate between perspectives of meaning and significance, between poles of musical import and deep spirituality. Ravi Shankar can empathize; he marks the same effect in his own music:

> We have this piece "Alap": it's without drums, very slow and serene, and is meant to be like an invocation or prayer—very, very spiritual. But if the listener listens without being told that this is the theme, it may give him a feeling of tranquility perhaps, but he would not necessarily be thinking in a Godly manner. What Coltrane felt in making *A Love Supreme* may not be exactly the same as what the listener gets. He might feel romantic or very sad. Or very spiritual, feeling God.

But at least *feeling.* For Coltrane, that was the bottom line. "The emotional reaction is all that matters," he stated weeks before recording his most famous work, "as long as there is some feeling of communication."

Four decades on, *A Love Supreme* continues to be felt and to matter, whether received as performance or prayer, or some subjective combination of the two. In sound, spirit, and name, its arc of influence and inspiration remains unbroken and, like the transitory elements that helped create it, poignantly unrepeatable.

Persistence of a Label

ABC . . . MCA . . . GRP . . . UMG . . . VMG . . .

The ticker above charts a series of record companies that map the up-and-down fortunes of the Impulse label and, by association, *A Love Supreme*. While the recorded legacies of, say, Miles Davis and Dave Brubeck enjoy the benefits that a long-standing label like Columbia Records can offer, Coltrane's Impulse catalog—especially in the seventies and eighties—bounced from one corporate parent to another, "an orphan child," as producer Esmond Edwards puts it.

Yet *A Love Supreme* has never fallen out of print since 1965. By the close of the sixties it was available in every commercial format—LP, cassette, reel-to-reel, even eight-track—and Impulse producer Ed Michel marked Coltrane's ongoing role and importance. "Impulse had a fairly sizable catalog with over a hundred records, and it was clear that sales pretty much broke down fifty-fifty between new releases and reissues. Something new might do OK, but Trane *always* did well. *A Love Supreme* was almost certainly the largest-selling single item on Impulse [and] his records were the backbone of the catalog."

A veteran of hopping between the rock, jazz, and hybrid sessions that were typical of that period (Albert Ayler with members of blues-rock band Canned Heat, for example), Michel recalls how a diverse music community came to look upon the label: "Impulse was absolutely 'The House That Trane Built.'"

After Coltrane's passing, changes swept Impulse. In 1968, the entire company—re-dubbed ABC-Dunhill after merging with a hit-heavy pop label—moved to Los Angeles, where Dunhill co-founder Jay Lasker took the helm from Larry Newton. The following year, Thiele, having knocked heads with his higher-ups for years, left the company. Impulse's course was left largely in the hands of Michel, who oversaw the continuing release of unissued material left behind by Coltrane, and regularly flew to New York to oversee sessions by the label's remaining stars—Pharoah Sanders, Archie Shepp, Alice Coltrane, and Albert Ayler.

In 1971, Michel was joined by a rock promotion specialist with a penchant for jazz. "Steve Backer is one of the great promotion men," says Michel. "He came out of being one of the top guys for Elektra." Fresh from a more youthful environment promoting the Doors, the Paul Butterfield Blues Band, and Carly Simon, Backer was unprepared for the boardroom dichotomy he encountered at ABC (by then abbreviated to a simple three-letter moniker):

Jay Lasker was an old-school tough guy, a Damon Runyon–esque individual, and he set the tone. At the conference room table there would be sharkskin suiters with pinky rings on one side, and the guys with long hair and beads on the other. Of course, it's been the same tightrope walk between art and commerce for the last forty years; only the hairstyles and dress codes have changed. But that was ABC then.

Backer entered the picture at a time when rock music was big business and getting bigger, yet was still open to creative influences like jazz. Coltrane's campus appeal, inferred by Thiele in the mid-sixties, had spread to an entire generation by the onset of the seventies. To promote wider label recognition, Backer created a number of Impulse samplers—in the label's standard gatefold covers—featuring trippy cover art and era-appropriate titles (*Irrepressible Impulses, Impulsively!, Energy Essentials*). He also produced a wildly popular national tour of rock and campus venues, placing Impulse's veterans (Sanders, Ayler, Alice Coltrane) and label newcomers (bassist Charlie Haden, keyboardist Keith Jarrett, saxophonist Gato Barbieri) in front of open-eared, youthful audiences.

Backer's tenure at Impulse proved a brief one: "It was quite a successful period, and it lasted two or three years." A paucity of bestsellers from the pop side of the company—Steely Dan was ABC's sole hit act during that period—meant "you feel it in the jazz end." By 1974, Backer had left Impulse to pursue a similar role at the newly formed Arista Records; a year later, ABC hired Esmond Edwards, then a twenty-year music business veteran, to take over Impulse. This time, the palpable spirit of Coltrane seemed to have disappeared. Edwards:

People weren't running around with banners saying, "Let's do something with John!" and I certainly didn't devote a lot of time to delving into the Coltrane catalog. By the mid-seventies, jazz was something that ABC did like going to church on the weekend. I only went there with a two-year deal, and when my contract was about to expire—when the label was about to expire—that's when ABC was sold to MCA [in 1979].

Once the dust of the takeover had settled, MCA, a massive rock-oriented company, called in a noted jazz producer to help them figure out what they had acquired. Michael Cuscuna, the teenage enthusiast whose passion had steered his career from FM deejay to record producer to independent reissue expert, had already taken a peek:

> When I first went into the Impulse vaults in 1978, they had been very mistreated. The tapes had been moved from New York to L.A., so as early as 1969 or '70 there was already stuff missing. I was able to find a lot of good Coltrane that was unissued, and of course I tore the place apart trying to find what I thought was an entire alternate version of [the] Love Supreme suite, with Archie Shepp and Art Davis, but found nothing.

Cuscuna did find an utterly depressing consequence of ABC's final, cost-cutting days:

> I'm ninety-nine percent sure that the master tapes of A Love Supreme were scrapped. This happened to a lot of popular recordings in the seventies, not only jazz. They would dub from the original tape, making new masters for fear that the old one was wearing out, oxide was falling off, or the splices were getting old and drying up. That's OK, but often they

A Love Supreme goes digital: the first CD version, 1986

> threw the original away because they didn't want to double the tape inventory they had!

With the use of the most pristine copies available, the reissue arc of A Love Supreme continued. MCA's 1980 reissue was a low-budget LP affair: wafer-thin, low-grade vinyl; no gatefold or Vic Kalin portrait; no poem to the Almighty. As the eighties progressed and the digital era arrived, listeners could finally enjoy the full suite uninterrupted, from gong to final "amen." The first CD version arrived in 1986, as Impulse was relaunched with new jazz titles by the likes of Henry Butler and Mike Metheny. A Love Supreme greeted the digital age with a fresh makeover: Coltrane's profile blown up as if ready to stamp on a coin, the angled title replaced by a two-toned approach favoring his name over the album's.

Four years later, MCA absorbed another jazz label, GRP, which took charge of the entire company's jazz efforts, again recruiting reissue specialist Cuscuna. In 1995, he produced GRP-155, the most recent issue of A Love Supreme, with additional liner notes, the album's original black-and-white design (translated to a two-fold CD package), and featuring the highest sonic standards to date:

> On the latest edition, we got into 20-bit rate of sampling, meaning that you get a fuller sound when it's taken from analog into the digital domain. A lot of the sonic characteristics that people complain about getting lost in digital—like the room sound, the overtones, the warmth—you now retain with 20-bit.

The arc of reissue: Impulse ads from 1977,
'86, and '97 reveal Coltrane's unbroken
legacy

For "a small audience that holds on to the LP, usually the ones with high-end equipment who can hear the difference between analog and digital," Cuscuna spearheaded a simultaneous reissue of the album on high-grade vinyl with the original cover and gatefold design intact. Almost forty years later, *A Love Supreme* continues to cross distinctions of genre and format.

Fast-forward to 2002. Tracing the current state of Coltrane's music—and *A Love Supreme*—necessitates navigating a dizzying series of mergers in the late nineties that created the global mega-media group Vivendi-Universal, which effectively joined MCA with Polygram, another jazz-rich major label. All music-oriented divisions in the conglomerate now operate under the rubric "UMG," for Universal Music Group, which in turn has placed all jazz-related activity in the hands of "VMG," the Verve Music Group.

Verve's activity is mainly the reissue business, with the majority of its efforts focused on securing unreleased material and developing new ways to package old titles from a wealth of vintage catalogs. All that was Verve, Mercury, and Emarcy now shares archival residency with Decca, Commodore, Chess, GRP, and Impulse. Part of the fallout of the MCA-Polygram merger in 1998 was Impulse's being relegated to reissue projects only. The last new releases were tenor saxist Donald Harrison's *Free to Be,* in February 1999, and *McCoy Tyner Plays John Coltrane,* in 2001, a title tailor made for the orange-and-black design.

Even as Verve's present-day jazz stars (singer/pianist Diana Krall, saxophonist Wayne Shorter, organist Jimmy Smith) add to Verve's coffers, it is the catalog that accounts for the majority of the company's income.

"It can range from roughly sixty to eighty percent, depending on the business year," states Michael Kauffman, Verve's senior sales vice president. "When we don't have a big release—Diana Krall or George Benson—the catalog sales are going to be higher." Accordingly, Verve makes sure their leading catalog titles are marketed with as high a profile as possible. In 2000, Kauffman reports,

We initiated what we call our top ten "Desert Island Discs." There's Ella and Louis, Getz/Gilberto, *Count Basie's* April in Paris, *Billie Holiday's* Lady Sings the Blues. *But the only person on the list twice is Coltrane—*Coltrane and Hartman, *and, of course,* A Love Supreme.

Today, hanging proudly in Verve's Manhattan offices is a legitimately certified gold record of *A Love Supreme.* In January 2001, with prodding from the Coltrane family, Verve secured the Recording Industry Association of America's gilded award for yielding $1 million in sales of the album, with 500,000 copies shipped. After almost four decades of sales and increasing renown, it's a designation that seems woefully inadequate.

Sadly, even a rough estimate of total sales from the past thirty-plus years seems out of reach. "You'd think it would've gone gold decades ago," Kauffman remarks. "I guess the only answer to why that didn't happen in the past is: (a) no one ever submitted it for certification, and (b) there were complexities between the sales reporting systems of the various companies that owned the music over the years. Sometimes the data was hard to find, or to merge, or maybe even it dropped

A surviving dub of the original assembled master reels

out." "It's always been a best-seller, because we knew it was," submits Verve's director of catalog development, Ken Druker, noting that *A Love Supreme* earned its current gold status for CD sales alone. "Those were all the numbers we had. Who knows about vinyl? It's almost certainly a platinum album [one million copies shipped, $2 million in sales], but those figures were probably all stashed in some file drawer that's in some used office supply store."

Whatever the figures, *A Love Supreme* impresses most as a long-distance runner, not a current reissue star. Its weekly sales figures are not a source of amazement, and an outside chance exists that one of Coltrane's older albums—*Blue Train*, *Giant Steps*, or *My Favorite Things*—might be a better seller simply by having been on retail shelves longer. But for Verve, more than any other catalog title, *A Love Supreme* functions as the star canvas in a popular gallery, consistently upholding the company's reputation, drawing consumers, and helping to pay the rent.

"In the best way possible, *A Love Supreme* defines our goal of representing jazz music that is both cre-

atively brilliant and commercially successful," states Ron Goldstein, Verve president and CEO. "It is probably the most important single album under the Verve Music Group umbrella of labels."

True to the spirit of Goldstein's words, Verve has prepared—with the support of the Coltrane family, with Cuscuna producing, and with Rudy Van Gelder mastering—a special two-disc edition of *A Love Supreme* that presents the most complete portrait of Coltrane's magnum opus to date. In an effort to secure the most pristine copy of the recording, Cuscuna had a brainstorm.

All previous digital incarnations of A Love Supreme *have been derived from a 1971 second-generation master tape [that added] equalization and compression to the original recording and had an inexplicable flaw in the left channel during the first three minutes of "Pursuance." The situation was a cause of great concern until it occurred to us that* A Love Supreme *was issued in 1965 in territories other than the United States.*

A quick call to EMI's tape vault, at the Abbey Road Studios in London, revealed a master reel, unused since EMI's licensing deal with Impulse had expired in the '70s, with no equalization or compression. Van Gelder's happy reaction:

This tape preserves the sonic details like the vivid accuracy of Elvin's cymbals, the deep intensity of the vocal chant, and the openness of the group's sound.

Released in October 2002, *A Love Supreme (Deluxe Edition)* features all of the musical performances recorded in Van Gelder's studio on December 9, 1964 (including various outtakes and breakdowns); the never-before-heard December 10 session (two takes of "Acknowledgement"); and the full live performance of the suite from Antibes on July 26, 1965 (including stage announcements).

Whatever the supplementary material or packaging, Cuscuna emphasizes an essential aspect to the new edition:

With anything that was recorded at Rudy Van Gelder's, I breathe a great sigh of relief, even if it's a second- or third-generation copy. When I hear the Love Supreme *tape, it's amazing how alive it is, how much [aural] information is actually on it. All I have to do is tie my hands behind my back and not mess it up. It's that easy.*

Near Los Angeles, on a Universal Studios backlot bordering on outdoor sets depicting a variety of historical settings, a small warehouse contains the majority of Verve's musical archive, including all Impulse recordings. There, in a darkened, climate-controlled environment, the most pristine version of *A Love Supreme* is stored, waiting to be pulled down for the next reissue project. "That is the best source for the music, but the object itself held no fascination for me," admits now retired Ed Michel. "I long ago gave up any sense of mysticism associated with it. It's just a plastic base with metal oxide on it—it's just a reel of tape."

Epilogue "Opening the Doors"

In one manner or another, all the forces that created *A Love Supreme* have moved on.

Jimmy Garrison's career was cut short in 1976 by lung cancer, after he contributed to a variety of groups and recordings with Alice Coltrane, Archie Shepp, Ornette Coleman, Sonny Rollins, and many others. During the early seventies, he took a three-year hiatus from performing and taught music at a number of northeastern campuses, including Bennington College and Wesleyan University. After returning to active duty in 1974, he created his first group as a leader—the New World Ensemble—a project for which he held high hopes but which never recorded. At the time of his death, he had returned to familiar company, teaming again with Elvin Jones. "It's a love affair," he said of his drumming companion in one of his last interviews. "It's been that way since the first time we played together. We've always been comrades."

Until he succumbed to kidney failure in 1996, producer Bob Thiele never stopped hustling. Through the seventies and into the nineties, he secured financing for a series of jazz labels with colorful names, such as Flying Dutchman (which introduced Gil Scott-Heron's pre–rap/jazz fusion), Dr. Jazz, and Red Baron. He occasionally resurrected familiar formulas: modeling the 1991 album *Sunrise, Sunset* on the Classic Quartet, and featuring David Murray with pianist John Hicks, bassist Cecil McBee, and drummer Andrew Cyrille. The title track was another waltz-time tune in the tradition of "My Favorite Things." It seemed Thiele was determined to acknowledge a debt. "Even to this day," he said toward the end of his life, "I thank Coltrane for being—because he carried me on into jazz music. I think I would have just faded away. I was a swing cat, you know."

A year before Thiele passed away, Bob Golden played his Boswell, co-writing Thiele's autobiography, *What a Wonderful World.* The task allowed Golden to witness an ardor that age and years in the music business could not diminish:

> **He was one of the great hobbyists, like [legendary jazz producer] John Hammond. From the time he was a teenager, he was always just fascinated with this world of jazz that accepted him and his formative excesses. And he never lost that enthusiasm.**

Ravi Coltrane personally encountered Thiele's indefatigability in the early nineties. A young arrival on the New York jazz scene, he was actively dodging a number of generous offers to record an album of his father's music:

> **A lot of guys came after me, all with dollar signs in their eyes. I had dinner with Bob a few times and he'd always bring it up, but with him it was different. He'd say, "Come on—it'll be neat." I'm sure he was thinking of the sales, too, but with him there was this sense of fun—that it'd really be an enjoyable project, too.**

In Englewood Cliffs, Rudy Van Gelder still sits behind the glass, beneath that same high ceiling he assembled more than forty years ago. His studio, while still impressively spacious, is now partially taken up by two isolation booths: for drummers and vocalists, respectively. In the control room, he now operates up-to-date digital equipment; for one who spent decades mastering every step in the analog recording process, there's little sense of loss:

> **The LP has disappeared altogether, and as far as I'm concerned, I'm glad . . . aside from any personal feeling about the finished product that process was never really comfortable. At the end of the day, that technology was primitive.**

Van Gelder's schedule book still fills up as he juggles recording dates and an increasing number of remastering projects. His renown is now marketable enough that his name has been moved from the back of albums to their front covers. Blue Note Records's popular RVG series features titles by Sonny Rollins, Art Blakey, Horace Silver, Grant Green, and others, many originally recorded by Van Gelder, and some not. Verve Music Group has likewise sought his remastering expertise. The startling clarity and definition in his resuscitative effort with the various tapes from the *Love Supreme* sessions are a tribute to the confluence of modern technology and a legendary set of ears.

Ironically, those ears, for all their experience and carefully honed taste, now hinder his ability to spin an old recording, settle back, and just enjoy: "I can't listen, really, to any recording without thinking technically about the balance, about the acoustics, about the medium." Even a recording like *A Love Supreme* can't pierce the professional filter. "If it's mine, what I would've done better . . . I'm afraid that I just can't totally get immersed in the music now, because there's a screen of technicality between me and music."

It would be too easy—and incorrect—to say the two surviving musicians who recorded *A Love Supreme* simply carry on Coltrane's legacy. Both McCoy Tyner and Elvin Jones continue to enjoy the exalted stature they first gained as part of the Classic Quartet. Tyner's highly individual piano style, identified by its vibrant chord voicings and climactic rhythmic drive, stands as one of the most influential in contemporary jazz. His prolific output—more than fifty albums to date—has featured him in a staggeringly wide array of settings, from solo to full orchestra.

Sticking to a more consistent context of quartets and quintets now collectively known as "Jazz Machine," Jones is today worshipped by generations of percussionists. A recent weeklong engagement at a New York nightclub found well-known rock, funk, and jazz drummers in attendance, lining up in the narrow hallway outside the dressing room for a moment with the master of explosive energy and polyrhythmic nuance.

Yet both Jones and Tyner realize that, for many, the aura of the past will forever compete with anything they might perform now. "I mean, some people, whenever they hear me they think of John immediately," complained Tyner. "[I'm] proud of my association with the Coltrane quartet, but right now I'm involved in—we have to continue, you know?"

Jones understands:

What I think is that people experienced so much, and enjoyed the music of Coltrane to such an extent, that they have almost a rever-

ence for it. And when they encounter me, it invokes all those memo-ries they have of that time. Perhaps they were some of the best times of their lives. I know it was certainly one of the best times of *my* life.

His current listening habits?

> I always like *Crescent,* for entertainment. I think there's a wide vari-ety of things on that particular album. *A Love Supreme* is always a more spiritual experience.

Jimmy Garrison's widow, Roberta, recalls her husband's listening tendencies. "*A Love Supreme* and *Crescent* were the ones he listened to the most."

Asked to name his favorite Coltrane recording, Bob Thiele offered, "I think *A Love Supreme* is probably the most important"—and recalled Coltrane's:

> I remember very definitely. I said, "Which album do you really dig the most?" and he said, "Well I like them all . . . after I listen to one for a few weeks, I stop listening and I forget about it."

Coltrane said it himself: he had an aversion to absolute choices. "I don't voice opinions much about anything because I'm usually in the middle, you know. I never make up my mind on anything." In a Tokyo hotel room in 1966, he mulled over the same question:

> The music I recorded that I like the best? I don't know. I'll tell you this though: some of the best wasn't recorded.

■ During the final phase of this book, I interviewed "Cousin" Mary Alexan-der. I had to speak with her. She had known Coltrane his entire life, longer than anyone alive.

A widow at seventy-four, the former Miss Lyerly still inhabits the same Philadelphia town house where Coltrane lived in the mid-fifties, where he wrote his first recorded compositions, and where he went cold turkey in 1957. That same address now houses the John W. Coltrane Cultural Society, the only organization serving to connect the saxophonist with the city he moved to so many decades ago. Mrs. Alexander *is* the Society: she answers the phone, she pushed the city for the plaque belatedly commemorating one of its favorite sons. Befitting her age, she agreed to talk early on a Sun-day: "I'm much better in the mornings."

She spoke of arriving in Philadelphia in 1946 and moving into the small starter apartment already being shared by Coltrane and his mother. It was a cramped situation, and through thin walls, the neighbors made it seem even more so. Everybody knew everyone's business because everybody heard everyone's business.

Fifty-five years later, Mrs. Alexander recounts the situation with a firm lock on detail:

> **When we first came from North Carolina we lived in a building where there were two-room apartments—we had the apartment on the second floor in the rear. Later on we got an apartment on the fourth floor in the front, which meant we had four rooms in that place. But that first apartment was small, John used to practice *all* the time, and we'd just go right past him, and go outside and let him sit there. He'd practice in front of a mirror [in the] bedroom set. In fact, I still have that vanity right here in the basement and it has the marks [on it where] John would put his cigarettes and let them burn. The neighbors were close by, and they kind of got tired of his practicing, and they'd talk in the street about it. So we sort of got wind of it.**

Coltrane's salvation—and his neighbors' peace—was not far away:

> **Just about a block from our apartment on 12th Street—that was 1450 North 12th Street—was this church we had joined on Oxford Street, the Walters Memorial AME Zion Church. On the corner was a big Baptist church, but right beside it was this small church, and that was our church. The pastor said that he would let John practice there, and gave him a key so he could go in and out whenever he wanted. And that's what John did.**

I had the sudden sense of peering into the wrong end of a telescope, glimpsing an intensely private moment from afar. Young John Coltrane, alone in a church with his saxophone and his thoughts, surrounded by sanctity and silence.

Mrs. Alexander caught my pause. I recall thinking that she must be used to such tongue-tied moments when the subject is her cousin, for she offered a quick disclaimer. "I just want people to know that John was a normal person, he was a man, you know, and not God like some people might think."

I asked her how she felt when she first heard *A Love Supreme,* if she was taken aback by its exposed spirituality. "He had done spiritual things before, but it was a big difference. I mean *really* spiritual. I felt he was doing the same thing Grandfather had done, but he was doing it through his music."

There it is, I thought, the perfect coda to the story. What more could be said? I was content, and thanked her for her time. But Mrs. Alexander was not done; one more memory begged retelling:

> **John was a normal child, fun and a practical joker. When we were little, you know—skating and playing and doing everything that everybody else was doing—we had to go to church every Sunday. *Had* to go. I remember one Sunday, after everything was over, they opened the doors of the church. In the Methodist church they call it "opening the doors of the church," that's when people come up from their seats to join the church after the pastor has preached. They still do that. Out of the clear blue sky John went up to join the church. I didn't even know what he was doing, he was so little.**

With a snap, it all seemed to come full circle. I immediately thought of how many rituals are built around that moment of religious acceptance, and how—though celebrating the most intimate moment between man and God—they tend to be thrust into an open, communal forum. I thought of *A Love Supreme* as the ultimate step of a public path John Coltrane began when, as a child, he first rose from that church seat in North Carolina. I recalled a passage Joe Goldberg had written of the saxophonist in 1965:

> **That he continues to progress in the inexorable glare of a scrutiny that invests his most casual acts with significance is evidence of unusual conviction. Coltrane is probably the first major soloist of the contemporary era whose development largely took place under such scrutiny.**

And, as one who was a little less assured in his agnostic or rationalist beliefs, I thought of that phrase "opening the doors." On the verge of standing up and stepping forward to celebrate the universally transcendent possibility in music, I find that *A Love Supreme* still opens the portal wider than any other recording I know.

Notes

John Coltrane was a reluctant interviewee, among the least-quoted of the giants in modern jazz. Couple that fact with the media's generally hesitant, inconsistent appreciation of his genius, and a researcher looks upon any recording of his thoughts—in text, on tape—as rare gifts. Gratitude is certainly due the few prescient reporters who afforded him the chance to get comfortable and expand at will: in many cases that happened overseas. As such, the job of re-translating valuable print interviews (mainly in French) when the original recordings of conversations have been lost does impose a strange double-filter on Coltrane's words—but hopefully not on his ideas.

All other interviews, unless otherwise stated, were with the author.

Introduction: "The First Time I Have Everything Ready"

xv *"I don't think people"* Leonard Feather, "Coltrane Shaping Musical Revolt," *New York Post* (October 18, 1964): 54.

xv *"It was late summer"* Alice Coltrane, interview, DAT recording, June 1, 2001.

xv *"It was like Moses"* Ibid.

xvi "A Love Supreme *reached out*" Miles Davis with Quincy Troupe, *Miles: The Autobiography* (New York: Simon & Schuster, 1989): 286.

xvi *"In the 1960s, we were in the age"* Archie Shepp, interview, DAT recording, July 14, 2001.

xvi *"I know there are so many people"* Alice Coltrane, interview.

xvi "A Love Supreme *is probably one of the most beautiful*" Moby, videotape, Rock and Roll Hall of Fame induction ceremony, March 19, 2001. Thanks to VH1's Matt Hanna.

xvii "A Love Supreme *wasn't a jazz record*" Ravi Coltrane, interview, DAT recording, November 8, 2001.

xvii *"Music . . . That's what I call it"* Elvin Jones, interview, DAT recording, December 4, 2001.

xvii *"Music shouldn't be easy to understand"* Randi Hultin, "I Remember 'Trane," *Down Beat* (Music 1968—year-end issue): 104.

xviii *Coltrane's album and Davis's best-seller* Unfortunately, incomplete and/or missing records make an accurate quantitative comparison impossible.

xviii *"I just remember the cumulative effect"* Frank Lowe, interview, DAT recording, April 4, 2001.

xviii *"To be honest, I didn't get any of it"* John McLaughlin, email to author, October 2, 2001.

xviii *"The first time I heard"* Carlos Santana, interview, DAT recording, June 23, 2001.

xix *"You have to come to the music yourself"* Hultin, "I Remember 'Trane."

xix *"We should challenge ourselves"* Alice Coltrane, interview.

xix *"It often seems the book was closed"* Francis Davis, *Like Young* (New York: Da Capo, 2001): 174.

xix *"John Coltrane: John the Baptist"* Curtis Fuller, interview, DAT recording, June 20, 2001.

xix *"You will get the message"* Reggie Workman, interview, DAT recording, August 10, 2001.

xix *"In your spirituality"* Alice Coltrane, interview.

xx *"When I saw there were so many religions"* Interview by August Blume, tape recording, June 15, 1958.

xx *"I don't really know what a listener feels"* Kitty Grimes, "John Coltrane Talks to Jazz News," *Jazz News* (UK) (December 27, 1961): 13.

xx *"I believe in all religions"* Nat Hentoff, liner notes to *Meditations,* Impulse A-9110, 1966.

xx *"Sheets of sound"* Ira Gitler, liner notes to John Coltrane, *Soultrane,* Prestige 7142, 1957.

xx *"Anti-jazz"* John Tynan, "Take 5," *Down Beat* (November 23, 1961): 40.

xxi *"By the time* A Love Supreme *hit"* Nat Hentoff, interview, DAT recording, June 15, 2001.

xxi *"I highly recommend it"* Tommy Flanagan, interview, DAT recording, August 8, 2001.

xxi *"This trombone player I was playing with"* Branford Marsalis, interview, DAT recording, November 1, 2001.

xxii *"I was just beginning to play saxophone"* Zane Massey, interview, DAT recording, June 17, 2001.

xxii *"a blast from another planet for me"* Alan Reder and John Baxter (eds.), *Listen to This!* (New York: Hyperion, 1999): 62. Thanks to the Dunton family library.

xxii *"it was 1968"* Gil Scott-Heron, quoted in Jon Bennett, "Gil Gets on the 'Trane," *Mojo* (August 2001): 31.

xxii *"I was at the top of the Grand Hotel in Chicago"* Bono, email to author, November 3, 2001.

xxiii *"Why is it that I hear this terrible inner turmoil"* Ravi Shankar, email to author, October 31, 2001.

xxiii *"I have been so moved by this record"* Ravi Shankar, interview, DAT recording, October 3, 2001.

xxiii *"The only thing I ask"* Alice Coltrane, interview.

Chapter 1/Miles Ahead, Miles Behind

1 *"Q: [Did Miles Davis have] a major stranglehold"* Interview by Carl-Erik Lindgren, tape recording, March 22, 1960.

1 *"It seemed like"* Jimmy Cobb, interview, DAT recording, August 28, 2001.

2 *"He grumbled and complained"* Davis, *Miles,* 246.

2 *the* Oakland Tribune *to read* Russ Wilson, "Coltrane May Quit Davis, Form Quintet," *Oakland Tribune* (June 14, 1959).

2 *"This made me real mad"* Ibid., 237.

2 *"As much as I liked Trane"* Ibid., 224.

3 *"It was hard for [Coltrane]"* Ibid., 232–33.

4 *"I remember very well this show"* Frank Tenot, interview, DAT recording, July 10, 2001.

4 *"That's the way he played every night"* Jimmy Cobb, interview.

4 *"the audience was completely with him"* Frank Tenot, interview.

5 *"So after the show"* Ibid.

6 *"For all their theoretical sense of freedom"* John S. Wilson, "Coltrane's 'Sheets of Sound,'" *New York Times* (August 13, 1967).

6 *John Coltrane was born in 1926* Much of the early biographical information on Coltrane is drawn from Lewis Porter, *John Coltrane: His Life and Music* (Ann Arbor: University of Michigan Press, 1998), 1–53; and the liner notes to John Coltrane, *The Heavyweight Champion: The Complete Atlantic Recordings,* Rhino R2-71984, 1995.

6 *"His father played violin and guitar"* Radio documentary, "Tell Me How Long Trane's Been Gone," part 1 of 5, Steve Rowland and Larry Abrams (co-prods.), 2001.

7 *"In my early years"* John Coltrane, interview, Blume.

7 *"My grandfather was instrumental"* "Tell Me How Long Trane's Been Gone," part 1 of 5.

7 *"He used to buy books"* Pharoah Sanders, interview, DAT recording, October 11, 2001.

7 *"I remember him reading the Bhagavad Gita"* Curtis Fuller, interview.

7 *"Those things John didn't like"* Porter, 19.

8 *"He kept that saxophone with him"* Ibid., 33.

8 *"The loss of his father"* Ibid., 17.

8 *"for a while, I don't think he had anything but that horn"* Ibid.

8 *"In my late teens"* John Coltrane, interview, Blume.

9 *"I think that the majority of musicians"* Ibid.

10 *"A big break with the dancing tradition"* John Coltrane, interview, Grimes.

10 *"The confidence with which Rabbit plays!"* John Coltrane, "Coltrane on Coltrane," *Down Beat* (September 29, 1960): 26.

10 *"He would have achieved his objective"* "Tell Me How Long Trane's Been Gone," part 1 of 5.

11 *"We were like second-string beboppers"* Jimmy Heath, quoted in interview with Howard Mandel for documentary *The World According to John Coltrane,* Tobey Byron (prod.), 1993.

11 *"was very important to the musicians"* Ibid.

11 *"Wherein some people would lay back"* Ibid. Heath adds: "One example of [Coltrane's ability to focus] was the fact that we observed that older saxophonists . . . like Coleman Hawkins, Ben Webster, Don Byas, and Lester [Young], they played a lot in D-flat. And Coltrane took it upon himself . . . to learn how to play in D-flat. And what he did was to zoom in on D-flat for I don't know, maybe six months, or a year . . . The result of that is obvious on a record by Miles Davis called 'Two Bass Hit' which is a fast blues in D-flat, [and] on which Coltrane played more in D-flat than most of his predecessors." (Ibid.)

11 *"Philadelphia Library together"* Ibid.

11 *"When Coltrane played in my band"* Porter, 64.

12 *"One had to earn a living"* Jimmy Heath, interview, *The World According to John Coltrane.*

12 *"Trane worked in some of those kinds of bands"* Ibid.

12 *"[What] I usually call my first"* John Coltrane, interview, Blume.

12 *"Coltrane's early experience"* Joe Goldberg, *Jazz Masters of the 50s* (New York: Da Capo, 1965): 192.

12 *"The blues, black clubs"* Dave Liebman, interview, DAT recording, April 16, 2001.

12 *"The thing about Coltrane's later Impulse work"* Branford Marsalis, interview.

13 *"Anything blues is good"* David Murray, interview, DAT recording, October 6, 2001.

13 *"A lot that was perceived as new"* Robert Palmer, liner notes to *Honkers & Screamers,* Savoy/Arista SJL 2234, 1979.

13 *"They played a song that had this tenor solo in it"* Porter, 74.

13 *"Before I switched from alto"* Coltrane, "Coltrane on Coltrane," 26.

15 *"I was fascinated by his arpeggios"* Ibid.

15 *"One night I happened to run into him in Cleveland"* Ibid.

15 *"There were two frustrations"* Porter, 78.

15 *"What I didn't know with Diz"* Ira Gitler, "'Trane on the Track," *Down Beat* (October 16, 1958): 16.

16 *"I stayed in obscurity for a long time"* François Postif, "John Coltrane," *Jazz Hot* (France) (January 1962). Translation by Jonathan Matz.

16 *"fabulous technical facilities"* Coltrane, "Coltrane on Coltrane," 26.

16 *"Then I worked with one of my first loves"* Ibid.

16 *"It was my education to the older generation"* Gitler, "'Trane on the Track," 17.

17 *"He was more than just a guy"* McCoy Tyner, interview, DAT recording, April 12, 2001.

18 *"I believe you could say"* John Coltrane, interview, Blume.

19 *"If you can get and keep a group together"* George Avakian, interview by Mark Masterson and author, videocassette, TV documentary-in-progress, November 13, 1999.

19 *"four year horror show"* Davis, *Miles,* 132.

19 *"His sound wasn't what I heard"* Ibid., 194.

19 *Philly Joe, who mentioned his home buddy* Years later, Red Garland claimed it was he who "got a telegram from Miles asking me if I knew anyone in Philadelphia who could play tenor sax. I told him I knew a cat named John Coltrane, and Miles asked me, 'Can he play?'" (Len Lyons, *The Great Jazz Pianists* [New York: Da Capo, 1983]: 147.) The story seems apocryphal given Miles's past familiarity with Coltrane, though the trumpeter did often poll all his sidemen when considering a new band member. Ultimately,

Davis handed the credit to his drummer: "Philly Joe brought up John Coltrane." Davis, *Miles,* 195.

19 *They had met a year later, according to Coltrane* Coltrane, "Coltrane on Coltrane," 26.

19 *"I used Sonny Rollins and Coltrane"* Davis, *Miles,* 155.

19 *"I could hear how Trane"* Ibid., 195.

20 *"I just played what the others expected from me"* John Coltrane, interview, Postif.

20 *"My silence and evil looks probably turned him off"* Davis, *Miles,* 195.

20 *"Trane was the only one"* Ibid.

21 *"After we started playing together"* Ibid.

21 *"We used to talk a lot about music"* Ibid., 223.

21 *"In November of 1955"* James Rozzi, "Bob Weinstock: Withstanding the Sands of Time," *Audio* (August 1994): 35.

21 *"I approached him"* Ibid.

22 *"one-take masters"* Tommy Flanagan, interview with Robert Palmer, *The World According to John Coltrane.*

22 *"what I can leave out"* Miles Davis, quoted in Amiri Baraka, "Homage to Miles Davis," reprinted in Gary Carner (ed.), *Miles Davis Companion* (London: Schirmer, 1996): 47.

22 *"it took that long to get it all in"* Barbara Gardner, "John Coltrane," *Down Beat* (Music 1962—year-end issue).

22 *"As a soloist, Coltrane appears"* Harry Frost, "Miles Davis in St. Louis," *Metronome* (May 1957): 30.

22 *"because some people couldn't understand"* Art Davis, interview, DAT recording, May 31, 2001.

22 *"He just played"* Ibid.

23 *"Why Miles picked me"* John Coltrane, interview with Grimes, *Jazz News.* Ravi Coltrane isolates one solo that was eventually released on the album *Steamin'* as a possible source of his father's embarrassment: "There's this unbelievable squeak on one of his solos—on 'Diane.' You can hear how it messes him up. He stutters for a minute, starts again, but that's the take. I don't think Trane was obsessive about that record date or anything, because usually guys will stop and redo a take like that. But the dates he did with Miles on Prestige were all one-takes. When I hear it my heart just aches, because you know that Miles wasn't going to stop." (Ravi Coltrane, interview.)

23 *ultimately yielded six albums* The six albums for Prestige: *Miles, Cookin', Relaxin', Miles Davis and the Modern Jazz Giants, Workin',* and *Steamin'.* The one for Columbia: *'Round About Midnight.*

23 *"Coltrane's what you hear on* that record" Goldberg, 198.

24 *"I just tell them if they work for me"* Nat Hentoff, *The Jazz Life* (New York: Da Capo, 1961): 93.

24 *"About that time I made a decision"* John Coltrane, interview, Blume.

24 *"During the year 1957"* John Coltrane, liner notes to *A Love Supreme,* Impulse A-77, 1965.

25 *"A few years ago I recovered faith"* Michel Delorme and Claude Lenissois, "Je ne peux pas aller plus loin," *Jazz Hot* (France) (September 1965). Translation by Dave Sinclair.

25 *"There was a time when I went through a personal crisis"* John Coltrane, interview with Ralph J. Gleason, tape recording, May 2, 1961. © 1989, Jazz Casual Prod., Inc., by permission. All rights reserved. This applies to all excerpts of same.

25 *"I'm sure that there was some sort of revelation"* Mary Alexander, interview, DAT recording, August 19, 2001.

25 *"Naima was with him all the time"* Ibid.

25 *"John was playing a club"* Ibid.

25 *"I never did go to the club"* Ibid.

26 *"definitely a turning point"* McCoy Tyner, interview.

26 *"It was the first time"* Ibid.

26 *"He had people around him that loved him"* Ibid.

26 *"I remember he told me he had a dream"* Ibid.

26 *"I kind of remember . . . it was before he joined Miles"* "Tell Me How Long Trane's Been Gone," part 3 of 5.

27 *"I remember I looked at him"* Jimmy Cobb, interview.

27 *"It was almost like he had something"* McCoy Tyner, interview.

27 *"I took the picture of him resting"* Esmond Edwards, interview, DAT recording, October 1, 2001.

27 *"There were certain musicians"* Bob Weinstock, interview, DAT recording, February 20, 2001.

28 *"John Glenn . . . showed me"* Coltrane, "Coltrane on Coltrane," 27.

28 *His wife reported him working for twenty-four hours a day"* Gardner, "John Coltrane."

28 *"ninety percent saxophone"* Jimmy Heath, interview, WBGO-FM, Newark, October 16, 2001.

28 *"A lot of the scalar material"* Joe Zawinul, interview, tape recording, January 26, 2000. Bill Perkins commented on just how challenging Slonimsky's exercises could be: "I looked at [Slonimsky's book] and it didn't mean anything to me. Even today I go to lesser books on scales because Slonimsky requires tremendous perseverance. It's strictly dry mathematics. John went through it and found scales he liked, maybe one out of a hundred that would work for him." (Bill Perkins, quoted by Doug Ramsey, liner notes to *John Coltrane: The Prestige Recordings,* Prestige 16 PCD-4405-2, 1991, 12.)

29 *"a musical architect of the highest order"* Coltrane, "Coltrane on Coltrane," 27.

29 *"Monk is exactly the opposite of Miles"* John Coltrane, interview, Postif.

30 *"Monk . . . showed me how to make"* Coltrane, "Coltrane on Coltrane," 27.

30 *recording for Riverside* During 1957, four classic albums were generated from four sessions of the brief Monk-Coltrane convergence: *Thelonious Himself, Blues for Tomorrow, Monk's Music,* and *Thelonious Monk with John Coltrane.*

30 *"I'd go by his apartment"* John Coltrane, interview, Blume.

30 *"Monk's music"* Tommy Flanagan, interview by Phil Coady, August 21, 1995, for enhanced CD *The Ultimate Blue Train,* CDP 7243-8-53428-0-6, 1997.

30 *"one has to know the melodies"* Martin Williams, *The Jazz Tradition* (New York: Oxford University Press, 1970): 227.

30 *"The scene that stands in my mind"* Radio documentary, "Remembering Trane," Steve Rowland (prod.), 1987.

31 *"When he played with Monk"* Steve Lacy, heard on "Tell Me How Long Trane's Been Gone," part 1 of 5.

31 *no fewer than ten* Porter, 113.

31 *" 'Blowing session'—that was the common term"* Kenny Burrell, interview by Larry Blumenfeld, 1995, for enhanced CD *The Ultimate Blue Train,* CDP 7243-8-53428-0-6, 1997.

31 *"Most recordings were just loosely organized jam sessions"* Bob Weinstock, interview.

31 *"To me [Blue Train] was well-schemed"* Curtis Fuller, interview by Phil Coady, July 3, 1995, for enhanced CD *The Ultimate Blue Train,* CDP 7243-8-53428-0-6, 1997. Though the label funded a session to go over the material, Fuller recalls complaining—and inadvertently titling one of the tracks: "I was getting on [Coltrane's] case, because he had written all the music for the record date. You get this one-day rehearsal that they give you at Blue Note, and he came up with all this hard music—'Lazy Bird' and everything. 'Man, you dropped this stuff on us at a moment's notice.' And he laughed, I mean, gave that half-smile . . . and ironically, the song came out as 'Moment's Notice.'" (Ibid.)

32 *"We came out of that"* Ibid.

32 *"I had this idea"* Davis, *Miles,* 217.

32 *"Cannonball's blues-rooted"* Ibid., 220.

32 *"That was interesting especially because Trane"* Cannonball Adderley, interview.

33 *"I found Miles in the midst"* Coltrane, "Coltrane on Coltrane," 27. For further discussion of modal jazz: John Litweiler, *The Freedom Principle: Jazz After 1958* (New York: Da Capo, 1984): 105–28; Barry Dean Kernfeld, "Adderley, Coltrane and Davis at the Twilight of Bebop: The Search for Melodic Coherence." Ph.D. thesis, Cornell University, 1981; and Ashley Kahn, *Kind of Blue: The Making of the Miles Davis Masterpiece* (New York: Da Capo, 2000): 66–71.

33 *"This was the first record"* Davis, *Miles,* 225.

33 *"Miles's music gave me plenty"* Coltrane, "Coltrane on Coltrane," 27.

34 *"I want to cover"* Ibid.

34 *"not so much commercially"* Adderley, quoted in Gardner, "John Coltrane." During this period, he had also grown into a session star, prominently featured on albums by composers George Russell (on the album *New York, NY*) and Michel Legrand (*Legrand Jazz*), bassist Wilbur Harden (*Tanganyika Suite*), tenor saxist Gene Ammons (*Big Sound*—on alto), Cannonball Adderley (*Cannonball Adderley Quintet in Chicago*), and Cecil Taylor (*Stereo Drive*). On a pair of collaborative efforts on Prestige, his name was big enough to command title billing, as he blew alongside tubaist Ray Draper (*The Ray Draper Quintet Featuring John Coltrane*) and guitarist Kenny Burrell (*Kenny Burrell & John Coltrane*). He led his own sessions seven times in 1958 for Prestige, yielding enough material to keep the label busy with fresh titles for a decade. One distinct measure of Coltrane's growth is that almost all of the albums derived from these sessions featuring the saxophonist as an incidental sideman have been reissued under his name alone, as if he had originally been the leader!

34 *his three-year contract with Prestige was running out* Bob Weinstock remains unhappy about the talent-poaching common in his field. "That went on in the jazz world—I didn't like it at all, and [Blue Note Records head] Alfred Lion didn't like it. Blue Note and Prestige were the main pioneers among jazz musicians, because we would record people that weren't that famous. And other companies—like Atlantic and CBS—they'd just take them away." (Bob Weinstock, interview.) Weinstock maintains that, though he could never match the contractual generosity of larger companies, the last laugh was his: "You know what the biggest joke of it all was? I had Gene Ammons—who outsold everybody two to one, Miles, Coltrane, Monk, all of them put together—since the year I started the company to the end when I sold it [to Fantasy Records in 1971]. Gene Ammons had the ability to reach the people, jukeboxes, everything. He appealed to the R&B audience and the pop audience with the pretty ballads, like he did 'My Foolish Heart,' which sold a million records. And these other companies didn't even go near Ammons. Gene would always say, 'Thanks for keeping my name in front of the people.' " (Ibid.)

34 *"This company was started by jazz lovers"* Ahmet Ertegun, interview, DAT recording, April 16, 2001.

34 *Atlantic's jazz interests* Jerry Wexler: "The comings and goings of whoever it was—John Coltrane, Ornette Coleman—it didn't create any stir up at the other end of the office. It sounds cold-blooded and very commercial and corporate, but we were very proud of what Nesuhi did, and of his roster. . . jazz is an art form, whereas rock 'n 'roll is merely a craft." (Wexler, interview, DAT recording, February 19, 2001.)

35 *"Coltrane was a project that Nesuhi brought in"* Miriam Bienstock, interview, DAT recording, February 26, 2001.

35 *$7,000 for a one-year* Porter, 140.

36 *"I sit there"* Nat Hentoff, liner notes to *Giant Steps*, ATL 1311, 1960.

36 *"that whole date"* Tommy Flanagan, interview, *Blue Train* enhanced CD. Flanagan adds: "Coltrane brought that by my place before the recording date, and played it for me on the piano, just the chords. Well, there wasn't any problem at all—until we got to the date. I didn't know what tempo he was going to play it at!" (Ibid.)

36 *"[The songs] didn't really resolve"* Tommy Flanagan, interview, *The World According to John Coltrane.*

36 *"Giant Steps—we sort of called it a family album"* Mary Alexander, interview.

36 *"That date was different"* Tommy Flanagan, interview, *The World According to John Coltrane.*

37 *"I didn't know where I was going to go next"* Benoit Quersin, "Entretiens: La Passe dangereuse," *Jazz* (France) (January 1963): 40.

38 *"what Ornette Coleman"* Martin Williams, liner notes to Ornette Coleman, *The Shape of Jazz to Come*, ATL 1317.

38 *"I feel indebted to him"* John Coltrane, interview, Quersin.

38 *"He was interested in non-chordal"* Peter Watrous, "John Coltrane: A Life Supreme," *Musician* (July 1987): 106.

39 *playing with pickup bands in variety of venues* Lewis Porter, liner notes to John Coltrane, *The Heavyweight Champion.*

39 *"Davis did Coltrane three great favors"* Doug Ramsey, liner notes to *John Coltrane: The Prestige Recordings.*

Chapter 2/The Classic Quartet

41 *"If you want a photographic"* Ralph Gleason, "Coltrane Not for Those Who Want Popular Tune," *Des Moines (Iowa) Register* (March 26, 1960).

41 *When* Newsweek *tackled* "Finally Made," *Newsweek* (July 24, 1961): 64.

41 *"You can play lighter things"* Ibid.

42 *scheduling all sessions* Dowd describes the cross-genre nature of his job: "There were times when, at two o'clock in the afternoon, I might be doing the Coasters—'Charlie Brown,' 'Yakety Yack,' or 'Poison Ivy'—and the phone would ring and it's Nesuhi and he says, 'We're doing Mingus tonight at midnight.' You want culture shock? Go from doing 'Poison Ivy' to doing *Pithecanthropus Erectus.* Give me a break!" (Tom Dowd, interview, DAT recording, February 19, 2001.)

42 *"I played in university bands"* Ibid.

42 *"Nesuhi would call me"* Ibid.

43 *performing publicly on the soprano* Porter reports that Coltrane was publicly experimenting on soprano in early 1959 while still with Miles Davis (Porter, 181), while Coltrane chronicler Yasuhiro Fujioka claims mid-May 1959 as the date when he began to play it on a regular basis: Yasuhiro Fujioka et al., *John Coltrane: A Discography and Musical Biography (Studies in Jazz; No. 20)* (London: Scarecrow, 1993): 141.

43 *first played it on a recording four weeks later* Neil Tesser, liner notes to *The Avant-Garde*, Rhino/Atlantic R2-79892, 2000.

43 *"The first time I saw Coltrane"* Frank Tenot, interview. A 1976 warehouse fire unfortunately destroyed most of Atlantic Records's original master tapes, so verification of this has not been possible. Tom Dowd recalls Coltrane switching between saxophones during the "My Favorite Things" session, even within one take—"such horn-hopping was par for the course"—but cannot remember which of these alternative takes took place when the tapes were rolling.

43 *"Some times we have to live"* John Coltrane, interview, Gleason.

44 *standard jazz practice* Many of the classic performances by Louis Armstrong, Billie Holiday, and Charlie Parker were borrowed from other productions. A few months after "My Favorite Things" hit, five recordings of the theme to the film *Exodus* graced the pop charts: tenor saxist Eddie Harris topping versions by Ferrante & Teicher, Mantovani, Pat Boone, and Edith Piaf. ("Exodus Movie Theme Racks Up 5," *Billboard* [May 15, 1961]: 11.)

44 *"I try to pick . . . a song"* John Coltrane, interview, Gleason.

44 *"I don't know how long"* Ibid.

44 *"I have several men in mind"* John Coltrane, interview, Lindgren.

45 *"I remember when he was writing"* McCoy Tyner, interview.

45 *"we had a sort of verbal understanding"* Len Lyons, *The Great Jazz Pianists* (New York: Da Capo, 1983): 238.

45 *"John's group is where I belonged"* Ibid.

45 *"Bud Monk" was Tyner's teenage nickname* Porter, 177.

45 *"When I began with John"* Lyons, 238.

45 "Kind of Blue *was a major influence"* McCoy Tyner, interview, tape recording, November 10, 1999.

45 *"I was very young"* McCoy Tyner interview, James Brown, tape recording, WBGO-FM, Newark, February 1982.

46 *"Our personalities complemented each other"* Lyons, 239.

46 *"When a man's faith is never tried"* Ibid.

46 *"I've known him a long time"* Nat Hentoff, liner notes to *Live at the Village Vanguard*, Impulse A-10, 1962.

46 *"We had to accept the fact"* McCoy Tyner, interview.

46 *"John told me about Elvin Jones"* Ibid.

46 *"It's hard for a young person"* Rick Mattingly, "Elvin," *Modern Drummer* (December 1982): 9.

46 *"There is nothing in his playing"* Branford Marsalis, interview.

47 *"I listened to* A Night at the Village Vanguard*"* Ravi Coltrane, interview.

47 *"When exchanging fours or eights"* Rick Mattingly, "Elvin Jones: Once More, with Feeling," *Modern Drummer* (May 1992): 26.

48 *"One time John called me"* Wayne Shorter, interview, Howard Mandel, June 26, 1990, for documentary *The World According to John Coltrane*, Tobey Byron (prod.), 1993.

48 *"You can get bogged down in clichés"* Mike Hennessey, "The Emancipation of Elvin Jones," *Down Beat* (March 24, 1966): 24.

48 *"to be more flexible where rhythm is concerned"* Coltrane, "Coltrane on Coltrane," 27.

48 *"It isn't necessary"* Don DeMicheal, "The Sixth Man," *Down Beat* (March 28, 1963): 18.

49 *"Some people are more sensitive"* Herb Nolan, "Rhythmic Pulsemaster," *Down Beat* (December 15, 1977): 13.

49 *"The more sensitive you are"* Ibid.

49 *"That first night Elvin was in the band"* J. C. Thomas, *Chasin' the Trane* (New York: Da Capo, 1975): 130.

49 *"That first night, Elvin said"* McCoy Tyner, interview.

49 *The dates eventually yielded three groundbreaking albums* My Favorite Things *was released in early 1961,* Coltrane Plays the Blues *in mid-1962, and* Coltrane's Sound *in summer 1964.*

49 *"I feel that we have every reason"* Coltrane, "Coltrane on Coltrane," 27.

50 *"It was revolutionary"* George Avakian, email to author, July 20, 2001.

50 *The saxophonist now merited a $10,000 advance* Thomas, 143.

50 *"Not too much now"* John Coltrane, interview, Gleason. By all indications (Thiele, Taylor, etc.), Coltrane's new contract called for two records a year. In stating "three," Coltrane might have been speaking of 1961 in particular, when he was due to produce two titles for Impulse and still owed Atlantic one.

51 *"I wasn't party"* Rudy Van Gelder, fax to author, October 31, 2001.

51 *"During the time [Coltrane]"* Ibid.

51 *"The Believer"* was actually a McCoy Tyner composition Coltrane heard in 1957 when the two performed at the Red Rooster, according to Neil Tesser, liner notes to *Olé Coltrane*, Rhino/Atlantic R2-79965, 2000.

51 *"Most recently I've been listening"* John Coltrane, interview, Gleason.

51 *"Coltrane was very interested"* "Tell Me How Long Trane's Been Gone," part 2 of 5..

55 *"I have an African record at home"* John Coltrane, interview, Gleason.

55 *"I like extended jazz works"* John Coltrane, interview, Grimes.

55 *"We play 'Greensleeves'"* John Coltrane, interview, Gleason.

58 *"That evening at the Gate"* Herb Snitzer, *Jazz: A Visual Journey* (Clearwater, Fla.: Notables Inc., 1999): 17.

58 *"I've been listening more"* John Coltrane, interview with Michiel deRuyter, London, November 11, 1961.

58 *"Reggie [Workman] and Art [Davis]"* Dom Cerulli, liner notes to *Africa/Brass,* Impulse A-6, 1961. Art, no relation to Steve Davis, who had then departed the group, explains his role: "Coltrane wanted me to play sort of in a solo capacity—that would drive him. Then another bassist would play the regular bass parts, having a drone sound, like in Indian music. For instance, on 'Africa,' he told me to play melody, where the other bass has that low sound. I played the same thing on the intro to 'Dahomey Dance.'" (Art Davis, interview.) Davis had become a favorite practice partner of Coltrane's, and would have been his bassist had Davis not been gainfully employed by the NBC-TV orchestra. "I actually wanted Art to join me as a regular bassist," Coltrane remarked. "So I had to get in Steve Davis, and when he left Art still couldn't make it, so I got Reggie." (Val Wilmer, "Conversation with Coltrane," *Jazz Journal* [January 1962]; reprinted in Carl Woideck [ed.], *The John Coltrane Companion* [New York: Simon & Schuster, 1998]: 106.) Originally from Harrisburg, Pa., Davis earned status among musicians for his accomplishments both on the bandstand (playing in a wide range of musical styles) and off (taking a strong, personal stand against Jim Crow practices of the day in New York's orchestral and studio music community). Davis currently teaches music at the University of California at Irvine and other colleges in Orange County. "My abilities have still not yet been fully challenged," he recently stated. (Nat Hentoff, "Art Davis and the Mystery of Making It," *Jazz Times* [March 2001]: 122.)

58 *"There are still quite a few avenues"* John Coltrane, *Newsweek.*

59 *"A growing anti-jazz trend"* John Tynan, "Take 5," *Down Beat* (November 23, 1961): 40.

59 *"Tynan's comments on the 'anti-jazz' trend"* Leonard Feather, "Feather's Nest," *Down Beat* (February 15, 1962): 17.

59 *"intonation trouble"* Don DeMicheal, "The Monterey Festival," *Down Beat* (November 9, 1961): 13.

59 *"I'll try to build things"* Don DeMicheal, "John Coltrane and Eric Dolphy Answer the Jazz Critics," *Down Beat* (April 12, 1962).

60 *"For his second album"* Ted Fox, *In the Groove: The People Behind the Music* (New York: St. Martin's, 1986): 192.

60 *"He had a lot of seichl"* Dan Morgenstern, interview, DAT recording, April 9, 2001.

60 *"I was apprehensive"* Ibid.

60 *"In fact, my first meeting"* Frank Kofsky, "The New Wave: Bob Thiele Talks to Frank Kofsky About John Coltrane," *Coda* (May 1968): 3.

60 *The eventual album* The complete recordings have, to date, yielded six albums and/or box sets, including the recent four-CD collection *The Complete 1961 Village Vanguard Recordings,* IMPD4-232, 1997.

61 *"a treadmill to the Kingdom of Boredom"* Ira Gitler, "Double View of Coltrane 'Live,'" *Down Beat* (April 26, 1962).

61 *"one of the noblest failures on record"* Pete Welding, "Double View of Coltrane 'Live.'" For a compelling study of this track, see Gary Giddins, *Visions of Jazz* (New York: Oxford University Press, 1998): 476.

61 *"start from nothing"* John Coltrane, interview, Grimes.

61 *"The melody not only wasn't written"* John Coltrane, liner notes to *Live at the Village Vanguard.*

61 *"Though I don't particularly"* John Coltrane, interview, Postif.

61 *not before recommending his replacement, Scott LaFaro* Per Jimmy Garrison: "I was with Bill Evans, and that's when Philly Joe Jones called, but anyway, Scott LaFaro and I changed up. I was with Bill Evans, Joe called, and I told Bill about Scott LaFaro, so he hired Scott, went with Philly Joe, and maybe after that is when I went with Stan Getz." (Jimmy Garrison, interview, tape recording, Herb Nolan, Chicago, 1974.)

63 *"I was with Ornette Coleman"* Ibid.

63 *"Being with Ornette"* Ibid.

63 *"When I was with Ornette"* Ibid.

63 *"I'll tell you, if you're strong"* Ibid.

64 *"I'm not sure, but it will probably revert"* Bob Dawbarn, "I'd Like to Play Your Clubs," *Melody Maker* (November 25, 1961): 8.

64 *"happen fortuitously"* John Coltrane, interview, Postif.

65 *"I said, 'John'"* McCoy Tyner, interview.

65 *"I remember Elvin used to get so wet"* Jimmy Cobb, interview.

65 *"Playing with these three"* "Tell Me How Long Trane's Been Gone," part 2 of 5.

66 *"I don't give these polls more than they deserve"* Jean-Claude Dargenpierre, "John Coltrane: Un Faust moderne," *Jazz* (France) (January 1962): 24; translated in Porter, 191.

66 *"Whenever I'd say to John"* Cecilia Foster, interview, DAT recording, September 6, 2001.

66 *"I came off the stage"* Elvin Jones, interview by Michael Shrieve for biography-in-progress.

66 *"When I was with the Count Basie orchestra"* Frank Foster, interview, DAT recording, September 6, 2001.

66 *"Coltrane brought a more intelligent"* Ibid. Foster adds: "I hadn't exploited my Coltrane influence too much while with the Basie band. But after I left in 1964, whenever Eddie 'Lockjaw' Davis wanted to take off, Basie had someone call me to substitute for him because I knew the book. My solos by that time had just gone hog wild into the Coltrane idiom. Everybody's head would be turning. [Alto saxophonist] Marshall Royal's brow would go up . . . he started calling me 'Johnny No-Trane.' " (Ibid.)

67 *"I never thought of myself"* Hultin, "I Remember 'Trane."

67 *"Horn players . . . gravitated to him"* McCoy Tyner, interview.

67 *"John was eleven years older than I am"* Archie Shepp, interview.

67 *"When we talk about the avant-garde"* Ibid.

68 *"At that time, he was listening"* Ibid.

68 *"It was like being in church"* Ibid.

68 *"In Chicago, he always played . . . at McKie's"* Ibid.

68 *"I like playing"* John Coltrane, interview, Grimes.

69 *"There were nights that I would hear him"* Archie Shepp, interview.

69 *"It was so intense"* Sy Johnson, interview, DAT recording, May 8, 2001.

70 *"Many nights he would come off the bandstand"* McCoy Tyner, interview, WKCR-FM.

70 *"One time we were at the Half Note"* McCoy Tyner, interview.

70 *"it requires some concentration"* Kofsky, *Coda,* 1968, 8.

71 *"[Coltrane] explained everything to me"* Fox, 193.

71 *"I think that he was less affected"* Bob Thiele, interview with Kofsky, *Coda,* 1968, 4. Thiele added: "In those days [1961–64], what *Down Beat* said with respect to sales records wrongly affected record people, and now I find that most of the things they said at the time, and even the things they say now, amount to nothing."

71 *"Impulse was interested in having"* John Coltrane, interview with Frank Kofsky, August 1966; reprinted in Pauline Rivelli and Robert Levin (eds.), *The Black Giants* (New York: World, 1970): 34.

71 *"He was our leading jazz artist"* Larry Newton, interview, DAT recording, February 19, 2001.

71 *"ABC was buying companies"* Bill Kaplan, interview, DAT recording, June 21, 2001.

72 *"See, Prestige had a following"* Bob Weinstock, interview, DAT recording, December 3, 2001.

72 *"I never considered"* Ibid.

72 *"I remember"* Robert Palmer, "From the Inside Out: Bob Palmer Interviews Bob Thiele," *Coda* (June 1971): 34.

73 *"And we were always trying"* Ibid.

73 *"I attended a fully integrated high school"* Patti Smith, email to author, November 26, 2001.

73 *"The pervasiveness of jazz in the ghetto"* David Rosenthal, *Hard Bop: Jazz and Black Music, 1955–1965* (New York: Oxford University Press, 1992): 68.

76 *"As of now, jazz is still quite colored"* "The Playboy Jazz Panel: Jazz—Today and Tomorrow," *Playboy* (February 1964); reprinted in Robert Walser (ed.), *Keeping Time* (New York: Oxford University Press, 1999): 289.

76 *"I heard many things in what Trane was doing"* "Remembering Trane," radio documentary.

76 *"John was much more than that era"* Sonny Rollins, "Remembering Trane," radio documentary.

77 *"it would seem to me"* Kofsky, *Coda,* 1968, 4.

77 *"Jazz is built on this notion"* Joshua Redman, interview, DAT recording, September 26, 2001.

77 *"They were a real band"* Ravi Coltrane, interview.

77 *"Elvin, I got to ask you"* Dave Liebman, interview.

78 *"If you listen to Miles's group"* Joshua Redman, interview. Miles's approach never quite connected with Coltrane's, according to Liebman, also a veteran of Davis's band. "I don't think Miles identified with the quartet at all—I don't think that he could understand how you can play for an hour and a half on an E-minor or a D-minor chord, or on less than that . . . But the funny thing is when you look at *Bitches Brew*—it's Coltrane's *Ascension* in rock 'n' roll. I mean it's a bunch of cats playing kind of everything or nothing—they're not really centered." (Dave Liebman, interview.)

78 *"That was a funny period in my life"* John Coltrane, Kofsky, *Coda,* 1968, 34.

78 *"How kind you are to me"* Poem dated January 7, 1964, reprinted in program to John Coltrane 75th Anniversary Tribute, September 29, 2001.

79 *"The song 'Alabama' came from a speech"* McCoy Tyner, interview.

79 *"Sometimes I go at it"* Delorme and Lenissois, *Jazz Hot.*

79 *"moments of contemplation"* Martin Williams, *Jazz Masters in Transition, 1957–1969* (New York: Da Capo, 1970): 228.

79 *"I think Crescent is one"* Frank Lowe, interview.

80 *"I think Crescent, which is my favorite of all Coltrane recordings"* Dave Liebman, interview.

80 *"I was still so much under its spell"* Michael Cuscuna, interview.

81 *"I was at Birdland one night"* Ibid.

Impulse: Creed's Vision

52 *"The late '50s"* June Bundy, "Late '50s Bid for Pos-

terity Fame as Real 'Jazz Age,' " *Billboard* (March 9, 1959): 1.

52 *"Wait a minute!"* Jerry Wexler, interview. Author Lewis Porter writes: "the LP version of *Peter Gunn* did include [jazzmen] Art Pepper, Ray Brown, Shelly Manne, Jimmy Rowles on various tunes—[it was] more jazz than people realize. Plas Johnson, a good tenorman, is soloist on the Peter Gunn theme."

52 *"In the fifties"* Larry Newton, interview.

52 *"We were in existence"* Sid Feller, interview, DAT recording, February 17, 2001.

53 *"After Ray came"* Ibid.

53 *"I would go to the record bins"* Creed Taylor, interview, DAT recording, February 22, 2001.

53 *"jazz was my mission"* Ibid.

53 *"It sold well for its time"* Ibid.

53 *"Cannonball and Nat [Adderley] came through the office one day"* Grachan Moncur, interview, DAT recording, February 19, 2001.

53 *"It just came out of nowhere"* Creed Taylor, interview.

53 *"I first tried to clear"* Ibid.

54 *"I tried to juxtapose the visual"* Ibid.

54 *"It was a landslide"* Ibid.

54 *"[Impulse] knocked me out"* Eliot Tiegel, interview, DAT recording, April 16, 2001.

54 *"Impulse was not major competition"* George Avakian, email to author, July 20, 2001.

54 *"At first there was"* Creed Taylor, interview

Chapter 3/December 9, 1964: Creating A Love Supreme

83 *"John used to"* Cecilia Foster, interview.

83 *"The week of December 7, 1964"* Rudy Van Gelder, fax to author.

84 *"This is the way it worked"* Ibid.

84 *"I was always over-budget"* Phil Johnson, "They Couldn't Help Acting on Impulse," *Independent* (UK) (February 3, 1995): 26.

85 *"That fact that [Coltrane] had the influence"* Rudy Van Gelder, interview, Coady.

86 *"There can only be a handful"* Thiele, *Coda,* 1971, 32.

86 *"I believe he had one way"* Rudy Van Gelder, fax to author.

86 *" 'Encouragement' is the word"* Kofsky, *Coda,* 1968, 9.

86 *"Bob was there, but he was never like"* McCoy Tyner, interview. Jones, however, recalls a time when he felt the producer overstepped his duties: "I had to straighten Bob Thiele out once. We were making this album *Ballads,* and he stopped one of the pieces, and said from the booth, 'You're using too much swish.' And I said, 'What the hell is he talking about? I'm using brushes—that's the way they're supposed to sound!' [laughs]. He shut up!" (Elvin Jones, interview.)

86 *"His job basically was"* Bob Golden, interview, DAT recording, June 22, 2001.

86 *"I remember something very unique"* McCoy Tyner, interview.

87 *"Everything I do is related to creating the perfect mood"* Daniel J. Levitin, "Interview with Rudy Van Gelder," *Recording-Engineer-Producer Magazine* (April 1992).

87 *"There was a joke among the musicians"* Bob Weinstock, interview.

87 *"When we got into the studio"* McCoy Tyner, interview.

92 *"When I walk into the studio"* Herb Nolan, "Rhythmic Pulsemaster," *Down Beat* (December 15, 1977): 14.

92 *"John said very little about what he wanted"* McCoy Tyner, interview.

92 *"He'd write down the symbols"* Ibid.

92 *"That first day"* Elvin Jones, interview.

92 *"In those sessions"* Ibid.

94 *"Once the form had been stated"* Mattingly, "Elvin," 53.

94 *"On A Love Supreme"* McCoy Tyner, interview.

94 *"It was definitely"* Ibid.

94 *"The long-playing record"* "Coltrane and I Played Without Preparation," *Crescendo International* (UK) (November 1970): 10.

94 *"An unusual thing that I recall"* Rudy Van Gelder, fax to author.

94 *"I usually ask them ahead of time"* Ibid.

95 *"All of them were two-track recordings"* Ibid.

95 *"I am certain there was no mixing involved"* Kevin Reeves, email to author, January 25, 2002.

95 *"There are only three possible degrees of separation"* Ibid. Reeves continues: "It is my guess, not having been granted permission to see the actual console, that Rudy did his equalization on the tracks on the channels of his board, each channel having its own set of processing knobs for equalization. Trane's mic had one channel, Elvin's another, and so on. Rudy would likely try and maximize each sound on each of these channels 'on the way in,' knowing that there would be no opportunity to go back and separately tweak each channel—as one would do if recording to a multitrack instead of live to two-track. Following that logic, that may also explain why Rudy chose to put Trane on one side of the room, and Elvin on the other—to minimize the leakage from one mic to another. Of course, with the advent of both the multitrack recorder and the isolation booth, these issues of separation are rarely broached by young engineers of today, and I fear that the fine art and skill of the 'live to two-track' session has been lost."

96 *"would run a master tape"* Rudy Van Gelder, quoted in Ben Sidran, *Talking Jazz: An Oral History* (New York: Da Capo, 1995): 317.

96 *"I made [lower-quality] 7½ ips mono tapes"* Rudy Van Gelder, fax to author.

96 *"I had a job"* John Slate, interview, DAT recording, September 4, 2001.

97 *"It's the signal of something different"* Ravi Coltrane, interview.

97 *"he didn't play soprano saxophone"* Elvin Jones, interview.

97 *"I don't know if it's because the tone"* Tommy Flanagan, interview.

99 *E major . . . an unusual key for Coltrane* Steve Reich offers his interpretation of Coltrane's opening key choice to *A Love Supreme* as one step in a suite-long harmonic journey: "Talk about modal jazz! That's really something, the way he starts with this little thing in E major, which is totally off the wall, jazz-wise, as a key. In jazz, you mainly have flat keys, [but] he's playing mostly in three flats, sometimes it's in five flats. I mean, *A Love Supreme*'s all over the place. I would say that by the end of the suite, he is definitely saying, 'OK, here we are—back in a five-tone scale.' It's very relaxed; the harmonic intensity and complexity is resolved in a five-note scale in C minor [in 'Psalm']." (Steve Reich, interview, DAT recording, October 12, 2001.)

99 *"If you say* A Love Supreme*"* Alice Coltrane, interview.

99 *"Mau Mau"* Thanks to Mike Fitzgerald for the tip on this musical antecedent.

99 *"You know Led Zeppelin's 'Whole Lotta Love'?"* Branford Marsalis, interview.

99 *"The blues is the common denominator"* Giddins, *Visions of Jazz,* 479.

100 *"Garrison's swing"* John Litweiler, *The Freedom Principle: Jazz After 1958* (New York: Da Capo, 1984): 44–45.

100 *"never slicing the rump roast"* Stanley Crouch, "Titan of the Blues: John Coltrane," *Village Voice* (October 6, 1987).

100 *"There are some musicians"* Herb Nolan, "Jimmy Garrison: Bassist in the Front Line," *Down Beat* (June 6, 1974): 41.

101 *"I used to listen to Xavier"* Mattingly, "Elvin," 27–53.

101 *"I always try to sustain"* Ibid.

101 *"I especially like his ability to mix"* Nat Hentoff, liner notes to *Live at the Village Vanguard,* Impulse A-10, 1961.

101 *"That section is always"* Ravi Coltrane, interview. The section begins 4:43 into "Acknowledgement."

102 *"he's telling us God is everywhere"* Porter, 242. As mystical as Porter's interpretation may seem, Coltrane applied his universalist sensibility to all aspects of his music-making, including the saxophone itself, as Alice Coltrane told *Ebony* magazine: "He liked to draw an analogy between mankind and his horn, explaining that one group might represent the upper register, another the mid-range and yet another the deeper notes, but that it took all to make the whole." (Phyl Garland, "Requiem for 'Trane," *Ebony* [November 1967]: 72.)

102 *"In a nutshell"* Steve Reich, interview.

103 *"It's deliberately random"* Ravi Coltrane, interview.

103 *"It's really looking towards"* Dave Liebman, interview.

103 *"brilliantly executed"* Porter, 242.

104 *"It's as if"* Alice Coltrane, interview.

104 *"I know that his grandfather"* Wayne Shorter, interview, DAT recording, August 11, 2001.

104 *"along with Elvin Jones"* Ibid.

104 *"900243—Part I—voice overdub"* Regarding the vocal overdub, Van Gelder writes: "I don't actually remember overdubbing it, Judge, but that doesn't mean it didn't happen, Your Honor! After listening to *A Love Supreme* years later, it sounds to me as if there are two voices on the vocal. Whether it's two people singing or John overdubbing, I don't know. If it was an overdub, it was not intended to replace anything, but to enhance what was already there." (Rudy Van Gelder, fax to author.)

105 *"When I first"* Frank Tiberi, interview, DAT recording, April 18, 2001.

105 *"I'd be sitting"* Ibid.

106 *"My man is definitely"* Bob Belden, interview, September 8, 2001.

106 *"to study the harp"* Reggie Workman, quoted by Porter, 273.

106 *"landmarks"* Coltrane used the term to describe mid-solo moments when he played or implied notes to clue his sidemen as to where they were: "I have several, couple landmarks there, that I know I'm going to get to, so I try to play something in between there that's different, and keep hoping that I hear something different on it. But it usually goes about almost the same way every night, every time." (John Coltrane, interview, Gleason.)

106 *"Hear how he puts extra emphasis"* Bob Belden, interview.

106 *no outtakes of "Pursuance/Psalm"* Why a modicum of in-studio dialogue on any of the *Love Supreme* tapes? Van Gelder responds: "It's always been like that. I don't believe in recording rehearsals or in recording without the musicians being aware of what is happening. Furthermore, I need to know the shape of the whole piece before I record, because it's a live situation." (Rudy Van Gelder, fax to author.)

107 *"You want to know what started me on that?"* Nolan, "Jimmy Garrison: Bassist in the Front Line," 41.

107 *"Coltrane would make 30 takes on a tune"* William Ruhlmann, "Bob Thiele Produced Them All," *Goldmine* (December 11, 1992): 4. To Thiele's defense, Impulse studio records do reveal Coltrane's perfectionist tendency on earlier sessions, viz., seven

complete takes of "It's Easy to Remember" for the 1963 *Ballads* album.

108 *"The thing about him"* Rudy Van Gelder, interview, Coady.

109 *"For me, when I go"* John Coltrane, interview, Delorme and Lenissois.

109 *"the central section"* Ibid.

109 *"a great set"* Pat LaBarbera, interview, DAT recording, June 19, 2001.

109 *"There's just so much"* Ibid.

110 *"McCoy is a beauty"* John Coltrane, interview, Gleason.

110 *"Excitement is there"* Goldberg, 195.

110 *"I'd tell him to begin in the middle"* Davis, *Miles*, 223.

110 *"You're allowing yourself"* Sidran, *Talking Jazz*, 234.

111 *"it's a very vocal "* Bob Belden, interview.

111 *"For a sax player"* Ibid.

111 *"I always liked that"* Ravi Coltrane, interview.

111 *"One day I was listening to Percy Heath"* Jimmy Garrison, interview with Herb Nolan, audiocassette, Chicago, 1974.

114 *"The trend I see taking place"* Don DeMicheal, "The Sixth Man," *Down Beat* (March 28, 1963): 17.

115 *"In my first trip to Europe in 1957"* Elvin Jones, quoted in Mike Joyce, "Elvin Jones: Interview," *Cadence* (February 1981): 9.

115 *"The conventional thing"* Elvin Jones, quoted in Herb Nolan, "Rhythmic Pulsemaster," *Down Beat* (December 15, 1977): 13.

115 *"didn't give me any instruction"* Elvin Jones, interview.

115 *"The drummer and horn"* Joyce, "Elvin Jones: Interview."

116 *Like similar melodies from his past recordings* Writer Francis Davis posits a possible source for the structure of "Pursuance" in a review of *A Love Supreme:* "Has anyone ever pointed out . . . that the eight-bar theme subtitled 'Pursuance' . . . borrows its intervals from [Miles's] 'Nardis,' much as 'Impressions' borrowed from Davis's 'So What.' " (Francis Davis, "A Love Supreme," in Keith Shadwick (ed.), *Gramophone Good Jazz CD Guide* [London: B. & W. Press, 1995]: 119.)

116 *"Perhaps my main fault"* Mike Hennessey, "Coltrane: Dropping the Ball and Chain from Jazz," *Melody Maker* (August 14, 1965): 6.

116 *"First, there is his melodic inventiveness"* Nat Hentoff, liner notes to McCoy Tyner LP *Inception,* Impulse A-18, 1962.

116 *"Invariably, in our group"* Ibid.

116 *"He's got the voicings!"* John Coltrane, interview, Gleason.

116 *"Tyner developed a particular type of voicing"* Porter, 177.

116 *"the reason why I may have used fourths"* Sidran, *Talking Jazz*, 234.

117 *"The more I listen"* Ravi Coltrane, interview. John Coltrane was well aware of the engineer's effect, especially of the need to balance fullness of sound with proximity of the microphone: "I've discussed this fault with engineers because the playbacks haven't sounded right," he told Valerie Wilmer in the UK's *Jazz Journal* in January 1962. "They get too close to the horn with the mikes and don't give the sound time to travel as they should. Consequently, they don't get enough of the real timbre and they miss the *whole* body of the sound. They get the inside of it, but not the outside of it as well."

118 *"That's basically the 'Giant Steps' cycle"* Ravi Coltrane, interview. Ravi Coltrane marks the "Giant Steps" cycle as beginning 6:23 into "Pursuance."

119 *"When I worked with John"* Les Tomkins, "Coltrane and I Played Without Preparation," *Crescendo International* 9:3 (1970): 10.

119 *"I was just as content"* Elvin Jones, interview.

119 *"There were certain people"* Dan Morgenstern, interview.

119 *"There was a kind of telepathy between them"* Ibid.

120 *"My broad concern"* Ron Carter, interview, DAT recording, August 11, 2001.

120 *"I like the idea"* Don Heckman, "After Coltrane: Jimmy Garrison," *Down Beat* (March 9, 1967).

121 *"I remember one time"* Mattingly, "Elvin," 27.

121 *"I wasn't so interested in jazz"* Randi Hultin, *Born Under the Sign of Jazz* (London: Sanctuary, 1998): 176.

122 *"I was always taught"* Herb Nolan, "I Play Drums That's Just What I Do," *Down Beat* (November 6, 1973): 18.

122 *"I thought some of the compositions"* Elvin Jones, interview.

122 *"You can pick anything in classical music"* Branford Marsalis, interview.

122 *"Ornette Coleman's 'Lonely Woman' "* Ibid.

123 *"You have your exclamation marks"* Sidran, *Talking Jazz*, 234.

123 *"The fourth and last"* John Coltrane, interview, Delorme and Lenissois.

123 *"I think he was . . . adding on"* Wayne Shorter, interview.

124 *" 'Psalm' is a psalm"* Reggie Workman, interview.

124 *"Somebody hipped me to that"* Branford Marsalis, interview.

124 *"You will find that he"* Porter, 247.

124 *"Elvin Jones indicated to me"* Porter, email to author, October 21, 2001.

124 *"It's the wear"* Bob Belden, interview.

126 *"The saxophone at the end of 'Psalm' "* Rudy Van Gelder, fax to author. Coltrane had employed over-

dubbing in 1963 on the *John Coltrane and Johnny Hartman* album, returning to the studio a few days after to record obbligatos, melodic phrases weaving in and around the vocal line.

126 *"The original saxophone"* Ibid.

127 *"In one sense, it seemed that"* Rick Mattingly, "Elvin Jones: Once More with Feeling," *Modern Drummer* (May 1992): 27.

Rudy Van Gelder

88 *"He had been in other studios"* Rudy Van Gelder, fax to author.

88 *"I used to buy a lot of records"* Phil Ramone, interview, DAT recording, March 8, 2001.

88 *"One of the things we were looking for"* Sidran, *Talking Jazz,* 465.

88 *mythic proportions* Another measure of Van Gelder's reputation is the long list of jazz tunes whose titles refer to his studios. Thelonious Monk's "Hackensack" from 1953 is probably the best-known reference to his first location, while the following saluted his newer studio: Pee Wee Russell's "Englewood" (1960); Jimmy Hamilton's "Route 9W" (1961); Cliff Jackson's "Blues in Englewood" (1961); Duke Pearson's "Ready Rudy?" (1966); Charles Earland's "Blues for Rudy" (1978); Jay McShann's "Rompin' at Rudy's" (1990); Valery Ponomarev's "High Voltage at Rudy's" (1991); and Charles Earland's "I'm Rudy's Blues" (1995). Thanks to Dan Skea.

88 *"Those great Blue Note . . . records"* Joel Dorn, interview.

88 *"meet the demands of the client"*: Rudy Van Gelder, interview, Phil Coady.

88 *"When you were with Rudy"* McCoy Tyner, interview.

88 *"I was examining eyes one day"* Rudy Van Gelder, interview with Bob Clark, October 12, 1996, for book-in-progress *Temples of Sound* (San Francisco: Chronicle Press). Much thanks to Bob and Jim Cogan for sharing their resources.

89 *"The pressure was on me"* Rudy Van Gelder, interview, Coady.

89 *"The reason he came back"* Rudy Van Gelder, interview, Clark.

90 *"He was just a very pleasant person"* Rudy Van Gelder, interview, Coady.

90 *"There was definitely a mutual admiration"* Creed Taylor, interview.

90 *"We all loved him"* McCoy Tyner, interview.

90 *"Well, that room was perfect"* Elvin Jones, interview.

90 *"I made a record there"* Joel Dorn, interview.

90 *"He was secretive"* Tom Dowd, interview.

90 *In a review of a 1957 Thad Jones album* The review of Blue Note's *The Magnificent Thad Jones, Vol. 3* was penned by Charles Robertson, "Jazz and All That," *Audio* (October 1957): 56–57.

91 *"he had a very unique way"* McCoy Tyner, interview.

91 *"Even though Columbia"* Phil Ramone, interview.

91 *"In my estimation"* Ibid.

91 *"It is my wish"* Robertson, "Jazz and All That."

91 *"I really don't like to think of it"* Rudy Van Gelder, interview, Clark.

91 *"What it is"* Chris Hovan, *All About Jazz* website, June 1999.

Chapter 4/December 10, 1964: A Second Try, a Year of Triumph

129 *"lost version"* John Litweiler, *The Freedom Principle: Jazz After 1958* (New York: Da Capo, 1984): 99.

129 *"original version"* Val Wilmer notes that "despite the fact that this was recorded the day following the released version by the regular quartet, it was Coltrane's original intention to play with Shepp and Davis added." Wilmer, *As Serious as Your Life: John Coltrane and Beyond* (London: Serpent's Tail, 1977): 37.

129 *"There's all kinds of stories"* Art Davis, interview.

130 *"I kind of remember that"* McCoy Tyner, interview.

130 *"You know, it's a funny thing"*: Elvin Jones, interview.

130 *"No recollection of that session"* Rudy Van Gelder, interview.

130 *"out of the blue"* Archie Shepp, interview.

131 *"You have what the French call"* Ibid.

131 *"Archie was there"* Art Davis, interview.

131 *"Yes, I was there"* Chuck Stewart, interview, DAT recording, April 20, 2001.

131 *"In those days"* Ibid.

131 *"Each studio has its own photographic sound"* Ibid.

133 *"Someone might say"* Alice Coltrane, interview.

133 *"He was always looking"* Ibid.

133 *"didn't know what was going to happen"* McCoy Tyner, interview.

133 *"It was a complete musical entity"* Elvin Jones, interview.

133 *"I felt daunted"* Archie Shepp, interview.

133 *"At that time"* Ibid.

136 *"As I look back"* Ibid.

136 *"had a small scrap of paper"* Ibid.

136 *"Jimmy was to play the bass notes"* Art Davis, interview.

136 *"Acknowledgement" only* Both Davis and Shepp recall only working on "Acknowledgement." Says the former, "We ran through it at least two times, but that was typical of John, he wanted not to over-record things, he wanted them to be fresh." Shepp adds, "It was all just one solo, unfortunately."

136 *Coltrane solidified* Of course, the concept of two tenors was not new to Coltrane, having recorded with Sonny Rollins, Johnny Griffin, and—at the request of Miles Davis in 1962—Hank Mobley on "Someday My Prince Will Come."

137 *"I had to sort of try to rise to the occasion"* Archie Shepp, interview.

137 *"He always showed an appreciation"* Alice Coltrane, interview.

137 *"Well, I wish I had listened more"* Archie Shepp, interview.

138 *"at first, I thought of this"* Ravi Coltrane, interview.

138 *"I think I was a sort of catalyst"* Archie Shepp, interview.

139 *"Trane's key-hopping"* Ravi Coltrane, interview.

139 *"I call it the two-bass concept"* Art Davis, interview.

139 *"Some of the things"* Archie Shepp, interview.

139 *"lyrical banshee"* Amiri Baraka, liner notes to *Four for Trane,* Impulse AS-71, 1964.

141 *"For both this date"* Ibid.

142 *the group appeared* Porter, 372.

143 *"Well, the first part"* John Coltrane, interview, Grant.

143 *"We talked about that"* Alice Coltrane, interview.

147 *"It's purely a question"* Rudy Van Gelder, interview, Coady.

147 *"This always frightens me"* Mike Hennessey, "Coltrane: Dropping the Ball and Chain from Jazz," *Melody Maker.* (August 14, 1965): 6.

147 *"People like Coltrane, or Duke Ellington"* Palmer, *Coda,* 1971, 32.

148 *"I tried . . . whenever possible to give him"* Kofsky, *Coda,* 1968, 9.

148 *Coltrane decided to use . . . an old black-and-white photograph* Given Thiele's lifelong devotion to Duke Ellington, it was most probably to the Coltrane-Ellington summit that he brought his own camera, arguing that September 26, 1962, would be the date of the *Love Supreme* cover photo. Thiele allowed *Jazz* magazine to use the portrait in an early issue (November–December 1962), and Shaw Artists employed the same image in an advertisement announcing Coltrane's European tour the following year.

149 *"I always get a kick"* Bob Thiele, interview for French TV documentary *Blue Trane,* Philippe Koechlin and Dominique Cazenare (prods.), Canal Plus, 1992.

149 *"Interestingly, there were two"* Alice Coltrane, interview.

149 *black-and-white acrylic portrait* By 1964, illustrator Victor Kalin's prodigious and arresting images—paintings, drawings, photographs—were a common sight on book covers, in magazines, and especially on jazz albums like *Mingus Plays Piano.* According to his widow, Kalin's portrait of Coltrane is based on a photograph Kalin himself took at the Newport Jazz Festival in 1961, an image he then translated to a color watercolor and a woodcut design. The black-and-white portrait he eventually gave to Coltrane; it now hangs in Alice Coltrane's home in California.

150 *a two-page spread in* Billboard February 6, 1965.

150 *"You know, ABC at the time"* "Tell Me How Long Trane's Been Gone," part 4 of 5.

152 *"His records were selling"* Ibid.

152 *Larry Newton reactivated Apt Records* "ABC-Paramount Will Reactivate Apt Label," *Billboard* (January 9, 1965): 3.

152 *ABC introduced a new budget classical label* "ABC-Para's Baroque Series," *Billboard* (January 30, 1965): 10.

152 *"The Big Drive in '65"* "ABC-Para Parley Sets New Mark," *Billboard* (January 30, 1965): 4.

153 *"It was up"* Sid Feller, telephone conversation with author, November 30, 2001.

153 *freelance "hit men"* As discussed at length in Frederic Tannen's book *Hit Men* (New York: Vintage, 1991), the stranglehold that independent promotion wielded in the music business of the late seventies—and to a degree through today—was born in the promotional practices of the fifties and sixties.

153 *"The record promotion guy's job"* Joel Dorn, interview, DAT recording, June 22, 2001. Disarmingly candid, Dorn elaborates on the subject of payola and its influence on jazz deejays: "I played what I wanted to play, because I had a certain style show. See, one of the protections against payola in the old days was, if guys just took money to play records, they'd lose their listenership. And not just in Philly. People are going to listen to the radio station that they like. If you're taking [payola] to play records, and you're not playing music that your audience likes, you've become ineffective. You were your own best cop." (Ibid.)

154 *"[Singer] didn't have to do"* Ibid.

154 *"Coltrane and* A Love Supreme" Chuck Niles, interview, DAT recording, June 11, 2001.

154 *"To the world outside"* Billboard (February 27, 1965): 30.

155 *"I was sort of in the circle"* Wayne Shorter, interview.

155 A Love Supreme *began to appear in stores at the end of February* Intensive research has failed to pinpoint the album's exact release date. The *Schwann Long Playing Record Catalog* of April 1965 affixes "3/65" to its first mention of the title. Judging by the normal two-month lag time for that publication, and the practice of placing advertisements in trade and jazz periodicals right around the time of an album's release, it follows that *A Love Supreme*'s debut fell in late January/early February 1965.

155 *"I used to work a lot for my grandfather"* David S. Ware, interview.

155 *"I was in high school at the time"* Michael Brecker, interview, DAT recording, October 19, 2001.

155 *"I didn't know his voice was so deep"* Tommy Flanagan, interview.

155 *"I fell even more in love"* Frank Foster, interview.

156 *"I think that was a pristine attitude"* Yusef Lateef, interview, DAT recording, June 28, 2001.

156 *"In those days in New York"* Dave Liebman, interview.

156 *"By the time* A Love Supreme *came out"* Patti Smith, email to author.

156 *"He said, 'Heard it?' "* Donald Fagen, interview, tape recording, November 5, 1999.

156 *"Crescent is like a perfect musical portrait"* Frank Lowe, interview.

156 *"Since I was the first person"* Sun Ra, quoted in Jean-Louis Noames, "Visite au Dieu Soleil," *Jazz* (France) (December 1965).

157 *"[After my group] moved to New York"* "Tell Me How Long Trane's Been Gone," part 4 of 5.

157 *"When that album came out"* Pat LaBarbera, interview.

157 *"I had no connection at that point"* Sy Johnson, interview.

158 *"While the religious celebration"* Henry Woodfin, "Coltrane's Progress," *Sounds & Fury* (October 1965): 6–7.

158 *"John Coltrane has made it very difficult"* Joe Goldberg, "A Love Supreme," *HiFi/Stereo Review* (July 1965): 84.

158 *"an enormous musical, emotional,* personal *statement"* John Sinclair, "A Love Supreme," *Jazz* (October 1965): 24–25. Dave Sinclair, brother to John, the Detroit-based activist and band manager famous for his association with the proto-punk group MC5, was himself manager of a group following in MC5's loud-and-angry path: the Up. Members of the Up— which lasted from 1969 to 1973— intermittently performed "Acknowledgement," including the chant, in their shows.

158 *"thoroughly a work of art"*: Don DeMicheal, "Spotlight Review: 'A Love Supreme,'" *Down Beat* (April 8, 1965): 27.

159 *"There were three ways"* Joel Dorn, interview.

159 *"There was a different"* Ibid.

159 *"In 1965"* Ibid.

160 *"When* A Love Supreme *was released"* Archie Shepp, interview.

160 *"I think that's what you hear in that music"* "Tell Me How Long Trane's Been Gone," part 5 of 5.

160 *"Most of the white"* Rick James, interview, DAT recording, December 14, 2001.

160 *"You gotta understand"* Joel Dorn, interview.

161 *"I'm attracted to music that frightens me"* Charles Perry, "Number Five with a Dildo: Steely Dan Comes Up Swinging," *Rolling Stone* (August 15, 1974): 32.

161 *"was assertive, it was strong"* Roger McGuinn, interview, DAT recording, March 8, 2001.

161 *"I did buy* A Love Supreme" Ibid.

161 *"I think [A Love Supreme]"* Ibid. In 1971, Ben Sidran compared the racial strata of the sixties spiritual flowering: "The difference between the Beatles' infatuation with the Maharishi and the spiritual content of Coltrane's music was as enormous as, let's say, the difference between the *verbal* glibness of a young man cut off from his culture, and the *physical* dedication of a mature man who is very much part of his. It is not superficial that the white counter-culture has had to rely so strongly on black culture for its spiritual direction." (*Black Talk*, 149.)

161 *"had pierced into the whole 'flower-child'"* David Murray, interview.

162 *"That's one of the"* Phil Lesh, interview, DAT recording, September 5, 2001.

162 *"I took LSD"* Sam Andrew, interview, DAT recording, June 23, 2001.

162 *Coltrane's extended improvisations* Drummer Michael Shrieve, who played in the first incarnation of the group Santana and tutored Carlos Santana in his appreciation of Miles Davis and John Coltrane, mentions another modal stepping-stone for San Francisco groups that arrived the year after *A Love Supreme.* "Paul Butterfield Blues Band's album *East-West*—the title track—was this long guitar jam that stayed on one Eastern-sounding scale. The sound of that particular piece was the sound of walking into the Fillmore." (Conversation with author, December 6, 2001.)

162 *"What is really amazing"* Carlos Santana, interview.

162 *"I had to be around fifteen"* Bootsy Collins, interview, DAT recording, January 23, 2001.

163 *"It was at this little jive jazz club"* Ibid.

163 *"I remember when"* Maurice White, interview, DAT recording, January 24, 2001.

163 *"I heard him several times in San Francisco"* Terry Riley, interview, DAT recording, October 8, 2001. Riley's fellow minimalist pioneer La Monte Young explains further: "John Coltrane was using what were elements of minimalism in his playing when he would take a fixed constellation of tones and these very interesting mathematical permutations on them . . . He had refined the process because of his exposure to Indian classical music and other Eastern traditions of modalism—you can hear it tied into his blues legacy and brought to a new level of refinement and understanding." (La Monte Young, in *The World According to John Coltrane.*)

165 *"most devoted followers are young listeners"* Leonard Feather, "Coltrane Shaping Musical Revolt," *New York Post* (October 18, 1964): 54.

165 *"I never even"* John Coltrane, ibid.

165 *"He did call every once in a while"* Kofsky, *Coda,* 10.

165 *"Eventually . . . the listeners"* Feather, "Coltrane Shaping Musical Revolt."

Poetry and Prayer

144 *"He was baring"* Elvin Jones, interview.

144 *"I think it was an instinctual . . . conviction"* Nat Hentoff, interview.

144 *"I'd call him up and say"* Ibid.

144 *"It's awfully hard to get words"* Ibid.

144 *well-established liner-note option* The question of just how far back musician-penned liner notes can be traced generated a flurry of discussion on Yahoo!'s jazz research group. Precedents of musicians explaining their own music were offered from the early sixties (Jackie McLean, Charles Mingus), the fifties (Gerry Mulligan, Jon Hendricks, Teddy Charles, Paul Desmond), and as far back as the era of 78s (Dave Brubeck).

145 *biblical terminology* By spiritual confluence, 1965 offered another example of popular music derived from Scripture. In November, the Byrds' "Turn, Turn, Turn"—borrowing lyrics from the Book of Ecclesiastes—went to number 1.

145 *"He is gracious and merciful"* Other biblical references to a merciful and gracious God: 2 Chronicles 30:9; Nehemiah 9:17; Psalms 103:8 and 116:5.

145 *"May I be acceptable in Thy sight"* Reggae enthusiasts will recognize Psalm 19, as well as Psalm 137, as having inspired the lyrics to the well-known tune "Rivers of Babylon" by the Melodians.

145 *"I remember her telling me"* Bobby Timmons, quoted by J. C. Thomas, *Chasin' the Trane* (New York: Da Capo, 1975): 186.

145 *In 1891* Henry Drummond, *The Greatest Thing in the World: Love: The Supreme Gift* (New York: Fleming H. Revell and Company, 1891).

146 *"a number of people"* Feather, "Coltrane Shaping Musical Revolt."

146 *"[They] did affect how I listened"* Joshua Redman, interview.

Suite by the Sea

166 *"If I went into a nightclub"* Don DeMicheal, "The Responsibilities of Success: Cannonball Adderley," *Down Beat* (June 21, 1962): 15.

166 *So why slight* Interestingly, an April 2, 1965, broadcast on WABC-FM from the Half Note includes announcer Alan Grant commenting, "By the way, his album is out now on Impulse—*A Love Supreme* . . . I would suggest that you make it your business to buy it." Then, Coltrane performs two familiar covers—"Afro Blue" and "I Want to Talk About You"—rather than anything from the suite. Hats off to Chris DeVito for the tip on—and copy of—this tape.

166 *"The Trane who was into the major . . . composition"* A. B. Spellman, heard on "Tell Me How Long Trane's Been Gone," part 4 of 5.

166 *"I think that"* Ravi Coltrane, interview.

166 *"Now there was a time"* John Coltrane, interview with Frank Kofsky, August 1966; reprinted in Pauline Rivelli and Robert Levin (eds.), *The Black Giants* (New York: World, 1970): 27.

166 *In 1960* The history of the Antibes Jazz Festival—one of the world's longest-running—was drawn from off-tape tales told (and reconfirmed) by many of those who were there from the outset: photographer Jean-Pierre Leloir, journalist Michel Delorme, broadcaster/emcee André Francis, and promoter/publisher Frank Tenot. The year-by-year list of artists who performed there is inserted in the festival's annual program.

167 *"I was the MC"* André Francis, interview, DAT recording, July 7, 2001. Massive thanks to Laurent Masson for assistance; translation by Jonathan Matz.

167 *"It was a little chilly at that time"* McCoy Tyner, interview.

168 *"None of us"* Elvin Jones, interview.

168 *Jef Gilson* "Jef Gilson" is the anglicized name adopted by pianist/arranger Jean-François Quiévreux, whose long career has largely kept him to his native country. He has written on jazz for decades, played with many touring and transplanted Americans (Steve Lacy, for example), and generations of French jazz players have passed through his groups, including violinist Jean-Luc Ponty.

168 *"When I finished"* Jef Gilson, interview, DAT recording, August 7, 2001.

168 "A Love Supreme *was my idea*" Ibid.

168 *"People didn't request suites that much"* Elvin Jones, interview.

168 *"I think that it's because Coltrane"* André Francis, interview.

168 *"The material really wasn't the challenge"* McCoy Tyner, interview.

168 *"That part of the Riviera"* Elvin Jones, interview.

169 *"He played only forty-eight minutes"* Michel Delorme, interview, DAT recording, July 14, 2001.

169 *"I opened my mouth"* Michel Delorme, interview.

170 *"You can feel the creative tension"* Dave Liebman, interview.

170 *"That's a very, very fast tempo"* Branford Marsalis, interview.

170 *"solo number 527"* Andrew White, interview, DAT recording, April 19, 2001.

171 *"A third of the audience"* Michel Delorme, interview.

171 *"You really had to be there"* Arrigo Polillo, "Successo a Juan-les-Pins," *Musica Jazz* (Italy) (October 1965): 15. Translation by Andrew B. Caploe.

171 *"His playing has developed"* Randi Hultin, "Coltrane det store trekkplasteret i Antibes," *Dagbladet* (Norway) (July 30, 1965). Translation by Wivi-Ann Wells.

171 *"the audience were a little puzzled"* Hennessey, *Melody Maker.*

171 *"The minority"* Marcel Carles, "Festival Antibes 65," *Aria Jazz* (Spain) (October 1965): 12. Translation by Maria Alford.

171 *"The audience who left the Pinède Gould"* Michel Delorme, "A Love Supreme," *Jazz Hot* (France) (June 1966): 29.

172 *"That's my boy . . ."* Michel Delorme, interview.

172 *performed more familiar material* On Tuesday, July 27, Coltrane also performed a tune alternately credited as "Blue Valse" and "Blue Waltz"; according to Delorme and other Coltrane scholars, it is actually a quartet version of "Ascension."

172 *Decades later* Coltrane's sole live rendering of *A Love Supreme* now survives in the memories of the lucky few in attendance and—fortunately—on tapes buried in the deep, sepulchral archives of France's National Audiovisual Institute (INA) in Paris, where they have acquired a mythic prestige. Though the audio recording has been released in a variety of formats on a variety of European labels, it has only now seen legitimate release in America courtesy of the Verve Music Group.

Long rumored yet rarely seen, the video recording has never been released publicly in any country; in fact, assiduous research hints that the original videotape is lost. Yet somehow, from some source, a number of multigenerational copies exist that include a mere twelve minutes of the total performance, cutting off midway through Tyner's "Resolution" solo. Frustrating, yes, but the cassettes do offer an exciting—if wavy and distorted—memento of a special evening in 1965.

INA's records do not reflect any videotape of the live performance of *A Love Supreme* currently existing in their archives. The assumption is that Jean-Christophe Averty—the director who oversaw many of the TV tapings at Antibes, and who was a fan of neither Coltrane nor modern jazz in general—kept his own copy, from which a few other copies were struck. It is also assumed that the original video recording was, sadly, erased for reuse.

172 *"I saw so many performances"* André Francis, interview.

172 *"I was just so shocked"* Michel Delorme, interview.

172 *"I remember it was a very exciting . . . performance"* McCoy Tyner, interview.

172 *"I did not play as I wanted last night"* Hultin, *Dagbladet.*

172 *"I want to get to a point"* Hennessey, *Melody Maker.*

Chapter 5/Avant-Garde, a Force for Good

175 *"Every time I talk about jazz"* Joe Goldberg, *Jazz Masters of the 50s* (New York: Da Capo, 1965): 212.

176 *"Suite" . . . First Meditations Recorded* on June 10, 1965, "Suite" was eventually released on the album *Transition* in 1970. *First Meditations,* recorded on September 2, 1965, featured the quartet, and was not released until 1977; *Meditations* was recorded on November 23 with the quartet plus Pharoah Sanders and Rashied Ali, and was released in late 1966.

176 *"Once you become aware of this force for unity"* Nat Hentoff, liner notes to *Meditations,* Impulse A-9110.

176 *"From A Love Supreme onward"* Alice Coltrane, in *The World According to John Coltrane.*

176 *"This was before I was working"* Pharoah Sanders, interview, DAT recording, October 12, 2001.

177 *"He was just very quiet and concentrated"* John Tchicai, interview, Phil Coady, 1995, for *Blue Train* enhanced CD.

177 *"I was so doggone busy"* John Coltrane, interview, Kofsky.

178 *"I had an ego bigger than this building"* Porter, 269.

179 *"I figured I could do two things"* John Coltrane interview, Kofsky.

179 *"I felt if I was going to go any further musically"* Len Lyons, *The Great Jazz Pianists* (New York: Da Capo, 1983): 239.

179 *"I think that I was. I don't think he was"* Mike Joyce, *Cadence,* 10.

180 *two Grammys* On March 15, 1966, *A Love Supreme* was passed over for both the Best Original Jazz Composition (won by Lalo Schifrin's *Jazz Suite on the Mass Texts*) and Best Jazz Performance, Small Group or Soloist with Small Group (garnered by the Ramsey Lewis Trio for *The "In" Crowd*). (William Ruhlmann, "Going to Extremes: John Coltrane on Record," *Goldmine* [June 23, 1995]: 42.)

180 *"Gold before it went gold"* Archie Shepp, interview. Producer Ed Michel, who succeeded Bob Thiele at Impulse, reports the same story: "In the late sixties, there was a gold record of *A Love Supreme* up on the wall in the ABC corporate offices, which doesn't mean at all that at that point the album had in fact sold enough copies to be granted a gold record. (Ed Michel, interview, DAT recording, June 24, 2001.)

180 *"That was really cataclysmic to me"* Dave Liebman, interview.

181 *"I recall the last part of the first half "* Ibid.

181 *"massive and startling"* John S. Wilson, "Jazz and the Anarchy of the Avant-Garde," *New York Times* (April 24, 1966).

181 *"was the torch that lit the free-jazz thing"* Dave Liebman, interview.

182 *"The main complaint"* Frank Foster, interview.

182 *"sound was changing dramatically"* Porter, 276–77.

183 *"one of the great drummers"* Nat Hentoff, liner notes to *Live at the Village Vanguard Again!,* Impulse AS-9124, 1967.

183 *"You can get almost as avant-garde as you want"* David S. Ware, interview.

183 "*the right colors*" Hentoff, liner notes to *Live at the Village Vanguard Again!*

183 "*human foundations of music*" Ibid.

183 "*This music . . . opens up*" Don DeMicheal, "Double Review: Trane's Mediatations," *Down Beat* (December 1, 1966): 28.

183 "*A caveat for the casual*" A. B. Spellman, liner notes to *Ascension*, Impulse A-95, 1965.

183 "*Listening to Coltrane*" Nat Hentoff, liner notes to *Kulu Se Mama*, Impulse A-9106, 1966.

183 "*It was certainly through Coltrane*" Kofsky, *Coda*, 6.

184 "*Let me make the necessary observation*" Nat Hentoff, liner notes to Pharoah Sanders, *Tauhid*, Impulse AS-9138, 1967.

184 "*I must say that you can't*" Cannonball Adderley, interview with Jack Winter, tape recording, KCFR-FM, Denver, 1972.

184 "The term '*free*' *was often a euphemism*" Archie Shepp, interview.

184 "*I think you'll find that the spirituality*" Robert Palmer, liner notes to Albert Ayler, *Live in Greenwich Village/The Complete Impulse! Recordings*, Impulse IMPD-2-273, 1978, 11.

184 "*It changed the whole scene*" Sidran, *Talking Jazz*, 413.

184 *Newsweek devoted a six-page study* "The New Jazz," *Newsweek* (December 12, 1966): 101–8.

185 "*You couldn't help but pick up on it*" Frank Lowe, interview.

185 "*It was a documentary*" Ibid.

185 "*Their predecessors*" Nat Hentoff, "The Jazz Revolution," *The Reporter,* May 20, 1965.

186 "*the audience and manager*" Porter, 275. Sonny Fortune has spoken of the same engagement and how he "was supposed to work with [Coltrane] in Newark, but the cat fired him first. I remember him telling me why himself—it was because the first night the place was packed, but after the first set the people kind of emptied the place and the owner couldn't understand why." (Bret Primack, "John Coltrane: A 65th Birthday Salute," *Jazz Times* [October 1991]: 35.)

186 "*Davis and Coltrane became giants*" Ben Sidran, *Black Talk,* (New York: Da Capo, 1971): 134.

186 "*It was like, boom!*" Frank Lowe, interview.

186 "*Sure, it was black music*" Ibid.

187 "*I lived on Sterling Place*" Cecil Payne, interview, DAT recording, June 13, 2001. Other jazz luminaries in that section of Brooklyn included Betty Carter and Carmen McRae, while many bars and clubs offered live jazz on a regular basis, including the Kingston Lounge, Brownie's Lounge, and the Blue Cornet, where Coltrane appeared intermittently.

187 "*I was at the house*" Curtis Fuller, interview.

187 "*In 1965–66, I was president of the PTA*" Earl Toliver, interview, DAT recording, June 15, 2001.

Toliver was also a pioneering black TV editor who became vice president of community relations at New York's Fox affiliate, Channel 5.

187 "*When the change came*" Ibid.

187 "*There was a lot of turmoil in the church*" Ibid. Toliver maintains that a local, but particularly active, community group was behind the disruptions, pushing for both involvement and monetary support from the church for various activities. Other, still-active church leaders, parents, and teachers confirm the unrest.

188 "*My father wanted to build a playground*" Zane Massey, interview.

188 "*It was not really publicized*" Earl Toliver, interview.

189 "*I remember it was pleasant*": James Dobson, interview, DAT recording, June 15, 2001.

189 "*The hall contained room*" Alice Coltrane, fax to author, August 3, 2001.

189 "*It was a hot day*" Earl Toliver, interview.

189 "*I think this was*" Ibid.

189 "*It was a whole afternoon of jazz*" Zane Massey, interview.

189 "*We were the only whites*" Daniel Berger, email to author, September 23, 2001.

189 "*They were just regular people*" Cecil Payne, interview.

190 "*He wanted to set up a place*" Kofsky, *Coda*, 8.

190 "*John made his own decision*" Alice Coltrane, fax to author.

190 "*I was very close to the front*" Zane Massey, interview.

191 "*When Trane came on*" Ibid.

191 "*spinet in good condition*" Alice Coltrane, fax to author.

191 "*I remember they just got up there and played*" Zane Massey, interview.

191 "*I remember at one point*" Ibid.

191 "*Coltrane was indeed reading a piece of paper*" Daniel Berger, email to author.

191 "*John did not perform the entire suite*" Alice Coltrane, fax to author.

191 "*The band was playing*" Zane Massey, interview. Berger's brief report on the church affair in France's *Jazz Hot* magazine (no. 234, August–September 1967, 5; translated in Porter, 275) claimed that Coltrane's performance began with the poem-reading, and silence accompanied it. When asked to confirm this, he responded, "It is possible that [the] audience chanted." (Daniel Berger, email to author.)

192 "*After having heard Ascension*" Natasha Arnoldi, email to author, September 23, 2001.

192 "*It was sort of melodic*" Earl Toliver, interview.

192 "*John spoke highly*" Alice Coltrane, fax to author.

192 "*I had to meet him*" James Dobson, interview.

192 "*I remember after the performance*" Daniel Berger, email to author.

192 "After the concert" Zane Massey, interview.

192 "The pastor [Thomas Haggerty]" Cecil Payne, interview.

192 "The playground was built" Zane Massey, interview.

192 "I want to be a force for real good" John Coltrane, interview, Kofsky.

192 "I want to discover a method" John Coltrane, interview, Jean Clouzet and Michel Delorme "Entretien avec John Coltrane," *Les Cahiers du Jazz* (France) (August 1963). Translation by Jonathan Matz.

193 "To speculate on why A Love Supreme" Alice Coltrane, fax to author.

Chapter 6/The Unbroken Arc of A Love Supreme

195 "I'll never forget that day" Zane Massey, interview.

195 "It was very loud so I came downstairs" Ibid.

196 [Albert] Ayler "Coltrane Is Given a Jazzman's Funeral Here," *New York Times* (July 22, 1967). Descriptions of this event are culled from this article, from Porter, and from conversations with various attendees. Though some contest that the *New York Times* reporter was in error citing "Truth Is Marching" (presumably "The Battle Hymn of the Republic") as being performed by Albert Ayler's group—he does indeed perform a different number on the French radio broadcast of the funeral ("Our Prayer" per Yasuhiro Fujioka, 301)—there was certainly ample time for the performance of other tunes.

196 Nine Coltrane LPs At the time of his death, Coltrane was aware of at least ten new titles (nine released, one on the way) since *A Love Supreme*: six on Impulse (*Quartet Plays . . . , Ascension, Kulu Se Mama, New Thing at Newport, Meditations*—with plans completed for *Expressions*); three on Prestige (*Bahia, Last Trane,* and *Plays for Lovers*); and one on Atlantic (*The Avant-Garde*).

196 "Instead of a eulogy, Mr. Coltrane's friend" "Coltrane Is Given a Jazzman's Funeral Here," *New York Times.*

196 "May we never forget" Ibid.

197 "the tone of the tenor" Wayne Shorter, interview.

197 "that he just had to get himself right with God" Frank Foster, interview.

197 clutching his side, and even secluding himself Porter, 289–91.

197 "at that time, he was trying to lose weight" Pharoah Sanders, interview.

197 "[with] all the energy of 125th Street" Lynda Rosen Obst (ed.), *The Sixties* (New York: Random House/Rolling Stone Press, 1977): 219–20.

198 "I have a feeling that he might have" Primack, *Jazz Times,* 35.

198 "There is never any end" Nat Hentoff, liner notes to *Meditations.*

198 "People could not follow that music" Dave Liebman, interview.

198 "Once I was standing against the wall" Charles Lloyd, liner notes to John Coltrane, *The Heavyweight Champion: The Complete Atlantic Recordings.*

199 "A Love Supreme is a very profound and special thing" Ravi Coltrane, interview.

200 "No matter what instrument" Ibid.

200 "Old Man Moses" More thanks to Mike Fitzgerald, and to the members of the Yahoo! jazz research group. Special credit to Robin D. G. Kelley for the reminder of ". . . And Then He Wrote Meditations" (produced by—who else?—Bob Thiele).

202 Even the simple three-word phrase The various albums sharing titular references are by John Handy and Dissidenten (worldbeat, the former's *Karuna Supreme* featuring Indian virtuosi Ali Akhbar Khan and Zakir Hussain); Diana Ross and Chante Moore (soul and R&B); Sonik Boom of Love (rap) and Gun Club (psychobilly). The 12" techno and house singles from Europe are by England's Ballistic Brothers, Dutch deejay Mellowman, and Finland's JS-16. The British fanzine cheers the Sunderland AFC.

202 "I was on the other side of the coin" Ravi Coltrane, interview.

202 Kenny G digitally inserting his soprano sax Guitarist Pat Metheny's online blasting of Kenny G launched a thousand emails in June of 2000. It should be noted that Alice Coltrane herself once faced similar charges when she overdubbed strings, percussion, and harp onto a Coltrane quartet recording, released as *Infinity* (Impulse 9225) in 1972. An interesting discussion on her motivations can be found in Edwin Pouncey, "Enduring Love: Alice Coltrane," *The Wire* (April 2002): 40.

202 "I was very intimidated" Frank Foster, interview.

203 "If I were going to do something of Coltrane's" David S. Ware, interview.

203 "It's an issue not of music" Branford Marsalis, interview.

203 "It's like any other music out there" David Murray, interview.

203 Few approach any of his Impulse material "Impressions" was also recorded live in 1967 by bassist Ike Isaacs and the Jazz Crusaders, while Jack DeJohnette recorded "Miles' Made" in '68 and Tony Williams covered "Big Nick" in '70. But Coltrane's Impulse catalog was largely uninterpreted until the seventies.

204 propelled by drummer Michael Shrieve When asked of this recording, Shrieve recalls "It was a humility thing—I definitely felt unworthy." McLaughlin's motivating response: "If not you, who?"

204 "It was, for all intents and purposes" John McLaughlin, email to author.

204 "If I did do it" Carlos Santana, interview.

205 *Santana and McLaughlin* Both guitarists carried their love of Coltrane's signature album well into their respective careers. In 1978, *Rolling Stone* magazine described McLaughlin and his band, pre-rehearsal, "gathering in a circle in the middle of their collection of amplifiers, synthesizers, drums, gongs, and other equipment . . . [reading] together from 'A Love Supreme,' the inspirational poem John Coltrane wrote." (Robert Palmer, "McLaughlin's Return to Electric," *Rolling Stone* [July 13, 1978]. Percussionist Hal Miller, a longtime friend of Santana's, writes: "To this day, Carlos often performs the 'a love supreme' chant of 'Acknowledgement' in his concerts, usually as a tag and/or add-on to another song, and the cap you will most likely see him wearing these days has 'A Love Supreme' (or 'Peace On Earth') emblazoned on it." (Hal Miller, email to author, January 28, 2002.)

205 *"I remember in San Francisco"* Pat LaBarbera, interview.

205 *"I wish I had stuck to my guns"* Frank Foster, interview.

205 *"We played it quite a bit in clubs"* Pat LaBarbera, interview.

205 *A few recordings of their performances* Recent CD versions of the Elvin Jones Quintet performing material from *A Love Supreme*—with Foster and LaBarbera—include *Very Rare*, Evidence ECD 22053-2 (from Tokyo in 1978); and *Live at the Village Vanguard, Volume 1*, Landmark LCD-1534-2 (from 1984).

205 *Andrew Cyrille* Cyrille's CD *Ode to the Living Tree*, Evidence ECD 22185-2, 1995, includes this performance.

206 *"When you go to a gig"* Ravi Coltrane, interview.

206 *When performed by Wynton* The Japanese club recording of *A Love Supreme* was released as *Elvin Jones "Special Quartet,"* SRCS 7376, by Sony Music in Japan in 1994; the broadcast by National Public Radio of a 1994 Lincoln Center performance took place in 1995.

207 *"You don't try to play"* Wynton Marsalis, interview, Howard Mandel, August 1994, for NPR's "Jazz at Lincoln Center: A Love Supreme," Murray Street Productions, 1995.

207 *"I always live in the hope"* Elvin Jones, interview, Mandel.

207 *Consider the past few years in New York* To avoid any charge of Apple-centrism, another tribute of note to add would be the carefully orchestrated 1987 performance of "Acknowledgement" at London's Fairfield Hall, featuring Sonny Fortune, Freddie Hubbard, McCoy Tyner, and Elvin Jones.

208 *"I still play* A Love Supreme" Pat LaBarbera, interview.

208 *"We were sitting at the [Village] Vanguard"* Branford Marsalis, interview.

208 *"I just try to evoke the mood"* Ibid.

208 *"That's* Coltrane's *prayer"* Wynton Marsalis, interview with Howard Mandel, *Jazz from Lincoln Center.*

209 *"I didn't have any spiritual trepidation"* Branford Marsalis, interview.

209 *"The young players coming in today"* Charles Tolliver, interview, DAT recording, September 25, 2001.

209 *"A Love Supreme is one of my favorite albums"* Kenny Garrett, interview, DAT recording, September 7, 2001.

209 *"I probably know all those solos by heart"* Michael Brecker, interview.

209 *"That quartet—they were so professional"* Dave Liebman, interview.

210 *"What stays with me"* Ibid.

210 *"was one of the first composed records"* Joe Lovano, interview.

210 *"He was the first, really"* Archie Shepp, interview.

210 *"At the time, guys like Miles dismissed us as bullshitters"* Ibid.

211 *"There's one song [on Pursuance]"* Kenny Garrett, interview.

211 *"If one chooses to emulate others"* Yusef Lateef, interview.

211 *"When I hear a musician"* Branford Marsalis, interview.

211 *"I actually had to stop listening"* Joshua Redman, interview.

211 *"I waited a long time to get to Trane"* David Murray, interview.

212 *"I had to stop listening to some Coltrane records"* Frank Lowe, interview.

212 *"I don't want it to sound so utilitarian"* Joshua Redman, interview.

212 *"I can't say why it is so popular"* Patti Smith, email to author.

212 *"How to praise God and be honest?"* Bono, email to author.

213 *"We have this piece 'Alap'* " Ravi Shankar, interview.

213 *"The emotional reaction is all that matters"* Leonard Feather, "Coltrane Shaping Musical Revolt."

Persistence of a Label

214 *"an orphan child"* Esmond Edwards, interview, DAT recording, October 1, 2001.

214 *"Impulse had a fairly sizable catalog"* Ed Michel, interview.

214 *"Impulse was absolutely"* Ibid.

214 *continuing release of unissued material* "People like Coltrane or Duke Ellington recorded so much, they almost forgot about what was recorded," Bob Thiele stated in 1971. "It literally piled up." (Bob Thiele, interview, *Coda*, 1971, 32.) Coltrane left behind music—studio recordings, live performances—that have kept the inheritors of the Impulse

catalog busy to this day. At times—such as the recent *Olatunji Concert* album—labels will license private recordings to add to their ever expanding catalog.

214 *"Steve Backer is one of the great promotion men"* Ibid.

214 *"Jay Lasker was an old-school tough guy"* Steve Backer, interview, DAT recording, September 6, 2001.

214 *"It was quite a successful period"* Ibid.

214 *"People weren't running around"* Esmond Edwards, interview.

215 *"When I first went"* Michael Cuscuna, interview. Cuscuna explained the fate of Impulse's Coltrane master tapes: "Coltrane used to record often, and a lot of the session tapes piled up at Rudy's. When he died, Thiele collected all the tapes and took them back to ABC, supposedly making copies for Alice. Some session reels survive: for instance, the actual outtake reels from '65 [from the sessions for *Coltrane Quartet Plays . . . , Transition,* and others]. But other session tapes didn't. I don't know whether they were just thrown away to make space in a warehouse somewhere, or whether they were mislaid. I would guess that they weren't stolen, because they would've surfaced in the European bootlegs if they had been."

As it turned out, Thiele had sat on a number of safety (simultaneous backup) reels from 1962, eventually donating them in the nineties to the library of the Lawrenceville School in New Jersey (his high school alma mater), which in turn bequeathed them to the Institute of Jazz Studies at Rutgers University. In 2000, Dan Morgenstern, head of the IJS, discovered them to be session recordings from the dates that generated *Ballads* and *Coltrane,* and returned the five reels to the Verve Music Group. Verve Music released these session tapes in April 2002.

215 *"I'm ninety-nine percent sure"* Ibid. Verve engineer Erick Labson agrees with Cuscuna's theory: "I was told by our vault master that ABC used to make decisions back then to discard the original master because they had a released version available. I found that to be the case with many albums, including *A Love Supreme.*"

215 *"On the latest edition"* Ibid.

216 *"a small audience"* Ibid.

216 *"It can range"* Michael Kauffman, interview, DAT recording, October 16, 2001.

216 *"We initiated what we call"* Ibid. The remaining four of Verve's "Desert Island Discs" are Tom Jobim's *The Composer Plays, Sarah Vaughan with Clifford Brown,* Dinah Washington's *What a Difference a Day Makes,* and *Ella in Berlin.*

216 *"You'd think it would've gone gold"* Ibid.

217 *"It's always been"* Ken Druker, conversation with author, October 15, 2001.

217 *"In the best way possible"* Ron Goldstein, email to author, 2001.

217 *All previous digital* Michael Cuscuna, liner notes, *A Love Supreme (Deluxe Edition),* Impulse 314-589-945-2, 2002.

217 *This tape preserves* Ibid.

217 *"With anything that was recorded"* Michael Cuscuna, interview.

217 *"That is the best source"* Ed Michel, interview.

Epilogue: "Opening the Doors"

219 *"It's a love affair"* Herb Nolan, "Jimmy Garrison: Bassist in the Front Line," *Down Beat* (June 6, 1974): 19.

219 *the 1991 album* Thiele had previously recruited Murray in 1988 as a lead voice on the Grammy-winning *Blues for Coltrane* when he briefly worked with a revived version of Impulse. To date, it's one of the most satisfying of many Coltrane tribute albums, featuring Murray alongside Pharoah Sanders, McCoy Tyner, Cecil McBee, and Roy Haynes.

220 *"Even to this day"* "Tell Me How Long Trane's Been Gone," part 2 of 5.

220 *"He was one of the great hobbyists"* Bob Golden, interview.

220 *"A lot of guys came after me"* Ravi Coltrane, interview.

220 *"The LP has disappeared altogether"* Rudy Van Gelder, interview, Phil Coady.

221 *"I can't listen, really"* Ibid.

221 *"[I'm] proud of my association"* McCoy Tyner, interview, *Talking Jazz,* 230.

221 *"What I think is that people"* Jones, Mattingly, "Elvin," 46.

222 *"I always like* Crescent*"* Elvin Jones, interview.

222 *"A Love Supreme and* Crescent *were the ones"* Roberta Garrison, interview, DAT recording, August 2, 2001.

222 *"I think* A Love Supreme*"* James Rozzi, "Bob Thiele: Once Again Flying Dutch," *Coda* (September–October 1992): 14.

222 *"I remember very definitely"* Bob Thiele, *Coda,* 1968, 9.

222 *"I don't voice opinions"* John Coltrane, interview, Gleason.

222 *"I don't know. I'll tell you this though"* John Coltrane, interview with Kiyoshi Koyama, Tokyo, July 9, 1966.

222 *"I'm much better in the mornings"* Mary Alexander, interview. The remainder of Mrs. Alexander's quotes derive from this telephone conversation.

224 *"That he continues to progress"* Joe Goldberg, *Jazz Masters of the 50s* (New York: Da Capo, 1965): 190.

Bibliography

Books

Balliett, Whitney. *Such Sweet Thunder.* Indianapolis: Bobbs-Merrill, 1966.

———. *Collected Works.* New York: St. Martin's, 2000.

———. *American Musicians II: Seventy-One Portraits in Jazz.* New York: Oxford University Press, 1986.

Cook, Richard, and Brian Morton. *The Penguin Guide to Jazz on CD.* New York: Penguin, 1998.

Crow, Bill. *Jazz Anecdotes.* New York: Oxford University Press, 1990.

Davis, Francis. *Like Young: Jazz, Pop, Youth and Middle Age.* New York: Da Capo, 2001.

Davis, Miles, with Quincy Troupe. *Miles: The Autobiography.* New York: Simon & Schuster, 1989.

Duckworth, William. *Talking Music: Conversations with John Cage, Philip Glass, Laurie Anderson and Five Generations of American Experimental Composers.* New York: Schirmer, 1995.

Erlewine, Michael, et al., eds. *All Music Guide to Jazz.* San Francisco: Miller Freeman, 1998.

Fox, Ted. *In the Groove: The People Behind the Music.* New York: St. Martin's, 1986.

Fujioka, Yasuhiro, et al. *John Coltrane: A Discography and Musical Biography (Studies in Jazz; No. 20).* London: Scarecrow, 1993.

Giddins, Gary. *Visions of Jazz.* New York: Oxford University Press, 1998.

Gleason, Ralph J. *Celebrating the Duke: And Louis, Bessie, Billie, Bird, Carmen, Miles, Dizzy and Other Heroes.* New York: Da Capo, 1995.

Goldberg, Joe. *Jazz Masters of the 50s.* New York: Da Capo, 1965.

Hentoff, Nat. *The Jazz Life.* New York: Da Capo, 1961.

Hentoff, Nat, and Albert J. McCarthy, eds. *Jazz.* New York: Da Capo, 1959.

Hultin, Randi. *Born Under the Sign of Jazz.* London: Sanctuary, 1998.

Jones, Leroi (Amiri Imamu Baraka). *Black Music.* New York: Da Capo, 1998.

———. *Blues People.* New York: Morrow Quill Paperbacks, 1963.

Jost, Ekkehard. *Free Jazz.* New York: Da Capo, 1994.

Kahn, Ashley. *Kind of Blue: The Making of the Miles Davis Masterpiece.* New York: Da Capo, 2000.

Keepnews, Orrin. *The View from Within: Jazz Writings, 1948–1987.* New York: Oxford University Press, 1988.

Kirchner, Bill, ed. *A Miles Davis Reader.* Washington, D.C.: Smithsonian Institution Press, 1997.

Kofsky, Frank. *Black Nationalism and the Revolution in Music.* New York: Pathfinder, 1970.

Litweiler, John. *The Freedom Principle: Jazz After 1958.* New York: Da Capo, 1984.

Lyons, Len. *The Great Jazz Pianists.* New York: Da Capo, 1983.

Obst, Lynda Rosen, ed. *The Sixties.* New York: Random House/Rolling Stone Press, 1977.

Porter, Lewis. *John Coltrane: His Life and Music.* Ann Arbor: University of Michigan Press, 1998.

Reder, Alan, and John Baxter, eds. *Listen to This!: Leading Musicians Recommend Their Favorite Recordings.* New York: Hyperion, 1999.

Rivelli, Pauline, and Robert Levin, eds. *The Black Giants.* New York: World, 1970.

Rolling Stone Raves: What Your Rock & Roll Favorites Favor. New York: Rolling Stone Press, 1999.

Rosenthal, David. *Hard Bop: Jazz and Black Music, 1955–1965.* New York: Oxford University Press, 1992.

Shadwick, Keith, ed. *Gramaphone Good Jazz Guide.* London: B. & W. Press, 1995.

Shipton, Alyn. *A New History of Jazz.* London: Continuum, 2001.

Sidran, Ben. *Black Talk.* New York: Da Capo, 1971.

———. *Talking Jazz: An Oral History.* New York: Da Capo, 1995.

Snitzer, Herb. *Jazz: A Visual Journey.* Clearwater, Fla.: Notables Inc., 1999.

Tannen, Frederic. *Hit Men.* New York: Vintage, 1991.

Taylor, Arthur. *Notes and Tones: Musician-to-Musician Interviews.* New York: Da Capo, 1993.

Thiele, Bob. *What a Wonderful World: A Lifetime of Recordings.* New York: Oxford University Press, 1995.

Thomas, J. C. *Chasin' the Trane: The Music and Mystique of John Coltrane.* New York: Da Capo, 1975.

Vail, Ken. *Miles' Diary: The Life of Miles Davis, 1947–1961.* London: Sanctuary, 1996.

Walser, Robert, ed. *Keeping Time: Readings in Jazz History.* New York: Oxford University Press, 1999.

Williams, Martin. *Jazz Masters in Transition, 1957–1969.* New York: Da Capo, 1970.

———. *The Jazz Tradition.* New York: Oxford University Press, 1970.

Williams, Martin, ed. *Jazz Panorama: From the Pages of* The Jazz Review. New York: Crowell-Collier, 1962.

Wilmer, Val. *As Serious as Your Life: John Coltrane and Beyond.* London: Serpent's Tail, 1977.

———. *Mama Said There'd Be Days Like This.* London: Women's Press, 1989.

Woideck, Carl, ed. *The John Coltrane Companion: Five Decades of Commentary.* New York: Simon & Schuster, 1998.

Articles

Coltrane (Contemporaneous)

Clouzet, Jean, and Michel Delorme. "Entretien avec John Coltrane." *Les Cahiers du Jazz* (France) (August 1963).

Coleman, Ray. "Coltrane: Next Thing for Me—African Rhythms." *Melody Maker* (July 11, 1964): 6.

Coltrane, John. "Coltrane on Coltrane." *Down Beat* (September 29, 1960): 26–27.

Dargenpierre, Jean-Claude. "John Coltrane: Un Faust moderne." *Jazz* (France) (January 1962): 24. Translated in Porter, 191.

Dawbarn, Bob. "I'd Like to Play Your Clubs." *Melody Maker* (November 25, 1961): 8.

Delorme, Michel, and Claude Lenissois. "Je ne peux pas aller plus loin." *Jazz Hot* (France) (September 1965).

DeMicheal, Don. "John Coltrane and Eric Dolphy Answer the Jazz Critics." *Down Beat* (April 12, 1962): 20–23.

———. "The Monterey Festival." *Down Beat* (November 9, 1961): 13.

Feather, Leonard. "Coltrane Shaping Musical Revolt." *New York Post* (October 18, 1964): 54.

———. "Feather's Nest." *Down Beat* (February 15, 1962): 17.

———. "For Coltrane the Time Is Now." *Melody Maker* (December 19, 1964): 10.

"Finally Made." *Newsweek* (July 24, 1961): 64.

Gardner, Barbara. "John Coltrane." *Down Beat* (Music 1962—year-end issue).

Gitler, Ira. "'Trane on the Track." *Down Beat* (October 16, 1958): 16–17.

Gitler, Ira, and Pete Welding. "Double View of Coltrane 'Live.'" *Down Beat* (April 26, 1962).

Gleason, Ralph J. "Coltrane Not for Those Who Want Popular Tune." *Des Moines (Iowa) Register* (March 26, 1960).

———. "Coltrane on Jazz Solos." *New York Journal-American* (July 15, 1961).

———. "Coltrane's Sax Blows Instant Art." *San Francisco Chronicle* (November 24, 1963): 30.

———. "John Coltrane Here: A Major Artist." *San Francisco Chronicle* (September 15, 1960).

———. "Weinstock vs. Gleason on Coltrane." *Los Angeles Mirror-News* (March 28, 1960).

Goldberg, Joe. "John Coltrane: Style and Circumstance." *Jazz & Pop* (April 1958): 4–157.

Grimes, Kitty. "John Coltrane Talks to Jazz News." *Jazz News* (UK) (December 27, 1961): 13.

Hendricks, Jon. "John Coltrane." *Saturday Review* (November 1964).

Hennessey, Mike. "Coltrane: Dropping the Ball and Chain from Jazz." *Melody Maker* (August 14, 1965): 6.

Hultin, Randi. "I Remember 'Trane." *Down Beat* (Music 1968—year-end issue): 104–5.

Kofsky, Frank. "John Coltrane: Interview by Frank Kofsky." *Jazz & Pop* (September 1967): 23–31.

———. "The New Wave: Bob Thiele Talks to Frank Kofsky About John Coltrane." *Coda* (May 1968): 2–10.

Nelsen, Don. "Trane Stops in the Gallery." *Sunday News* (New York) (May 15, 1960).

———. "Exploring the Jazz Legacy of John Coltrane." *New York Times* (September 29, 1974): 8–10.

Pekar, Harvey. "Impressions." *Down Beat* (August 29, 1963): 22.

Postif, François. "John Coltrane." *Jazz Hot* (France) (January 1962).

Quersin, Benoît. "Entretiens: La Passe dangereuse." *Jazz* (France) (January 1963): 40.

Spellman, A. B. "Trane + 7 = A Wild Night at the Gate." *Down Beat* (December 30, 1965): 15–44.

Tynan, John. "Take 5." *Down Beat* (November 23, 1961): 40.

Welding, Pete. "My Favorite Things." *Down Beat* (June 22, 1961): 30–31.

Williams, Martin. "Africa/Brass." *Down Beat* (January 18, 1962): 29–32.

———. "Coltrane Triumphant." *Saturday Review* (January 16, 1965): 73–74.

———. "Coltrane Up to Date." *Saturday Review* (April 30, 1966): 67.

Wilson, John S. "Coltrane's 'Sheets of Sound.'" *New York Times* (August 13, 1967).

Wilson, Russ. "Coltrane May Quit Davis, Form Quintet." *Oakland Tibune* (June 14, 1959).

Woodfin, Henry. "Coltrane's Progress." *Sounds & Fury* (October 1965).

Coltrane (1967–Present)

Christon, Lawrence. "This Trane Keeps A-Rollin': Twenty-Five Years After John Coltrane's Death, Jazz and Pop Musicians Remain in the Long Shadow of the Saxophonist's Innovation and Influence." *Los Angeles Times* (July 12, 1992).

Cook, Richard. "John Coltrane: A Spiritual 'Trane Ride from the Birdland Blues to A Love Supreme." *New Musical Express* (December 25, 1982): 60–77.

Crouch, Stanley. "Titan of the Blues: John Coltrane." *Village Voice* (October 6, 1987): 90.

Davis, Francis. "Coltrane at 75: The Man and the Myths." *New York Times* (September 23, 2001).

Donloe, Darlene. "Living with the Spirit and Legacy of John Coltrane." *Ebony* (March 1989): 46–50.

Garland, Phyl. "Requiem for 'Trane." *Ebony* (November 1967).

Giddins, Gary. "Metamorphosis: Chasing 'Chasin' the Trane' Down the Corridors of Its History." *Village Voice* (October 7, 1997): 67–68.

Heckman, Don. "A Legacy Supreme: John Coltrane Broke the Bounds of Traditional Improvisation. Three Decades After His Death, When You Listen to Jazz of the '90s, You Can Still Hear the Influence of This Tenor Legend." *Los Angeles Times* (July 13, 1997).

Kopulos, Gordon. "John Coltrane: Retrospective Perspective." *Down Beat* (July 22, 1971): 14–40.

McDonald, Michael Bruce. "Traning the Nineties, Or the Present Relevance of John Coltrane's Music of Theophany and Negation." *African American Review* (vol. 29, no. 2, 1995): 275–82.

Norris, John. "The Final Legacy." *Coda* (May–June 1968): 18–20.

Palmer, Robert. "A Tribute to John Coltrane's Spirit." *New York Times* (September 25, 1987).

Priestley, Brian. "Countdown to Ecstasy." *The Wire* (December 1985): 39.

Primack, Bret. "John Coltrane: A 65th Birthday Salute." *Jazz Times* (October 1991): 35.

Rozzi, James. "Bob Weinstock: Withstanding the Sands of Time." *Audio* (August 1994): 35.

Ruhlmann, William. "Going to Extremes: John Coltrane on Record." *Goldmine* (June 23, 1995): 18–144.

"Still a Force in '79: Musicians Talk About John Coltrane." *Down Beat* (July 12, 1979): 20–45.

Tomkins, Les. "Coltrane and I Played Without Preparation." *Crescendo International* 9, 3 (1970): 10.

Watrous, Peter. "John Coltrane: A Life Supreme." *Musician* (July 1987): 106.

A Love Supreme

Bennett, Jon. "Gil Gets on the 'Trane." *Mojo* (August 2001): 31.

Boomer, Stu. "A Love Supreme." *Coda* (October–November 1965).

Boyd, Herb. "Ravi, Alice Coltrane Have 'A Love Supreme.'" *New York Amsterdam News* (June 24, 1988).

"Breakout Albums: 'A Love Supreme.'" *Billboard* (March 13, 1965): 26.

Davis, Clive. "Lost in the Sound System/Review of Coltrane Memorial." *Times* (London) (November 14, 1987).

Delorme, Michel. "A Love Supreme." *Jazz Hot* (France) (June 1966).

DeMicheal, Don. "Spotlight Review: 'A Love Supreme.'" *Down Beat* (April 8, 1965): 27.

Feather, Leonard. "CD Jazz Library: Swing to Avant-Garde." *Los Angeles Times* (June 12, 1988).

Giddins, Gary. "Between Intermissions" (includes review of Misako Kano's performance of *A Love Supreme*). *Village Voice* (June 22, 1999).

Goldberg, Joe. "A Love Supreme." *HiFi/Sterio Review* (July 1995): 84.

"Jazz Spotlight: 'A Love Supreme.'" *Billboard* (February 27, 1965): 30.

"John Coltrane: 'A Love Supreme'" [two reviews]. *Coda* (October–November 1965): 32.

"'A Love Supreme' Goes Gold." *Downbeat.com* (January 21, 2001).

Porter, Lewis. "John Coltrane's *A Love Supreme*: Jazz Improvisation as Composition." *Journal of the American Musicological Society* (no. 3, 1985).

Pringle, Doug. "A Love Supreme." *Coda* (October–November 1965).

Sinclair, John. "A Love Supreme." *Jazz* (October 1965): 24–25.

ABC/Impulse

"ABC-Paramount Bows Jazz Label—Impulse." *Billboard* (December 5, 1960): 3–14.

"ABC-Paramount Success Saluted." *Music Reporter* (August 24, 1959): 1–14.

"ABC-Paramount Will Reactivate Apt Label." *Billboard* (January 9, 1965): 3.

"ABC-Para Parley Sets New Mark." *Billboard* (January 30, 1965): 4.

"ABC-Para's Baroque Series." *Billboard* (January 30, 1965): 10.

"ABC to Step Up Buying Pace; Re-signs Newton." *Billboard* (December 23, 1967): 4.

Cuscuna, Michael. "The Story of Impulse!" Liner notes to two-CD package *Impulse! Jazz: A 30 Year Celebration.* GRD-2-101, 1991.

Hoefer, George. "The Record Men: Creed Taylor." *Jazz* (January 1965): 19–21.

Johnson, Phil. "They Couldn't Help Acting on Impulse." *Independent* (UK) (February 3, 1995): 26.

Kofsky, Frank. "The New Wave: Bob Thiele Talks to Frank Kofsky." *Coda* (May–June 1968): 3–10.

Milkowski, Bill. "Irons in the Fire." *Pulse!* (June 1990).

Palmer, Robert. "From the Inside Out: Bob Palmer Interviews Bob Thiele." *Coda* (June 1971): 31–34.

Rozzi, James. "Bob Thiele: Once Again Flying Dutch." *Coda* (September–October 1992): 11–16.

Ruhlmann, William. "Bob Thiele Produced Them All." *Goldmine* (December 11, 1992): 44–50.

Sutherland, Sam. "Steve Backer Still Bucking the System." *Billboard* (September 11, 1982): 10–31.

Tan, Kelvin. "Act on Impulse!" *Lindy Hop Ensemble* (Singapore) (http://www.lindyhopensemble.com/blackspeak/impulse.htm).

Tesser, Neil. "Steve Backer: Arista's Jazz Godfather." *Radio Free Jazz* (November 1978): 11–12.

Watrous, Peter. "Bob Thiele, 73, Record Producer for Jazz Legends" [obituary]. *New York Times* (February 1, 1996).

———. "Steve Backer: One Man's Faith in Jazz, in Words and Action." *New York Times* (February 18, 1997): Sec. 1, 15.

Antibes 1965

Carles, Marcel. "Festival Antibes 65." *Aria Jazz* (Spain) (October 1965).

Comolli, Jean-Louis. "Antibes 65." *Jazz* (France) (August 1965).

Hennessey, Mike. "Coltrane: Dropping the Ball and Chain from Jazz. *Melody Maker* (August 14, 1965).

Hultin, Randi. "Coltrane det store trekkplasteret i Antibes." *Dagbladet* (Norway) (July 30, 1965).

Polillo, Arrigo. "Successo a Juan-les-Pins." *Musica Jazz* (Italy) (October 1965).

Other Musicians, Influences

Baraka, Amiri. "Homage to Miles Davis." In Gary Carner (ed.), *Miles Davis Companion* (London: Schirmer, 1996): 47.

Bashier, Ahmed. "McCoy Tyner." *Jazz Journal* (UK) (December 1966): 29–30.

DeMicheal, Don. "The Sixth Man." *Down Beat* (March 28, 1963): 16–18.

———. "The Responsibilities of Success." *Down Beat* (June 21, 1962): 15.

Ellis, Don, and Harihar Rao. "An Introduction to Indian Music for the Jazz Musician." *Jazz* (April 1965): 20–22.

Heckman, Don. "After Coltrane: Jimmy Garrison." *Down Beat* (March 9, 1967): 18–40.

Hennessey, Mike. "The Emancipation of Elvin Jones." *Down Beat* (March 24, 1966).

Hentoff, Nat. "Art Davis and the Mystery of Making It." *Jazz Times* (March 2001).

"Indian Music May Prove Boon to Electronic Sound." *Billboard* (October 14, 1967): 14.

Jones, Leroi (Amiri Imamu Baraka). "Archie Shepp Live." *Jazz* (January 1965): 8–9.

Mattingly, Rick. "Elvin." *Modern Drummer* (December 1982).

———. "Elvin Jones: Once More, with Feeling." *Modern Drummer* (May 1992).

Noames, Jean-Louis. "Visite au Dieu Soleil." *Jazz* (France) (December 1965).

Nolan, Herb. "I Play Drums That's Just What I Do." *Down Beat* (November 6, 1973).

———. "Jimmy Garrison: Bassist in the Front Line." *Down Beat* (June 6, 1974): 18, 41.

———. "Rhythmic Pulsemaster." *Down Beat* (December 15, 1977).

Palmer, Robert. "Alice Coltrane's First Concerts Here in 7 Years." *New York Times* (September 21, 1984): Sec. C, 28.

———. "McLaughlin's Return to Electric." *Rolling Stone* (July 13, 1978): 17.

Perry, Charles. "Number Five with a Dildo: Steely Dan Comes Up Swinging." *Rolling Stone* (August 15, 1974): 32.

Pouncey, Edwin. "Enduring Love: Alice Coltrane." *The Wire* (April 2002).

Robertson, Charles. "Jazz and All That." *Audio* (October 1957): 56–57.

Smith, Steve. "The Sound and the Fury: Archie Shepp." *Jazz Times* (May 2001): 46–165.

Varga, George. "Shankar Opened Western Ears to Eastern Music." *San Diego Union-Tribune* (November 12, 2000).

Wild, David. "McCoy Tyner: The Jubilant Experience of the Classic Quartet." *Down Beat* (July 12, 1979): 18–49.

Wilmer, Val. "Elvin Talk: An Interview with Elvin Jones." *Down Beat* (March 16, 1972): 14–15.

Jazz, Avant-Garde, the Youth Movement, and Politics in the Sixties

Chernus, Roy. "Coltrane/Tyner and the 'New Thing.'" *New York Arts Journal* (no. 12, November–December 1978).

"Down Beat: Music 1962—7th Annual Yearbook."

"Down Beat: Music 1966—11th Annual Yearbook."

Feather, Leonard. "Feather's Nest" [column on "anti-jazz"]. *Down Beat* (February 15, 1962): 40.

Hyams Ericsson, Marjorie. "Experimentation in Public: The Artist's Viewpoint." *Down Beat* (April 8, 1965): 15.

"Jazz Is Mugged by 'New Thing'" [a response]. *Jazz* (April 14, 1965): 49.

Kofsky, Frank. "Revolution, Coltrane and the Avant-Garde." *Jazz* (Part I: July 1965): 13–26; (Part II: August 1965): 18–22.

"Music on Campus: The College Market for Records and Talent" [special insert]. *Billboard* (March 28, 1964).

"Music on Campus" [special insert]. *Billboard* (March 27, 1965).

Qamar, Nadi. "Titans of the Saxophone." *Liberator* (April 1966): 21–22.

"Racial Prejudice in Jazz—Part I." *Down Beat* (March 15, 1962): 20–26.

"Racial Prejudice in Jazz—Part II." *Down Beat* (March 29, 1962): 22–25.

Schoenfeld, Herm. "Jazz Mugged by 'New Thing.'" *Variety* (April 24, 1965): 49.

Wilson, John S. "Jazz and the Anarchy of the Avant-Garde." *New York Times* (April 24, 1966): 30–31.

St. John Will-I-Am Coltrane African Orthodox Church

Boulware, Jack. "A Church Supreme: After Three Decades of Feeding the Homeless, the World's Only Church Devoted to John Coltrane Now Finds Itself Without a Home." *Dallas Observer* (February 3, 2000).

"Coltrane's Widow Sues." *New York Times* (October 24, 1981).

Wong, Wesley "Soul Music: John Coltrane Is Their Patron Saint." *Image* (March 6, 1988): 18–20.

Radio

Rathe, Steve (prod.). "A Love Supreme" (live performance by Wynton Marsalis, Marcus Roberts, Reginald Veal, and Elvin Jones). National Public Radio—"Jazz from Lincoln Center" (April 17, 1995).

Rowland, Steve (prod.). "Remembering Trane." 1987.

Rowland, Steve, and Larry Abrams (co-prods.). "Tell Me How Long Trane's Been Gone" (five-part series). 2001.

Westervelt, Eric. "A Love Supreme." National Public Radio—"The NPR 100" (October 23, 2000).

Wright, David. "Church of St. John Coltrane." National Public Radio—"Weekend All Things Considered" (April 22, 2000).

Video

Blue Trane, VHS copy of TV documentary prod. Philippe Koechlin and Dominique Cazenare. Canal Plus (France), 1992, videocassette.

The Coltrane Legacy, prod. and dir. Burrill Crohn. Video Artists International, 1985, videocassette.

John Coltrane Quartet live in Antibes, France. Unreleased VHS copy (July 26, 1965), videocassette.

Ralph Gleason's Jazz Casual: John Coltrane, prod. Ralph Gleason. Rhino Home Video, 1995, videocassette.

The World According to John Coltrane, prod. Toby Byron. BMG Video, 1993, videocassette.

Discography

When all is said and written, the subject at hand is and should remain the music. All titles listed below were compiled selectively with an eye toward references within this book, as well as space and budget limitations. All are the most recent, compact disc editions. Happy listening!

A Love Supreme

A Love Supreme (Deluxe Edition). Impulse 314-589-945-2, 2002.

Coltrane with Miles Davis

1955–56
Miles (The New Miles Davis Quintet). Prestige OJC-006-2, 1992.
Cookin'. Prestige OJC-128-2, 1990.
1957–62
'Round About Midnight. Columbia 65359, 1997.
Milestones. Sony 65340, 1997.
Kind of Blue. Columbia/Legacy CK64935, 1997.
En Concert avec Europe 1: Olympia March 1960 (France). Sony Trema 71044 (disc 1 of 4), 1994.
Collections
Miles Davis Chronicle: The Complete Prestige Recordings. PCD-012-2, 1987.
Miles Davis with John Coltrane: The Complete Columbia Recordings. Columbia/Legacy C6K 6583, 2000.

Coltrane with Cannonball Adderley

Cannonball Adderley Quintet in Chicago. Verve 314-559-770-2, 1999.

Coltrane as Leader

1957–59
Coltrane. Prestige OJCCD-020-2 (P-7105), 1987.
Soultrane. Prestige OJCCD-021-2 (P-7142), 1987.
Blue Train. Blue Note CDP 7460952, 1996.
1959–61
Giant Steps. Rhino 75203, 1998.
Coltrane Jazz. Rhino 79891, 2000.
Coltrane's Sound. Rhino 75588, 1999.
My Favorite Things. Rhino 75204, 1998.
1961–67
The Complete Africa/Brass Sessions. Impulse IMPD-2-168, 1995.
Live at the Village Vanguard. Impulse MCAD-39136, 1992.
Duke Ellington & John Coltrane. Impulse IMPD-166, 1995.
John Coltrane & Johnny Hartman. Impulse GRD-157, 1995.
Impressions. Impulse 314-543-416-2, 2000.
Crescent. Impulse IMPD-200, 1996.
The John Coltrane Quartet Plays. Impulse IMPD-214, 1997.

Love Supreme: Juan-les-Pins Jazz Festival, Antibes, July 26–27, 1965. Giants of Jazz (Italy) CD 53068, 1996.

Ascension. Impulse 314-543-413-2, 2000.

Transition. Impulse GRD-124, 1993.

Sun Ship. Impulse IMPD-167, 1995.

Meditations. Impulse IMPD-199, 1996.

Live in Seattle. Impulse GRD-2-146, 1994.

Kulu Se Mama. Impulse 314-543-412-2, 2000.

The Olatunji Concert: The Last Live Recording. Impulse 314-589-120-2, 2001.

Collections

The Classic Quartet: Complete Impulse! Studio Recordings. Impulse IMPD-8-280, 1998.

The Complete 1961 Village Vanguard Recordings. Impulse IMPD-4-232, 1997.

The Last Giant: The John Coltrane Anthology. Rhino R2-71255, 1993. Includes such early Coltrane recordings as his 1946 Navy session, and dates with Dizzy Gillespie (1951) and Johnny Hodges (1954).

The Heavyweight Champion: The Complete Atlantic Recordings. Rhino R2-71984, 1995.

Spiritual. Impulse 314-589-099-2, 2001. A brilliant overview of Coltrane's spiritually oriented recordings from 1961 through 1965.

Music Inspired by A Love Supreme

Qualification—lest a never-ending list ensue—is necessary: the titles listed below feature musically obvious, if not titular, reference to the music on John Coltrane's signature album.

Ayler, Albert. *Love Cry*. Impulse GRD-108, 1991.

Coltrane, Alice. *Eternity*. Warner Bros. Masters 9362-47899-2, 1976.

———. *World Galaxy*. Impulse IMPD-19142, 1998.

Cyrille, Andrew. *Ode to the Living Tree*. Evidence ECD 22185-2, 1997.

Garrett, Kenny. *Pursuance: The Music of John Coltrane*. Warner Bros. 46209, 1996.

Green, Grant. *Iron City*. 32 Jazz 32048, 1998.

Handy, John, with Ali Akbar Khan and Zakir Hussain. *Karuna Supreme*. MPS G22719, 1976.

Herwig, Conrad. *The Latin Side of John Coltrane*. Astor Place TCD 4003, 1996.

Johnson, Marc. *Bass Desires*. ECM 1299, 1986.

Jones, Elvin. *Very R.A.R.E.* Evidence ECD 22053-2, 1993.

———. *Elvin Jones "Special Quartet" featuring Wynton Marsalis: Live at the "Pit Inn," Tokyo, Japan*. SONY SRCS 7376, 1994.

Kaiser, Henry. *Eternity Blue*. Shanachie 6016, 1995.

Liebman, Dave, with Wayne Shorter, others. *Live Under the Sky*. Epic EPC 4625802, 1987 (CD, also available in DVD format).

Lloyd, Charles. *Soundtrack/In the Soviet Union*. Collectables COL-CD-6237, 1999.

Marsalis, Branford. *Footsteps of Our Fathers*. Rounder/Marsalis Music 1161-3301-2, 2002.

Murray, David. *Octet Plays Trane*. Justin Time JUST 131-2, 2000.

Pittston, Suzanne. *Resolution: A Remembrance of John Coltrane*. Vineland VLCD 7755, 1999.

Roney, Wallace. *No Room for Argument*. Stretch SCD 9033-2, 2000.

Sanders, Pharoah. *Karma*. Impulse IMPD-153, 1995.

Santana, Carlos, and John McLaughlin. *Love Devotion Surrender*. Columbia CK 32034, 1973.

Scott-Heron, Gil. *Free Will: First Editions*. RCA 63843, 2001.

Smith, Wadada Leo. *Kulture Jazz*. ECM 1507, 1993.

Tyner, McCoy. *Remembering John*. Enja 79668, 1991.

Collections

Various artists, including McCoy Tyner, Roy Haynes, David Murray, and Pharoah Sanders. *Blues for Coltrane*. Impulse MCAD-42122, 1988.

Various artists, including John Coltrane, Yusef Lateef, McCoy Tyner, Alice Coltrane, and Pharoah Sanders. *Impulse Jazz: A 30 Year Celebration*. GRD-2-101, 1991.

Various artists, including Branford Marsalis, Alice Coltrane, and Pharoah Sanders. *Red Hot + Cool*. Red Hot GRD-9794, 1994.

Index

FOR THE BEST IN PAPERBACKS, LOOK FOR THE 🐧

In every corner of the world, on every subject under the sun, Penguin represents quality and variety—the very best in publishing today.

For complete information about books available from Penguin—including Penguin Classics, Penguin Compass, and Puffins—and how to order them, write to us at the appropriate address below. Please note that for copyright reasons the selection of books varies from country to country.

In the United States: Please write to *Penguin Group (USA), P.O. Box 12289 Dept. B, Newark, New Jersey 07101-5289* or call 1-800-788-6262.

In the United Kingdom: Please write to *Dept. EP, Penguin Books Ltd, Bath Road, Harmondsworth, West Drayton, Middlesex UB7 0DA.*

In Canada: Please write to *Penguin Books Canada Ltd, 10 Alcorn Avenue, Suite 300, Toronto, Ontario M4V 3B2.*

In Australia: Please write to *Penguin Books Australia Ltd, P.O. Box 257, Ringwood, Victoria 3134.*

In New Zealand: Please write to *Penguin Books (NZ) Ltd, Private Bag 102902, North Shore Mail Centre, Auckland 10.*

In India: Please write to *Penguin Books India Pvt Ltd, 11 Panchsheel Shopping Centre, Panchsheel Park, New Delhi 110 017.*

In the Netherlands: Please write to *Penguin Books Netherlands bv, Postbus 3507, NL-1001 AH Amsterdam.*

In Germany: Please write to *Penguin Books Deutschland GmbH, Metzlerstrasse 26, 60594 Frankfurt am Main.*

In Spain: Please write to *Penguin Books S. A., Bravo Murillo 19, 1° B, 28015 Madrid.*

In Italy: Please write to *Penguin Italia s.r.l., Via Benedetto Croce 2, 20094 Corsico, Milano.*

In France: Please write to *Penguin France, Le Carré Wilson, 62 rue Benjamin Baillaud, 31500 Toulouse.*

In Japan: Please write to *Penguin Books Japan Ltd, Kaneko Building, 2-3-25 Koraku, Bunkyo-Ku, Tokyo 112.*

In South Africa: Please write to *Penguin Books South Africa (Pty) Ltd, Private Bag X14, Parkview, 2122 Johannesburg.*

3

God Loves

May I Be acceptable in Thy sight

we are all one in his grace

The Fact That we are is

Acknowledgement of Thee O Lord

T. Y. L.

God will wash away all our

tears - He always Has - He always

will

Seek Him Everyday. In all ways

seek God everyday.

Let us sing all songs to God

To whom all praise is Due. Praise

God